Taking power, making change

I WEEK

University Campus **Oldham**

Higher Education at Oldham College

First published in Great Britain in 2013 by

Policy Press
University of Bristol
Fourth Floor
Beacon House
Queen's Road
Bristol BS8 1QU
UK
t: +44 (0)117 331 4054
f: +44 (0)117 331 4093
tpp-info@bristol.ac.uk
www.policypress.co.uk

North America office:
Policy Press
c/o The University of Chicago Press
1427 East 60th Street
Chicago, IL 60637, USA
t: +1 773 702 7700
f: +1 773-702-9756
sales@press.uchicago.edu
www.press.uchicago.edu

UNIVERSITY CAMPUS
OLDHAM

We must believe that it is the darkest before the dawn
of a beautiful new world.
We will see it when we believe it.

Saul Alinsky

Contents

List of tables, figures and boxes

Tables

Figures

Boxes

About the authors

Dave Beck initially trained as a primary school teacher and has worked in community development in the voluntary and statutory sectors since the mid-1980s, both in Nottingham and Glasgow. He has also developed a wide range of community-based adult education programmes within further education and the UK government's City Challenge initiative.

He writes on a wide range of issues related to community development, including the place of radical education in supporting community change, community development approaches to dealing with drug addiction, social capital and social change, and higher education and community partnerships to develop participation.

Currently, he manages the post-graduate programmes in community development at the University of Glasgow. He is also a board member of International Association for Community Development and the Federation for Community Development Learning.

Rod Purcell has degrees from the Universities of Wales, Glasgow and London. He trained as a community development worker and has practised in a range of communities in the West of Scotland, including a multi-ethnic community in the inner city of Glasgow. He then worked as community development consultant before coming to the University of Glasgow to establish their community development programme. He was head of the Department for Adult and Continuing Education and is currently director for community engagement. Rod is the author of a range of community development-related publications, and he has particular interest in urban culture and psychogeography.

Rod is a past chair of the Federation for Community Development Learning and board member of the International Association for Community Development. He is also a Fellow of the Royal Geographical Society.

Note: For purposes of attribution Dave Beck is the author of Chapters One, Six and Ten and Rod Purcell is the author of Chapters Two, Three and Five. Chapters Four, Seven, Eight and Nine were co-written.

Introduction

Power concedes nothing without a demand. It never did and it never will. (Frederick Douglass)

Community organising has a diverse history going back to the social welfare movements of the 19th century, and it first came to prominence through the work of Saul Alinsky in Chicago in the US in the late 1930s and 1940s. Alinsky wanted to build what he called 'organisations of organisations' that would enable poor communities to claim power. In doing so they would have more control over their own lives, bring increased resources and improved services to their community and engage more fully in the democratic process. His book, Rules for radicals, outlining how this process would work, is subtitled *A pragmatic primer for realistic radicals* (1971). It is a book about radical change to make the system work for the dispossessed; it is not about revolutionary change. This is the objective of community organising, and we have taken his phrase, 'realistic radicals', as the theme of this book.

The promise of community organising saw its rapid expansion in the US through Alinsky's organisation, the Industrial Areas Foundation (IAF), until recently through ACORN (Associations of Community Organizations for Reform Now) established by Wade Rathke, and other organisations such as Gamaliel (see www. gamaliel.com). Community organising has spread to Canada, the UK, Australia, the Indian Sub-continent, South East Asia, Africa and South America. It has taken many forms, from international networks such as Slum Dwellers International (SDI) to small and more localised operations.

This book seeks to explore the diverse history of community organising, to tell some of the stories of how it developed, its successes and failures, and the lessons that can be applied today. People always have, and always will, struggle to improve their living conditions, their quality of life, to bring hope for their children's future and to make democracy a reality. At the time of writing the Arab Spring is still working through, with improved freedom and optimism in Tunisia and Libya to resistance to continued violent oppression in Syria. In other countries the Occupy Movement expresses the same desires and motivations. Community organising offers a realistic way forward for many communities. While it is not a magic bullet for progressive change, it is a tried and tested way of improving people's lives. This book will hopefully be useful for many engaged in such struggles.

In producing the book we made field visits and conducted interviews in the US, Australia, Cambodia, India, South Africa and the UK. We wish to thank the many people, community organisers and local people who made us welcome, told us their stories and gave us the benefit of their experience and analysis. We hope we have done justice to their work.

About the book

In Chapter One we explore the basic ideas of community organising as developed by Alinsky. We ask what was he trying to do, what are the values, principles and processes that underpin community organising, and crucially, why we should organise communities in this way.

Chapter Two asks the question, what is community organising for in the 21st century? The US has changed greatly since the first community organisation was established in the Back of the Yards, the meat packing district of Chicago, in 1939. Community organising takes place in developed, developing and very poor countries across the world. What issues should community organisations be focusing on and what processes should they use? Can we develop criteria to examine the effectiveness of community organisations? This chapter discusses a range of factors from leadership development to building social capital, from the Millennium Development Goals of the United Nations (UN) to ideas around quality of life and wellbeing. These factors are used later evaluate the contribution of community organising.

In Chapter Three we further explore the early work of Alinsky and the IAF model of community organising. In particular we analyse the development and operation of the first community organisation, the Back of the Yards Neighborhood Council. We then consider the neighbouring community organisation in Chicago, The Woodlawn Organization. This is followed by a broader analysis of the IAF and their current activities.

Chapter Four explores the international dimension to the IAF. We discuss the current IAF affiliate in the UK (Citizens UK) compared to the government-related 'Big Society' initiative. These discussions are located within the context of how community work and community action has developed in the UK over the past 50 years. This is followed by the example of the Sydney Alliance, an IAF affiliate in Australia that was formed in 2007 with support from the New South Wales Trades and Labour Council.

To broaden out the story of community organising from the IAF, Chapter Five looks at the development of ACORN in the US from its founding in Arkansas in 1970, through its rapid national growth and diversification into housing and union activities, to its demise (at the hands of its political opponents) in 2010. The organisation lives on in other ways in the US and more directly through ACORN International. Two case studies in India (Delhi and Mumbai) are discussed.

Chapter Six further explores the international dimension to community organising by looking at the multinational network of SDI. This network operates in Asia, India and South America linking up poor communities in an operation that has both similarities and significant differences from community organisations in the US. We look at the Community Healing Network and SDI operation in Cape Town, South Africa. This is followed by the Indian Alliance, comprised of the National Slum Dwellers Federation, Mahila Milan (Women Together) and SPARC (Society for the Promotion of Area Resource Centres) in Mumbai. Finally, we move on to Cambodia for the case study of the Urban Poor Development Fund (UPDF) in Phnom Penh.

Chapter Seven considers a range of current and diverse community organising through an online survey of community organisations in several countries. We then return to the US to look at a current faith-based model of community organising, that of Gamaliel. Finally, this chapter explores what some practitioners are seeing as the new alternative to community organising, the comprehensive community development programmes. Here we consider the work of the Institute for Comprehensive Community Development (ICCD), the Local Initiatives Support Corporation (LISC) and the approach to community organising adopted by the Tea Party in the US.

In Chapter Eight we compare and contrast the various models of community organising, IAF versus ACORN versus SDI versus ICCD. Their similarities and differences are explored from a variety of perspectives relating to organising, partnership, power, leadership development and so on.

Chapter Nine continues this macro analysis to explore what the various models of community organising have and have not achieved in terms of our contemporary development perspectives outlined in Chapter Two. How useful are community organisations, what have they really delivered for the poor and oppressed communities, how relevant are they in the early years of the 21st century, and what might their future contribution be in both the developed and developing world?

Chapter Ten takes on board one of the major criticisms of community organising, that it may be operationally effective to some degree but that it is undermined by its lack of critical and structural analysis of modern societies. We discuss community organising in the context of hegemony and Antonio Gramsci's theory of counter-hegemony. Are community organisations a counter-hegemonic force that promote the development of organic intellectuals, or could they be? We then discuss the work of Paulo Freire in order to address the criticism of community organising which suggests that it sees local people as 'troops to be mobilised' and does not pay enough attention to the critical development of individuals. Is it possible to link the ideas of Freire to community organisation to produce a broader and deeper model of practice?

Finally, in the Endnote we think about the possible future of community organising. Where does it go from here, how different might this be in the US and developed countries compared to Asian and India? Is a unified community organisation model possible, and would that be desirable?

ONE

The roots of community organising

> The first step in community organization is community disorganization. The disruption of the present organization is the first step toward community organization. Present arrangements must be disorganized if they are to be displaced by new patterns.... All change means disorganization of the old and organization of the new. (Saul Alinsky)

This chapter explores and analyses the roots of community organising as seen in the work of Saul Alinsky. Reference is made to Alinsky's classic texts, *Rules for radicals* (1971) and *Reveille for radicals* (1989), as well as commentaries on Saul Alinsky by Nicholas von Hoffman (2010) and Sanford D. Horwitt (1989). The chapter seeks to understand and critique the underlying ideas and practices that informed the development of community organising through the initial development of the Industrial Areas Foundation (IAF), and explores the contribution that Alinsky as an individual made to that process.

Definitions of community organising

Community organising is a term that describes an approach to organisation building and social action developed in the US from the late 1930s onwards. Within this approach organisations of organisations are established. These are usually made up of block clubs, associations, churches and labour unions, but could also include families and individuals. Their intention is to build power in order to achieve changes in policy and practice within institutions that have an impact on the community, by deploying a range of electoral and non-electoral strategies and tactics that allow them to enter into negotiations with institutional decision makers. In the absence of mutually acceptable agreements, more confrontational approaches, such as non-violent disruption, public shaming, economic action (strikes and boycotts) and mass lobbying for reform programmes and legislation, are also deployed (Miller, 2010). The power of mass participation is also used to develop mutual aid projects and alternative institutions such as co-ops, credit unions and support groups.

> In theory, community organizing provides a way to merge various strategies for neighborhood empowerment. Organizing begins with the premise that (1) the problems facing inner-city communities do not result from a lack of effective solutions, but from a lack of power to implement these solutions; (2) that the only way for communities

to build long-term power is by organizing people and money around a common vision; and (3) that a viable organization can only be achieved if a broadly based indigenous leadership – and not one or two charismatic leaders – can knit together the diverse interests of their local institutions. (Obama, 1988)

Early life

Saul Alinsky is widely recognised as the founder of this approach to practice: 'Alinsky is to community organizing as Freud is to psychoanalysis' (Slayton, 1986). Alinsky was born in Chicago in 1909 into a middle-class, Jewish immigrant household. He studied sociology and criminology at the University of Chicago, during which time his observation of the systemic nature of poverty and growing dissatisfaction about the ameliorative approaches of social work led him to look for alternative ways to achieve social change. The Depression and the growing turbulence of the 1930s politicised both him and his wife Helene, a social worker, who was also an organiser, and was highly regarded within the labour movement (Horwitt, 1989).

The Back of the Yards neighbourhood, where he had earlier researched organised crime and juvenile crime, provided the opportunity for Alinsky to develop his theory and practice of community organising (Valley, 2008). Informed by the organising practices he observed in the Congress of Industrial Organizations (CIO) under the leadership of John L. Lewis (Horwitt, 1989), his methodology developed intuitively in response to the issues he was dealing with. Only later did he develop an analysis that made sense of what he did. This is illuminative of his ongoing approach that is action-focused and reflective, where knowledge production is a result of experiential learning.

His pragmatic approach to building power organisations based on individual self-interest is illustrated in the following:

> When we were building our organization in the Back of the Yards, the Polish Roman Catholic churches in Chicago joined us because they were concerned about the expanding power of the Irish Roman Catholic churches. The Packing House Workers Union was with us – so their rival unions joined, trying to counteract the potential membership and power pickup. We didn't, of course, care why they'd joined us – we just knew we'd be better off if they did. (Alinsky, 1971, p 74)

We can see that Alinsky's primary concern was not the ideological position of individuals and organisations involved, but how they could add to the creation of a power organisation based on people power that could effectively challenge the politically and economically powerful organisations that were oppressing people within the community. As Alinsky puts it, he was:

… concerned with how to create mass organizations to seize power and give it to the people; to realize the democratic dream of equality, justice, peace, cooperation, equal and full opportunities for education, full and useful employment, health, and the creation of those circumstances in which man can have the chance to live by values that give meaning to life. We are talking about a mass power organization which will change the world into a place where all men and women walk erect, in the spirit of that credo of the Spanish Civil War, "Better to die on your feet than to live on your knees." (Alinsky, 1971, pp 18-19)

Alinsky the man

There can be no doubt that Alinsky had a huge influence on how community organising developed. He was charismatic, fearless, brash and larger than life. He described himself as a professional outside agitator, revelled in the notoriety and relished the conflict and the drama of the organising encounter. He said, 'I'm one of those lucky guys who gets paid for doing what he wants to do, I'm having a ball!' (Alinsky, undated).

It would be fair to say that Alinsky traded on his reputation. For example, on one occasion he had planned to deliver some lectures at a university in Houston, Texas. When his plane arrived he was met by a delegation from the Ku Klux Klan in full regalia, the mayor was on the front page of the local newspaper saying he was going to investigate the university for inviting this radical, and the right-wing John Birch Society was running a picket line. The next morning, a delegation from the black community met with Alinsky and asked him to come and work with them; they had never seen all the people who hated them so agitated.

Alinsky was also a product of his time; growing up in the Depression, alarmed by the rise of fascism and operating during the civil rights struggles in the US shaped the way he thought and practised. In Rochester, New York there were severe 'race' riots in 1964; the National Guard was called in and a number of lives were lost. In response to that, the Rochester Area Council of Churches, a coalition of all the white churches in the area and some of the 'respectable black churches', called on Alinsky to come and work in the black ghettos. Alinsky refused on the grounds that they had no right to speak on behalf of the black people of that community. However, even Alinsky's initial involvement with the group came to the notice of the press who started running campaigns denouncing his involvement, saying that it would stir up bad relationships between the black and white communities. At the same time Malcolm X advised the black communities in Rochester that Alinsky could be trusted and did have some useful things to teach them. In response to both the media campaign and Malcolm X's endorsement, black churches, street gangs and individuals in the black communities petitioned Alinsky to work with them.

There is no doubt that he had a flair for the dramatic. This can be seen, for example, when he organised people in a particular neighbourhood to dump their rubbish on the doorstep of the alderman who had failed to get it collected! This personalised and theatrical approach to campaigning is typical of the flamboyant way in which Alinsky mobilised people to get results.

A further example can be seen in the conflict against the Eastman Kodak Company, which had reneged on an agreement to give jobs in their factory to local people. Alinsky and members of FIGHT (Freedom, Independence, God, Honor, Today), the community organisation in Rochester, managed to buy some of the company's stock and gain control of some others by proxy from sympathetic shareholders. This gave them the right to attend the shareholders' meeting. Alinsky himself gave a number of press and television interviews, stirring up interest and tension about the issue. On the day of the meeting several hundred people from Rochester protested outside. Meanwhile Alinsky and a number of black leaders from the organisation marched into the shareholders' meeting. This in itself was a dramatic act – black people walking into a situation dominated by white power was almost unheard of in 1960s America. In the middle of the proceedings they stood up and made their case, "Will you agree to honour these agreements that you signed?" When they didn't get a satisfactory answer they gave the meeting an ultimatum, "We give you one hour to agree or not agree to honour the agreement you signed!" With that they marched out, followed by the press and television.

The publicity that this dramatic act produced coupled with the people power that the Rochester organisation had created eventually led to Eastman Kodak backing down and giving 600 jobs to local, Rochester people. This elaborate process which included the development of strategic alliances, use of the media, clearly identifying and fearlessly going after an issue, making organisations live up to promises, deploying public shame and mobilising local people, exemplifies well Alinsky at the top of his game.

There is little doubt that without Alinsky community organising as we see it today would not have happened. The centrality of leadership and personalities is an issue that we will return to later in the book. However, the IAF that he established continues to this day, and a community organising approach still informs practice all across the world. In other words, even without Alinsky at the centre there are a set of ideas, values and principles that remain compelling in the 21st century, and it is to these ideas that we now turn.

Foundational ideas

Although, as we have seen, the Alinsky organising approach is rooted in tactics and practice, it is also built on a clear set of underpinning ideas and analysis which he explores in his seminal book, *Rules for radicals* (1971).

Inequality of the status quo

The first plank of this analysis is the recognition that we live in an unequal world. Alinsky expressed this inequality in terms of the 'haves' and the 'have-nots' – those who had access to power, influence, money and other social and cultural benefits and those who did not. He outlined the hegemonic nature of the 'haves', noting their deployment of the various mechanisms of civil society, including literature and the media. This was coupled with their ability to dispense rewards and the threat of sanctions that flowed from amassed economic and political power. The impact of these forces working together was the maintenance of the status quo within which the haves protected their positions of power.

This could also be understood in terms of social and cultural capital, as discussed by Bourdieu (1986), who explored how social inequality was reinforced and replicated through generations by the relationships that people in power developed and by their cultural investments. His definition of social capital was 'the sum of resources, actual or virtual, that accrue to an individual or a group by virtue of possessing a durable network of more or less institutionalizes relationships of mutual acquaintance and recognition' (Bourdieu and Wacquant, 1992, p 119). An example he cited was that membership of a private golf club both signalled a particular social position and developed a network of contacts that could facilitate business deals, which in turn led to better economic outcomes for the individual members.

Bourdieu further noted that people used cultural symbols to indicate their place in the social order, observing that some types of cultural taste enjoyed more status than others, for example, listening to opera music and going to the theatre indicated a higher social position than playing darts and going to bingo. These cultural practices and the significance given to them serve as a demarcation point between those who have power and those who do not. From this, people in power develop cultural investment strategies that further develop their social and economic advantage. An example of this can be seen in parenting practices within middle-class families. They deploy particular cultural investment strategies that lead to their children optimising their yield from the education system, which includes the types of books read, trips to museums and art galleries and so on. These types of cultural activities are in accord with the culture of schooling and therefore give the child an advantage in that setting since they are both more comfortable with its practices and perceived as being more acceptable to their teachers. This early advantage leads to better qualifications, better jobs and better economic outcomes.

Alinsky went on to describe the have-nots, who were 'caged by color, physical or political, they are barred from an opportunity to represent themselves in the politics of life. The Haves want to keep; the Have-Nots want to get.' Alinsky saw within this contradiction both an explanation of the ongoing, uneasy status quo and the potential impetus for change: 'Thermopolitically they (the Have Nots) are a mass of cold ashes of resignation and fatalism, but inside there are glowing embers of hope which can be fanned by the building of means of obtaining power' (Alinsky, 1971, p 29).

Alinsky then described a third category, the 'have-a-little, want mores'; from this group, situated in the middle of the contradiction described above, came potential leaders, and he cited: Moses, Paul of Tarsus, Martin Luther, Maximilien Robespierre, Georges Danton, Samuel Adams, Alexander Hamilton, Thomas Jefferson, Napoleon Bonaparte, Giuseppe Garibaldi, Nikolai Lenin, Mahatma Gandhi, Fidel Castro, Mao Tse-tung, and others (Alinsky, 1971, p 30). However, as we will see later, community organising practice is strongly based on a network of local leaders who are drawn from the 'have nots'. Alinsky envisaged a process whereby although action was catalysed by leaders (organisers), it was shaped, operationalised and ultimately carried by local leaders. Alinsky said that most world leaders had come from the have-a-little, want more class. In stark contrast, this category also produced a mass of people committed to the ideas of social justice but not prepared to do anything about it for fear of losing the limited status they already had. And so we see three groups of people with the potential to act locked into a status quo shored up by self-interest and fear.

In all of this, Alinsky was hopeful that the possibility for individuals to act and the contradictions inherent with the status quo meant that there was always the potential for action. He stated, however, that for this potential for action to be realised, the prerequisite was for an organiser to develop a community in such a way that their 'Curiosity becomes compulsive'. His most frequent word was 'why?' (Alinsky, 1971, p 24). This echoes the idea expounded in Freire's *Pedagogy of freedom* (2001) of critical curiosity that is the foundation for developing critical consciousness. Freire said, 'The more critically one exercises one's capacity for learning, the greater is one's capacity for constructing and developing what I call "epistemological curiosity," without which it is not possible to obtain a complete grasp of the object of our knowledge' (Freire, 2001, p 12), and without this understanding of our present conditions and envisioning a different world, the scope for change is limited.

In the end Alinsky had one unshakeable belief, that if people had the power to act, in the long run they would, most of the time, reach the right decisions. However, he was a political pragmatist, committed to seeing the world as it is: an arena of power politics moved primarily by perceived immediate self-interests, where morality was rhetorical rationale for expedient action and self-interest (Alinsky, 1971, p 25). It is to his ideas about power that we now turn.

Power

Alinsky deliberately used the word 'power' with all its connotations of conflict, determined not to detour around reality. This has particular importance these days when much of the language and the practice of development in all its forms has been depoliticised and neutralised (Harriss, 2002; Bunyan, 2010; Gaynor, 2011). Within the UK, for example, notions of power and conflict have increasingly been replaced by the rhetoric of stakeholders and fairness. Unfortunately, more inclusive decision-making processes have not materialised to match that rhetoric. Bunyan (2008, p 5) warns us that there has been a 'gradual realization that beneath the rhetoric, the emphasis has been more about centralized managerially led targets rather than commitment to people-centred processes … the profession now finds itself at a critical juncture, at risk of losing its identity and soul.'

Margaret Ledwith (2011, p 2) contends that one of the key elements of practice is 'an analysis of power and discrimination in society.' Unfortunately, even community workers who have a stated aim of working towards empowerment and social justice, can feel uncomfortable with the confrontational use of power found in Alinsky's work. Alinsky, however, refused to deal with the unreality that we were all on the same side as 'stakeholders' in society, but provocatively he spoke truth to power. His simple statement was that power was the 'ability, whether physical, mental, or moral, to act' (Alinsky 1971 p 50). Power was an inescapable fact of life, and Alinsky posited only two forms – organised or disorganised: 'only organised power will achieve lasting social change. Every organization known to man, from government down, has had only one reason for being – that is, organization for power in order to put into practice or promote its common purpose' (1971, p 56). From this flowed the idea that aggregated self-interest was the only foundation for genuine collective power.

Self-interest

Many community workers would like to think that people are motivated by altruism, and it is to this that we must appeal if we are to engage in social change. Alinsky's view was that to recognise that people were motivated primarily by self-interest was to see humanity as it is, not what we would like it to be. Self-interest intersects with self-reliance and self-management to produce possibilities for development (Kaufman and Alfonso, 1997, p 14).

This is not to say that community organising is an individualised practice. On the contrary, it recognises that the wellbeing of individuals is interwoven with that of others. This viewpoint is echoed in rational choice theory, which is based on the assumption that individuals maximise their self-interest. Since it is clear that an individual has limited potential to influence the wider world, it is rational and self-serving to create relationships and to support people who in turn will support you, thereby developing stocks of social capital that you can draw on in the future (Brown, 2002). This is similarly explored in Coleman's work on social capital (1988) where he theorised that social capital was the unintended outcome of individual action – individuals were driven by self-interest. The outcome of this collectivised self-interest was a social capital that was 'productive, making possible the achievement of certain ends that in its absence would not be possible' (1988, p 98). When the collective self-interest is linked to the self-interest of power holders, the result is greater influence and access to resources for the local community (Beck, 2007).

Conflict

As discussed above, Alinsky's view of society was that there was a power relationship between the haves and the have-nots; any change in this status quo would clearly result in conflict in some form or other. Again this has particular relevance and resonance within our current culture that emphasises partnership and consensus. There is a great fear of conflict, even with those in community development. In the UK an over-emphasis on inclusion and participation has made workers reluctant to act in a way that might cause conflict in the government-sponsored community partnerships they increasingly have to work within, since to do so would jeopardise jobs and future project funding. Alinsky took the contrary view, advocating that organisers should agitate to the point of conflict since it was only at the point of conflict that power was challenged and creative solutions developed.

His thinking on conflict is clearly expressed in his tactics of organising that he codified into his 13 rules, as outlined below:

1. Power is not only what you have but what the enemy thinks you have.
2. Never go outside the experience of your people.
3. Whenever possible, go outside of the experience of the enemy.
4. Make the enemy live up to their own book of rules.
5. Ridicule is man's most potent weapon.
6. A good tactic is one that your people enjoy.
7. A tactic that drags on too long becomes a drag.
8. Keep the pressure on with different tactics and actions, and utilize all events of the period for your purpose.
9. The threat is usually more terrifying than the thing itself.
10. The major premise for tactics is the development of operations that will maintain a constant pressure upon the opposition.
11. If you push a negative hard and deep enough, it will break through into its counterside.
12. The price of a successful attack is a constructive alternative.
13. Pick the target, freeze it, personalize it, and polarize it.

It is important, however, to understand that he envisaged these rules operating in the context of a clear set of values: equality, justice, freedom, peace and a concern for the preciousness of human life, which Alinsky saw as the goal of participative democracy and therefore the organising process. Without an unswerving commitment to these values, the approaches and tactics employed by an Alinsky organiser could easily become a tool for oppression in the hands of despots.

Alinsky was scathing in his criticism of people who he described as 'the do-nothings', who, from a position of comfort and security, moralised about the ethics of action while claiming a commitment to the ends of social change but doing nothing. Again this echoes Freire's (1972) statement that to do nothing was to side with the oppressor. Alinsky describes it in more graphic terms. 'Liberals in their meetings utter bold words; they strut, grimace belligerently, and then issue a weasel-worded statement "which has tremendous implications, if read between the lines." They sit calmly, dispassionately, studying the issue; judging both sides; they sit and still sit' (Alinsky, 1971, p 4). Alinsky's viewpoint is ably summed up in his rules pertaining to the ethics of means and ends (1971, pp 37-51):

1. One's concern with the ethics of means and ends varies inversely with one's personal interest in the issue.
2. The judgment of the ethics of means is dependent upon the political position of those sitting in judgment.
3. In war the end justifies almost any means.
4. Judgment must be made in the context of the times in which the action occurred and not from any other chronological vantage point.
5. Concern with ethics increases with the number of means available and vice versa.
6. The less important the end to be desired, the more one can afford to engage in ethical evaluations of means.
7. Generally, success or failure is a mighty determinant of ethics.
8. The morality of means depends upon whether the means is being employed at a time of imminent defeat or imminent victory.
9. Any effective means is automatically judged by the opposition to be unethical.
10. You do what you can with what you have and clothe it in moral garments.
11. Goals must be phrased in general terms like "Liberty, Equality, Fraternity, and Of the Common Welfare, Pursuit of Happiness, or Bread and Peace."12.

Compromise

Despite his emphasis on power and conflict, Alinsky saw compromise as a central strategy of the organising process – when developing an issue it was important to express it in terms of the community being 100 per cent right and the enemy being 100 per cent wrong. People would not be prepared to sacrifice time and energy for something that was not life or death, win or lose, all or nothing; however, the reality is that very few issues are 'black-and-white'. As he said, 'If you start with nothing, demand 100 per cent, then compromise for 30 per cent, you're 30 per cent ahead' (Alinsky, 1971, p 61).

The process

> Change comes from power, and power comes from organization. In order to act, people must get together. (Alinsky, 1971, p 100)

Organisers

Community organisers are at the heart of the Alinsky model. As previously discussed, they are generally from outside the community, which gives them the space and objectivity to be able to initiate action. It must be stressed again that the ongoing success of the organisation is based on the development of a strong network of local leaders who are organically embedded within their community. If this does not happen, the organisation will be dependent on the organiser and will ultimately fail. However, in the early stages process they have a key role. They must shake up the prevailing patterns of people's lives – 'agitate, create disenchantment and discontent with the current values, to produce, if not a passion for change, at least a passive, affirmative, non-challenging climate' (Alinsky, 1971, p 14).

Formal and informal training for organisers has always been a key feature of the community organising process. In 1969 Alinsky formalised training for community organisers through the IAF Training Institute, which he called a 'school for professional radicals'. The IAF currently runs a range of training programmes including 10 leadership courses and 90-day internships.

Characteristics of a community organiser

Alinsky described in detail the various characteristics that must be possessed by these exceptional people:

Curiosity: they are constantly curious about the way things are and how things could be different. They are also the provokers of curiosity in others; "for a people asking 'why' are beginning to rebel" (p 71).

Irreverence: they have a profound dissatisfaction with dogma and all repressive ideas and practices. This attitude is rooted in a deep reverence for the enigma of life, and an incessant search for its meaning.

Imagination: they have the ability both to imagine a better future and to enter into the experience of other people. It is important to understand the experience of community and also to understand the experience of the enemy, thereby being able to anticipate their actions and reactions.

A sense of humour: they have the ability to recognise and come to terms with the contradictions in the world. It is also an invaluable tool in the hands of the organiser since satire and ridicule are potent weapons in the organiser's armoury. It also helps the organiser keep a balanced sense of who they are.

A bit of a blurred vision of a better world: they have the ability to see how small actions and projects link into broader movements for social change.

An organised personality: within the chaotic and multi-issue context of community organising, the organiser must be both reflective and reflexive; "constant examination of life and of himself he finds himself becoming more and more of an organized personality" (p 75).

A well-integrated political schizoid: one part in the arena of action where he polarizes the issue to 100 to nothing, and helps to lead his forces into conflict, while the other part knows that when the time comes for negotiations that it really is only a 10 per cent difference – and yet both parts have to live comfortably with each other. "Only a well-organized person can split and yet stay together. But this is what the organiser must do" (p 75).

- Ego: "unreserved confidence in one's ability to do what he believes must be done"(p 76).

A free and open mind and political relativity: recognising the values are relative and being secure in one's own identity in a world of uncertainties; a flexible personality adapts well to changing circumstances.

Constantly creating the new from the old: recognising that new ideas arise from conflict, they use each situation as an opportunity to create power. This creative urge is the mainspring of the organiser's personality. In his constant striving for the new, he finds that he cannot endure what is repetitive and unchanging. "For him hell would be doing the same thing over and over again" (p 76).

Von Hoffman (2010, p 21) points out that 'the gifted outside organisers do have advantages. They come with fresh eyes and new ideas, enabling them to see possibilities those already there may not realise. They can bring hope and excitement because they are not like the people they have come to organise.'

Issues

As the organisation is beginning to build, the next key element of the organising process is choosing the issue that they will initially take on. Not every problem that exists in a community or that has an impact from outside is construed to be an issue in community organising terms. Bobo, Kendall and Max (1990, p 28) outline comprehensive criteria for deciding on an issue that will form the basis of community organising and action:

1. The issue meets the principles of direct action organising – that is, it leads to a real difference in people's everyday lives, it gives people a sense of their own power, and it changes the relations of power.
2. The issue is worthwhile, widely and deeply felt, non-divisive, and consistent with the organization's values and vision. Many

people in your constituency must find it important enough to take some action on it.

3. The issue suggests clear demands. The changes you propose address the negative conditions you've identified.

4. The issue is winnable. You have determined the likelihood of getting your solutions adopted by a particular agency or institution; precedents in other places, the affordability of your plan, the strength of your legal arguments, a clear strategy, or some other advantage raises your chances of winning.

5. The issue is easy to understand. The common rule is that you should be able to explain it in one paragraph on a flyer.

6. The issue has a clear target. In organizing, the target is always an individual who can agree to meet your demands.

7. The issue has a clear time frame that works for you. Issue campaigns, like good novels or movies, should have a beginning, middle, and end, and you should know roughly how long each of those phases will last.

8. The issue gives you opportunities to build leadership. An issue campaign should have many roles for people to play because the issue itself lends itself to many different creative tactics. For example, an issue that can be won only through a lawsuit is not the kind that builds leadership, as the key decision-making and negotiation roles tend to be limited to lawyers and judges.

9. The issue sets up your organization to tackle additional and related issues. The issue should help build a track record, a base of people and knowledge that the organization can easily transfer to other arenas.

Leadership

For the organising process to work, the organiser must identify local leaders. These are people who, although they may have no formal title or role, are in contact with people and have an influence on them. It is they who will engage small groups of people in conversations, get their ideas, enlist their support and feed all of that information back into the organisation. Alinsky (1989) observed that, with few exceptions, real local leaders were completely unknown outside of the community. They must be discovered by participating in informal situations, and being constantly alert to every word or gesture, which would both identify and raise the role of certain individuals within the community, for it was these people who would develop participation within the community and who would ensure both the power and the relevance of the action. In contrast, Alinsky critiqued approaches to regeneration where professionals decided what was to be done for underprivileged areas without any real participation by or even sustained consultation with the people of the area. He believed this approach to be fundamentally authoritarian and undemocratic, not leading to sustainable social change.

Local leadership would be consistently and systematically developed as an integral part of the community organising process. Local leaders would be given roles and responsibilities that would increase as they grew in experience and confidence. All action would be planned and reviewed; within this process leaders could review their own performance and enhance their thinking and practice.

Communication

> One can lack any of the qualities of an organiser – with one exception – and still be effective and successful. That exception is the art of communication. (Alinsky, 1971, p 77)

Communication is only effective when you speak within the experience of the people. It is a two-way process and therefore the organiser needs to understand the experience of people through dialogue. In order to communicate for persuasion it is imperative to understand the person's main values or goals and couch your discussion in terms that relate directly to them. Otherwise there is no point of connection between what you say and what the other person wants. Alinsky illustrated this point with the following anecdote:

> I walked around, trying to give the ten-dollar bill away. The reactions were all "within the experiences of the people." About three of them, seeing the ten-dollar bill, spoke first – "I'm sorry. I don't have any change." Others hurried past saying, "I'm sorry, I don't have any money on me right now," as though I had been trying to get money from them instead of trying to give them money. One young woman flared up, almost screaming, "I'm not that kind of a girl and if you don't get away from here, I'll call a cop!" Another woman in her thirties snarled, "I don't come that cheap!" There was one man who stopped and said, "What kind of a con game is this?" and then walked away. Most of the people responded with shock, confusion, and silence, and they quickened their pace and sort of walked around me. (Alinsky, 1971, p 82)

This is an important observation in our contemporary world where approaches to health improvement, education and so on seem predicated on the idea that all people lack is the facts. If, however, our messages do not speak to people's culture, experience and self-interest, the message will simply not be heard, first, due to internal issues – self-belief (for example, self-efficacy, self-esteem, locus of control) has been shown to be closely related to adoption/adherence to physical activities and healthy eating behaviours (Briggs et al, 2003, p 342), and second, for example, there is no point telling someone they should go to the gym because it's good for their health if they have never been – if it is not part of their cultural norm their friends would just laugh at them.

As with all aspects of the Alinsky approach, communication is also a value-driven practice, not merely adherence to a set of techniques. His methods of communication were in line with the attributes of participatory communication models, as outlined by Singhal (2001, p 12):

- The participation communication model begins with a belief in the potential of people. Everyone has the right and duty to influence decision making and to understand the results.
- The participatory communication model recognizes, understands, and appreciates the diversity and plurality of people. It believes in upholding and enhancing the dignity and equality of people. Ordinary people are viewed as the key agents of change, and hence their aspirations and strengths are engaged in culturally appropriate ways.
- The participatory communication model emphasizes the local community rather than the nation state, dialogue rather than monologue, and emancipation rather than alienation.
- The participatory communication model emphasizes the strengthening of democratic processes and institutions at the community level, and a redistribution of power.
- The participatory communication model recognizes that authentic participation, while widely espoused, is not in everyone's interest, especially those vested in guarding their privileged positions, that is, the elite.
- The participatory communication model also recognizes that participatory programs are not easily implemented or replicated, nor are they highly predictable, or readily controlled.

This intention to communicate within the experience of the audience works both within the organisation itself and with the various stakeholders and influencers with whom the organisation must work.

Internally, communication works through a network of formal and informal leaders:

> In community organizing, communication at the individual, group and official levels is understood to be central to the individual sense of ownership and is practiced in face-to-face meetings, group (or house) meetings, large assemblies and informal communication between meetings. These are organized by leaders and the organiser. (Bischof, 2009)

Externally, communication needs to be targeted and focused, recognising the language and concern of the various audiences who will hear the message:

> Message development is a matter of polarizing the issue, speaking to shared values, and maintaining discipline. One should not underestimate the power of a well-stated, strategic message to redefine the debate. Every media campaign has two targets, one being the institutions of power and their power brokers, who should be challenged and exposed, the other being the people whom progressives want to win over to their side. The message should put pressure on the power brokers but be directed toward the sympathies of the people. From one strategic message, people should be able to figure out exactly what happened and what the proposed solution is. This message should always be grounded in issue development and in campaign goals. (Sen, 2003, p 155)

Research, action, evaluation

According to Ed Chambers (2010, p 82), 'IAF organizations understand the digested actions are worth more than a University degree because they result in social knowledge.' This process of grounded learning, learning that takes place in the context of action, has always been a major feature of the organising process. Chambers identifies three phases in that process: research, action and evaluation.

The research process begins with an internal power analysis. This phase consists of a process whereby relational and small group meetings identify winnable issues, assess whether the organisation has the internal capacity to work on those issues and consider whether or not the action will build the organisation. Following on from this an external power analysis is carried out. In this key decision makers are identified and opposition and support is assessed.

Building from the research process, the action phase mobilises the community to personalise and polarise the issue. Chambers likens this action to a public drama. First, rather than nameless organisations, individuals are identified and held to account. Second, the issue is polarised. This means creating public tension around an issue by confronting the target with a large, diverse, disciplined crowd that expects the individual to respond favourably to their proposals (2010, p 85). In all of this people are assigned roles that both recognise their capacity and talents and stretch their limitations.

Finally, all action must be evaluated. Within this process participants discuss their feelings, analyse their behaviour and analyse the behaviour of their opposition. Questions such as 'Was there an exchange of power?' 'What did we do well?' 'What did we learn from them?' 'Did we have the right research?' 'What we do now?' (Chambers, 2010, p 87) all ensure that the action is analysed, social knowledge is produced and a clear rationale for future action is established.

Critiques

Many critiques have been levelled at the Alinsky approach to community organising and these have contributed to the development of practice that can be seen in the world today.

Social capital

Alinsky's approach was to build an organisation of organisations, which would include churches, trades unions and other associations. However, we know, from the work of Robert Putnam and others, that there has been a dramatic decline in the membership of exactly the type of organisations to which Alinsky referred. This therefore calls into question both the effectiveness and legitimacy of Alinsky's approach.

McGaffey and Khalil (2005, p 5) suggest that 'New strategies must stress an organizing process that enhances and builds community, and that focuses on developing a neighborhood's own capacities to do for itself what outsiders will or can no longer do. Taking neighborhoods seriously in their current condition means building social, political, and economic structures at the local level that recreate a space for these people to act and decide, challenging the internalized oppression that the system depends upon.'

Politics of place

Given Alinsky's simple, polarised typology of the internal neighbourhood and the external enemy, and the centrality of winnable local issues, structural issues are both unseen and unaddressed. For example, structural issues of 'race' and gender, that do not lend themselves to winnable issues in Alinsky's terms, get left off the agenda.

Feminism

Despite a rich and proud heritage of female organisers and movement leaders, the field of community organisation, in both its teaching models and its major exponents, has been a male-dominated preserve, where, even though values are expressed in terms of participatory democracy, much of the focus within the dominant practice methods has been non-supportive or antithetical to feminism. Strategies have largely been based on 'macho-power' models, manipulativeness and zero-sum gamesmanship (Weil, 1986, p 192).

It has been suggested that Alinsky's use of conflict as a primary method of organising was antithetical to feminist approaches based on models of cooperation. Feminists argue that women-centred organising is not motivated primarily by self-interest, an idea that was paramount in Alinsky's theory, but by compassionate sympathy for vulnerable members of the target community and the community as a whole (Sen, 2003, p Iiv).

Women don't participate for the sake of their own good....They wish to see the social environment improved to realize social justice.... They have a merciful heart that sustains participation. The seed of revolution inside is not violence but a kind of humanism. (Suet–Lin and Kwok–Kin, 2010, p 430)

A focus on the public rather than private sphere ignores the contribution of women in the organising process which includes processes of building, nurturing and compassionate relationships among participants and offering learning opportunities (Stoecker and Stall, 1997).

Sen (2003) highlights four area of critique from the feminist perspective: community organising over-emphasises intervention in the public sphere, it does not allow organisers to balance work and family, it focuses on narrow self-interest as the primary motivator and relies on conflict and militaristic tactics.

From this critique rises a model of practice that is typified by peace, empowerment and respect, where power is shared through inclusion, consensus-building and skills development which validates women's experiences and embraces diversity (PACSW, 2012). This model of organising claims a history of success which has challenged and changed both private and public gender relationships, having an impact on women's healthcare and women's knowledge of their own bodies, cultural practices around dating and relationships and the relationship between work and family; these continue to have a transforming affect in society (Stoecker and Stall, 1997). This work is being continued through organisations such as PILOT in Chicago whose mission is 'to strengthen the voice of parents in communities in order to create and build more family friendly, family supportive communities' (Smock, 2004, p 26).

Pluralism

Alinsky could be described as adopting a pluralist approach to community organising. This approach that is common to a range of community development practices across the world has been widely criticised. Ledwith (2011) describes this approach as having at its base an understanding of community as a range of power bases mediated by the state. Within this, community development is a force for amelioration, achieving change at the level of the neighbourhood and bringing about piecemeal reforms. Since the gains of one group are at the expense of other, less well-organised sections of the community, this approach is critiqued as having a zero-sum gain in terms of developing community power.

Critical analysis

It is argued that Alinsky's action-focused approach to organising, even though it had a central role for training and evaluation, had little space for the type of critical reflection that sited action within a broader analysis and critique of society. We explore this critique in more depth when we discuss Freire's possible contribution to community organising's thinking and practice in Chapter Ten.

Multiculturalism

Traditional community organisations reflect the inequality of wider society by the dominance of white males in their power structures. They are also often reluctant to go after issues around 'race' that might divide communities, preferring to go for winnable goals that have cross-community support. Calpotura and Fellner (1996), however, made a plea for multicultural organising that would include practice that was specifically anti-racist, anti-sexist and anti-homophobic. In their view the primary goal of community organising should be the development of equitable, multicultural communities. For this they called for the deployment of a wider range of approaches, practices and techniques than had been customarily seen in traditional community organising.

Rinku Sen is critical of community organising that does not take account of the cultural sensitivities of sections of the community, resulting in them being effectively excluded for the organising processes. She states that, 'many of the rules of community organizing run counter to the political traditions, cultures and realities of communities of color' (2003, p li).

Conclusion

The person, practice and ideas of Saul Alinsky remain influential in development practice across the world. The man and his ideas remain controversial, but as he himself said, all issues and all change are controversial. And Alinsky is still able to stir up trouble, as seen in the reaction of the right wing in the US to Barack Obama's presidential campaign and Obama's links to community organising.

Alinsky's legacy is not a uniform approach. Rather, the thinking and practice is dynamic, adapting to history and culture as they should since this is a practice rooted in the experience and the aspirations of people. And yet the central ideas remain true. As we will see, the experience and the opportunities of poor people around the world are greatly enhanced if they are organised. The power that comes from such organisations enables marginalised voices to be heard and a place at the table found for those who have been excluded. Although the emphasis will change from context to context (some more about conflict and others about partnership, some more centrally organised and some organic), the central aim remains constant. Practitioners, organisers and local leaders are all working towards one goal, and that is, a more just world.

TWO

The 21st-century context of community organising

Vision without action is merely a dream
Action without vision just passes the time
Vision with action can change the world. (Joel Barker)

It is now more than a generation since Saul Alinsky developed his model of community organising focused on developing leaders, building organisations and claiming local power. One of the key themes of this book is to ask how far the community organising model has evolved over the years to take on board changing perspectives on development practice. We now accept that we are living in a globalised world and that ultimately our futures are linked together. This is a long way from a world where the focus of development work could be limited to what happened in one ghetto in one city. We now know that the global affects the local, and global perspectives and lessons from elsewhere must inform what we do. Indeed, the basic ideas of community organising have been taken up, explicitly or otherwise, and adapted to a variety of contexts in many countries outside of North America.

As well as specific local and global development goals, development practice is now informed by the ideas of fundamental rights and sustainability, by quasi-technical concepts around capacity building, social capital creation and developing capability. In addition, many practitioners are also thinking about seemingly more esoteric, but actually fundamentally important, ideas around human needs, quality of life, wellbeing and happiness.

This chapter briefly outlines these basic issues and ideas, which are used to provide a context from which to consider the relevance of the original community organising model. The case studies later in the book provide practice examples on how far the ideas and practice of community organising have responded to these broader agendas. (See Chapter Nine for a discussion on how successful the community organisations have been in delivering on these agendas.)

Current issues: global and local

According to the United Nations Development Programme (UNDP 2006), around 1.2 billion people in the world go to sleep at night hungry; 70 per cent of these people are women and children. A similar number of people do not have access to minimum standards of sanitation and clean drinking water. Over 500,000 women die at childbirth or within six weeks of delivery. Children, especially girls, born into poverty are likely to drop out of school or leave without basic literacy and numeracy.

To try and make more progress on development issues world leaders agreed at the UN Millennium Summit meeting in September 2000 to a series of development goals, to be achieved by 2015, to tackle world poverty through specific actions. The UN believes that if these Millennium Development Goals (MDGs) were to be achieved, poverty levels would be cut by 50 per cent. Eight of the MDGs are outlined in Box 2.1, that in turn are broken down into 21 quantifiable targets and 60 indicators (for more details see www.undp.org/mdg/basics.shtml).

Progress on the MDGs has been patchy to date. Although the numbers in absolute poverty are falling, as China, India and Brazil are continuing to develop their economies, in terms of decreasing hunger, improving access to health and education and helping mothers and children, little overall progress is being achieved.

Any community organisation in the developing world, and the poorer parts of the developed world, are likely to be concerned, directly or indirectly, with some or all of the MDGs. One of the assessments of the effectiveness of community organisations is how far they have taken on this agenda, and what they are delivering locally. Some of the key issues within the MDGs are explored in more detail later in this chapter.

Urban development and global slums

The MDGs exist in the context of rapid global urbanisation. At the time of writing (2012) the world population is in excess of seven billion. In order to understand what this might mean we need to break down the distribution of the world population into understandable categories. The University of Wisconsin – Green Bay (Erickson and Vonk, 2006) suggest that the composition of the world population may look as shown in Table 2.1.

Of this seven billion, over 50 per cent currently live in cities, and increasingly in sprawling mega-cities. The UN Population Fund (UNFPA, 2007) calculated that 93 per cent of urban growth was in the developing world, driven forward by continued high rates of migration from the countryside. No one really knows the exact populations of the mega-cities in the developing world, and there are competing definitions of where to draw the city boundaries to attempt to make such a calculation: on its administrative boundary, its urban sprawl or the metropolitan travel-to-work area? The exact number of people living in the mega-cities does not really matter; what is important is the general size of the urban area. To illustrate the current state of urban development, Table 2.2 shows the figures of the largest 20 metro areas ranked to the nearest million (although please note that the figures are drawn from various sources and should only be taken as a general guide).

Box 2.1: UN Millennium Goals

Goal 1: Eradicate extreme poverty and hunger
- Reduce by half the proportion of people whose income is less than US$1 a day.
- Reduce by half the proportion of people who suffer from hunger.

Goal 2: Achieve universal primary education
- Ensure that all boys and girls complete a full course of primary schooling.

Goal 3: Promote gender equality and empower women
- Eliminate gender disparity in primary and secondary education, preferably by 2005, and in all levels of education no later than 2015.

Goal 4: Reduce child mortality
- Reduce by two thirds the mortality of children under-five.

Goal 5: Improve maternal health
- Reduce maternal mortality by three quarters.

Goal 6: Combat HIV/AIDS, malaria and other diseases
- Halt and reverse the spread of HIV/AIDS.
- Halt and reverse the incidence of malaria and other major diseases.

Goal 7: Ensure environmental sustainability
- Integrate principles of sustainable development into country policies and programmes; reverse the loss of environmental resources.
- Halve the proportion of people without access to safe drinking water and basic sanitation.
- Improve the lives of at least 100 million slum dwellers by 2020.

Goal 8: Develop a global partnership for development
- Develop further an open, rule-based, predictable, non-discriminatory trading and financial system.
- Address special needs of the least developed countries, landlocked countries and small island developing states.
- Deal with developing countries' debt.
- In cooperation with developing countries, develop and implement strategies for decent work for youth.
- In cooperation with the private sector, make available the benefits of new technologies, especially information and communications.

Source: UNPD (2012)

Table 2.1: Possible/projected composition of the world population, 2013

50% would be female 50% would be male 20% would be children 14% would be 65 years and older	61% would be Asian 12% would be European 13% would be African 14% would come from the Western Hemisphere	31% would be Christians 21% would be Muslims 14% would be Hindus 6% would be Buddhists 12% would practice other religions 16% would not be aligned with a religion
17% would speak a Chinese dialect 8% would speak Hindustani 8% would speak English 7% would speak Spanish 4% would speak Arabic 4% would speak Russian 52% would speak other languages	82% would be able to read and write; 18% would not 1% would have a college education 1% would own a computer	75% would have some supply of food and a place to shelter them from the wind and the rain; 25% would not 1% would be dying of starvation 17% would be undernourished 15% would be overweight 83% would have access to safe drinking water; 17% would not

Source: Based on Erickson and Vonk (2006)

In Western cities there are adequate financial and organisational resources to manage urban growth, but in developing countries this is less so. The exception is China, and to a lesser extent India, where considerable amounts of money are being invested in urban development. In many of the mega-cities basic services are not adequately reaching poorer communities. Clean drinking water, sewerage disposal, affordable housing, employment opportunities, health, schooling and welfare provision all fall short of what is required. The result of inadequate planning and investment is the growth of mega-slums as the urban populations continue to expand.

The UN define 'a slum' as an area where the residents are missing durable walls on their dwelling, a secure lease or title to their home, adequate living space, access to clean drinking water and sanitation. Many people living in slums are in work but simply cannot afford anywhere better to live. Many slums are now so large that they have their own local economy, often providing work in recycling or simple manufacture, and basic services (for example, food and recreation).

The UN Habitat report (2008) comments that in the last decade, 125 million people have escaped from living in slums partly due to urban redevelopment, but mainly from their own increases in income. But the UN estimate that the total slum population has increased by 55 million over the decade, and there are now around 830 million slum dwellers in the world.

Mike Davis (2007, p 28) estimated from various sources the following league table of slums (a further 20 slums are listed in addition to Table 2.3, with populations in excess of 5,000,000).

What should be done about the prevalence and growth of mega-slums, or more realistically, what can be done? Davis is critical of the failure of both international institutions (the International Monetary Fund, The World Bank, for example) and national governments to seriously attack the problem, relying instead on the supposed 'trickle-down' effects from general economic growth. Non-governmental organisations (NGOs) have a role here, and Davis is equally scathing about their approach and performance.

Davis cites John Turner (1976) and what he calls the 'amalgam of anarchism and neoliberalism' (page 72) as the new orthodoxy for urban development. The argument was that the traditional blitz and rebuild strategy had not worked as it simply moved the poor to new locations while the construction industry got rich. Turner argued that it was no longer the responsibility of government and top-down urban redevelopment programmes to solve the slum problem. The solution lay with the people in the slum, and for them to recognise the functionality and development potential within the slums themselves.

A major plank of Turner's argument was the importance of land ownership. Most people living in slums did not have the title deeds to their home, usually because they were built informally on what was marginal land. Turner argued that with the rapid increase in land prices as the city expanded, ownership of even a small piece of land was an

Table 2.2: Largest urban agglomerations

City	Population (millions)	Country
Tokyo	37	Japan
Delhi	22	India
Mexico City	20	Mexico
New York – Newark	20	USA
Sao Paulo	19	Brazil
Shanghai	19	China
Mumbai	19	India
Beijing	15	China
Dhaka	15	Bangladesh
Kolkata	14	India
Karachi	13	Pakistan
Buenos Aires	13	Argentina

Source: United Nations Department of Economic and Social Affairs (2012)

Table 2.3: Slum populations, selected countries

Country	Estimated slum population (millions)	% of urban population
Angola	4	86
China	174	33
Democratic Republic of Congo	14	76
India	110	35
Laos	1	79
Nigeria	42	66
Pakistan	26	47
Phillipines	23	44
Peru	7	36
South Africa	8	29

Source UN Habitat (2009)

economic asset if systems could be found to realise it. Therefore, one of the main campaigns must be to grant title deeds to slum residents. At another level this was an important development as in many regeneration programmes the government refused to rehouse those (the majority) who did not have title deeds to their homes on the grounds they should not have been living there in the first place.

It is hard to sort out the ideology from the pragmatism and abdication of state responsibility here, but the UN and The World Bank took up the idea. Put simply, the role of development agencies was to help the poor to help themselves. With some assistance people could improve their own homes, local projects could deal with sanitation and improve access to local services (health, schooling), and the local slum economy could grow to improve standards of living.

This sounds like a fertile environment for NGOs to make a difference. However, there are problems in this approach – as well-funded international NGOs move into an area, the local organisations may become marginalised or co-opted. Local leaders may be recruited by the major international NGOs and the local NGOs become starved of funding and expertise, with political opposition neutralised by the movement towards partnership development. In some cases, Davis argues, it is less the case of local empowerment and more an influx of soft imperialism, the lesson for local people being that nothing can be done unless an international NGO is present.

There is some truth to these criticisms, although clearly NGOs do have positive impacts in the slum areas. The broader question is how any approach, whether it be top-down regeneration, international NGOs or local organisations, can turn around the lives of half a million people in a single community. In the truly mega-slums the problem may now be out of control and beyond any attempt to effectively change the situation for the majority of residents.

How relevant are community organisations in this debate? Are they simply a variant of the NGOs working away in their own corner of the slum, or do they bring something new to the table? One of the emerging issues within the slums is the nature of power. Who represents the residents within the slums – is it the formal political structure, NGOs acting as intermediaries, left-leaning social movements, functional organisations (for example, small traders, rag pickers) or emerging local representative organisations? Community organisations, with their core belief in local people claiming power, should have a contribution to make here. These questions are picked up in the discussion of SDI and the India and Cambodia case studies later in the book (Chapter Six).

Sustainability

It is now generally agreed by development agencies that all development should be inherently sustainable, that is, seeing economic and social development within an environmental framework that conserves resources and is carbon neutral. The UN General Assembly (UNGA, 1987) defined the challenge thus: 'sustainable development is development that meets the needs of the present without compromising the ability of future generations to meet their own needs.'

Exploring the concept of sustainability in more detail produces a number of key areas for attention. A possible classification for the urban communities under discussion in this book could be:

- reducing consumption of luxury goods, air travel and carbon-based ground transport, energy and manufacturing processes
- recognising the 'carrying capacity' of the planet and the need for individuals and cities to reduce their ecological footprint and to improve recycling
- conserving and improving fresh water and land use; effectively dealing with waste products
- moving to healthy diets
- promoting peace, security and social justice
- rebuilding the relationship between people and the environment, so that we see ourselves as living in the environment rather than separate from it
- poverty reduction.

Figure 2.1 shows the interrelationships between these social, economic and environmental factors.

These raise the question of what MDGs mean for poor people in mega-cities and marginalised communities elsewhere. It is generally accepted that the MDGs

Figure 2.1: Environmental and economic factors

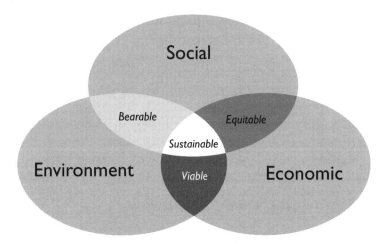

have to be delivered within this interdependent framework, but how do you move to effectively implement such programmes in a city of 10 million people? And how do you do this in a slum of half a million? The environmental footprint of slum dwellers is usually considerably less than that of the middle classes who may be living nearby. Simply increasing income to end poverty (the traditional economic growth solution) is likely to make the environmental situation worse as increased income leads to higher consumption of manufactured goods.

The World Bank Development Report (2010) suggests that it is possible to reduce poverty and to promote sustainability. The report proposes that we 'Act now, act together and act differently'. Success, the report argues, is tied to an effective climate change deal, the shift of public opinion so that individuals act in more environmentally conscious ways, and the reform of public policy and programmes. This approach is certainly aspirational, but it lacks hard policy for implementation. In any case it is difficult to see how the demand for consumer goods, produced by an expanding globalised economy, is going to decrease.

Figure 2.2, taken from the Global Footprint Network (2008), maps the ecological footprint of countries against the Human Development Index (HDI). The ideal is expressed as a society that meets both the baseline for high human development and that sits below the ecological capacity limit. Only Cuba meets both criteria. This is a challenging finding given that Cuba is effectively a single

Figure 2.2: Human welfare and ecological footprints compared

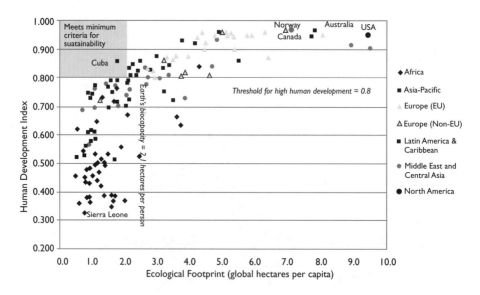

Source: Global Footprint Network (2008); UN Human Development Index 2007/08

party dictatorship with a poor human rights record and a relatively low level of income (per capita income in 2010 was US$4,500).

How far do the activities of community organisations attempt to promote the agenda of balancing human development with sustainability? Or are community organisations primarily concerned with meeting the immediate issues of poor communities, such as housing, employment, potable water and sanitation? A broader view of these questions will, of course, include questions of sustainability, but this can appear somewhat esoteric when you are living in a slum.

Building capacity, capability and needs

Community capacity

Originally promoted by the World Bank, community capacity is something that almost all development agencies and many governments now see as a prime objective. It is, however, a contested and confused concept. The underpinning idea of capacity building is that individuals and community organisations often inhibit development potential by not having the necessary skills and experience to undertake the tasks required for development. This raises a number of questions – for example, building capacity for what purpose? Which skills are required? How will they be delivered? Are local people/organisations passive recipients of prescribed training programmes or active developers of training? Who decides on these questions? From what perspective? Informed by what values?

As might be expected, local practice for capacity building varies considerably. To take examples from within Scotland, one local authority identified first aid training as a capacity building priority, another saw training volunteers to take pre-defined roles in local partnerships as the priority, and in a third area, the capacity training team were offering a range of pre-written training programmes. All these providers claim that their capacity building programme promotes individual and community empowerment, but with offering predetermined training it is hard to see how this is the case in any significant way. As Tedmanson (2005) suggests, implicit in this approach is 'an entrenchment of notions of what constitutes capacity, who defines capacity and what constitutes the relationship between the dominant culture *capacity-builders* and those identified as *capacity deficient*.'

The UNPD (2009) differentiates between capacity development and capacity building. In their view, capacity development is based on building out from existing skills, experience, organisation and capability. In contrast, capacity building assumes a minimal starting point of skills and experience. The UN talks about the latter approach being appropriate in post-disaster situations where existing capacity has indeed been wiped out. In Scotland for example (and no doubt elsewhere; see, for example, Craig, 2007), the implicit assumption can be that either local people do not know very much, or that they need to be retrained to fit the policies and priorities of the local authority. In either case, the capacity building programme operates on a deficit model, and existing skills and knowledge of people is often undervalued or simply ignored.

In contrast, the UNDP comment,

> Capacity development is seen as a long term effort that needs to be embedded in broader change processes that are owned and driven by those involved, that are context specific and that are as much about changing values and mindsets through incentives, as they are about acquiring new skills and knowledge
>
> While external actors may be able to facilitate and promote local processes, they can also serve to undermine ownership and local capacity. External actors may pay careful attention to play a more facilitative role related to the management of change processes, rather than a more interventionist role that has been played in the past' (UNPD, 2009, p 5).

In working through this more sophisticated view of capacity development, the UNPD identifies three levels of activity (2009, p 8):

- Enabling environment: the broader system within which individuals and organizations function and one that facilitates or hampers their existence and performance. This level of capacity is not easy to grasp tangibly, but it is central to the understanding of capacity issues. They determine the "rules of the game" for interaction between and among organisations. Capacities at the level of the enabling environment include policies, legislation, power relations and social norms, all of which govern the mandates, priorities, modes of operation and civic engagement across different parts of society.
- Organisational level: the internal policies, arrangements, procedures and frameworks that allow an organisation to operate and deliver on its mandate, and that enable the coming together of individual capacities to work together and achieve goals. If these exist, are well resourced and well aligned, the capability of an organisation to perform will be greater than that of the sum of its parts.
- Individual level: skills, experience and knowledge that are vested in people. Each person is endowed with a mix of capacities that allows them to perform, whether at home, at work or in society at large. Some of these are acquired through formal training and education, others through learning by doing and experience.

This is a more rounded and thought-out approach to capacity building and acknowledges the complexity of effective development activity, in particular, the requirement for an enabling environment. For social progress to be made, action needs to be taken on all three fronts. Simply training people and slotting them into pre-defined roles can only have limited value.

Capability

An alternative way of considering capacity development is through increasing individual and community capability. The idea of capability has been derived from that of human capital (see, for example, Becker, 1976) as an aid to increasing production. Briefly, capability can be described as developing knowledge, building collaboration between people, improving processes to develop knowledge and build collaboration, increasing motivation.

The welfare economist Amartya Sen (1985, 2001) evolved the ideas of human capital into capability. In Sen's view, people needed not only to develop their skills and ability (their functioning), but also to have the freedom and opportunity to apply these abilities. An individual's quality of life depended on realising what they had the potential do in terms of employment, developing social relationships and so on. The outcomes from this were partly determined by motivation and opportunity to act, or in Sen's term, agency.

The idea of capability comes from a free market position, so it is not surprising that its advocates argue that people who live in a free society have a range of personal choices that can maximise their opportunities to make a better life. Freedom in society comes in two basic forms: negative and positive. Negative freedom is based on minimal state intervention, whereas positive freedom implies an active state involved in social and economic change to improve the life of its citizens. Positive freedom can be enacted in various ways, from state encouragement for people to act compared to state prohibition and direct mobilisation. The more people live in a controlled society, the less the potential outcomes for their life.

For Sen, improved quality of life therefore came from increasing capability, better functioning and improved human agency, the potential for which was increased by a positive free environment. These ideas are currently very influential in policy terms and have been adopted by the UN and form the basis for the HDI.

In an attempt to operationalise these ideas, Martha Nussbaum (2000) identified 10 capabilities that should be fundamental to all societies:

- Life: being able to live to the end of natural life
- Bodily health: enjoying good health, an adequate diet, having adequate shelter
- Bodily integrity: freedom of movement, freedom from physical harm, choice over sexual activity and reproduction
- Senses, imagination and thought: access to education, religious freedom, cultural freedom
- Emotions: to love and care without freedom or anxiety
- Practical reason: thinking through and taking control of your life

- Affiliation:
  - being able to recognise and show concern for other humans
  - having the social bases of self-respect and non-humiliation. This entails provisions of non-discrimination on the basis of 'race', sex, sexual orientation, ethnicity, caste, religion, national origin and species
- Other species: living with concern for and in relation to animals, plants, etc
- Play: being able to laugh, to play, to enjoy recreational activities
- Control over one's environment
- Political: being able to participate effectively in political choices that govern one's life; having the right of political participation, protection of free speech and association
- Material: being able to hold property (both land and movable goods), and having property rights on an equal basis with others; having the right to seek employment on an equal basis with others; having the freedom from unwarranted search and seizure. In work, being able to work as a human, exercising practical reason and entering into meaningful relationships of mutual recognition with other workers.

It is noticeable that the subjects on the above list far exceed the limited and often technical agenda that is the usual fare for capacity building, and to a lesser extent, capacity development. Much of the capability agenda relies on positive action by an effective democratic government and is therefore beyond the scope of community-based organisations to deliver, although they can be campaigning objectives. It does suggest, however, the limits of what can be achieved in communities if the macro conditions are unfavourable to individuals and community organisations being able to work on and implement their desires. Although a challenging agenda, we need to explore how far community organisations can make a significant contribution to extending the capabilities of individuals and organisations.

Human needs

Closely linked with Nussbaum's list is the discussion on human needs. One of the key works in trying to understand human needs and wellbeing is Abraham Maslow's hierarchy of needs (1943) (see Figure 2.3). The most basic levels need to be provided for people to live a satisfying life, and the goal of self-actualisation can only be achieved if the preceding four levels of need have been met; these needs are usually presented as a pyramid.

Although this model may be a useful listing of needs, there are criticisms of expressing needs as a hierarchy, and many people argue that it is ethnocentric by ordering the categories to reflect an overt individualistic society such as the US (Hofstede, 1984). In contrast, Max-Neef (1987) suggested that human needs were interrelated, rather than hierarchical, and built on Maslow's categories to propose a matrix of nine needs, which could be analysed through being, having, doing

Figure 2.3: Maslow's hierachy of needs

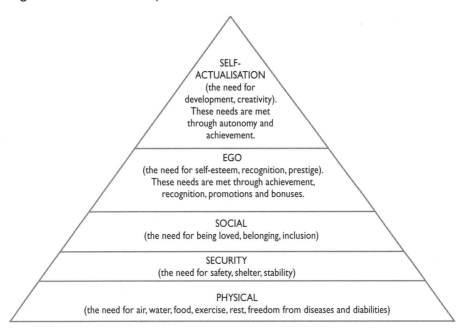

and interacting. He commented that what he called human scale development was a praxis that was,

> ... focused and based on the satisfaction of fundamental human needs, on the generation of growing levels of self-reliance, and on the construction of organic articulations of people with nature and technology, of global processes with local activity, of the personal with the social, of planning with autonomy, and of civil society with the state. (Max-Neef et al, 1987, p 12)

Table 2.4 outlines the Max-Neef model of human scale development.

Quality of life, wellbeing and happiness

Quality of life

Another way of considering human needs is to explore how people define quality of life in their communities. Coming from a health context, this is a difficult concept to nail down, being composed of a range of subjective factors and attempts

Table 2.4: Max-Neef model of human scale development

Fundamental Human Needs	Being (qualities)	Having (things)	Doing (actions)	Interacting (settings)
subsistence	physical and mental health	food, shelter, work	feed, clothe, rest, work	living environment, social setting
protection	care, adaptability, autonomy	social security, health systems, work	cooperate, plan, take care of, help	social environment, dwelling
affection	respect, sense of humour, generosity, sensuality	friendships, family, relationships with nature	share, take care of, make love, express emotions	privacy, intimate spaces of togetherness
understanding	critical capacity, curiosity, intuition	literature, teachers, educational policies	analyse, study, meditate, investigate,	schools, families universities, communities,
participation	receptiveness, dedication, sense of humour	responsibilities, duties, work, rights	cooperate, dissent, express opinions	associations, parties, churches, neighbourhoods
leisure	imagination, tranquillity, spontaneity	games, parties, peace of mind	day-dream, remember, relax, have fun	landscapes, intimate spaces, places to be alone
creation	imagination, boldness, inventiveness, curiosity	abilities, skills, work, techniques	invent, build, design, work, compose, interpret	spaces for expression, workshops, audiences
identity	sense of belonging, self-esteem, consistency	language, religions, work, customs, values, norms	get to know oneself, grow, commit oneself	places one belongs to, everyday settings
freedom	autonomy, passion, self-esteem, open-mindedness	equal rights	dissent, choose, run risks, develop awareness	anywhere

Source: Max-Neef et al (1987)

at statistical analysis – Schalock (2000) identified more than 100 attempts at a definition. One definition focusing on community development (Barr et al, 1996) argued that high quality of life was dependent on the complimentary interaction of economic, social and environmental factors in much the same way as Adams described sustainability above.

A further useful example produced for the Scottish Government (Galloway, 2006), also focusing on the social rather than specific health factors, saw quality of life as the outputs derived from environmental and policy inputs, mediated by individual choices and actions.

Wellbeing

One way of thinking about quality of life is through exploring the questions under the concept of wellbeing. This is mostly a subjective interpretation of personal experience (how we feel about ourselves and our lives), but there are also attempts to produce more objective ways of measuring wellbeing linked to the needs/capability factors discussed above.

Adrian White (2007) produced a meta-study of global data to create an international satisfaction with life index. This study ranked subjective satisfaction with life across 178 countries. The US was ranked 23rd and the UK 41. Although Denmark, Sweden and Austria were in the first three places, countries with lower per capita GDPs ranked highly. For example, Bhutan (see below) was ranked 8th, Costa Rica 13th and Malaysia 17th. What this study illustrates is that simply having more money does not necessarily lead to increased feelings of wellbeing. How much stress, anxiety and uncertainty comes along with the extra income? Acute poverty, however, does not produce high wellbeing scores. What can be concluded from White's work is that once a certain (country and cultural-influenced) level of income is reached and basic needs have been met, social factors have an increasing impact on how people feel about their lives.

For our purposes a more applicable example comes from Med Jones (2006) who identified seven measures of 'wellness'. There are macro indicators to suggest how well a society is, or is not, doing, in promoting the overall wellness of its population. They can, of course, be scaled down to look at particular urban areas, and it would be reasonable to ask how far the work of community organisations has had an impact on these indicators, which are:

• Economic wellness: consumer debt, average income to consumer price index ratio and income distribution
• Environmental wellness: pollution, noise and traffic
• Physical wellness: measurement of physical health metrics such as severe illnesses
• Mental wellness: usage of anti-depressants and rise or decline of psychotherapy patients
• Workplace wellness: job change, workplace complaints and lawsuits

- Social wellness: discrimination, safety, divorce rates, complaints of domestic conflicts and family lawsuits, public lawsuits and crime rates
- Political wellness: quality of local democracy, individual freedom and foreign conflicts.

Happiness

Another way of approaching the question of needs and wellbeing is through happiness. This is generally defined as a mental state of wellbeing and as such is again a subjective entity. However, it is possible to identify indicators to explore how far public policy and the social life of a country leads to increasing or decreasing happiness.

An underpinning area of work is that of the Genuine Progress Index (GPI). This set out to analyse the costs and benefits of social, economic and environmental assets within an area (neighbourhood, city, region or country). One of the main proponents of GPI is Ronald Colman and his work with GPI Atlantic (www.gpiatlantic.org). In this version GPI is split into two parts:

- the development of indicators and measures of progress
- assessments of value for social and environmental assets (human, social and environmental capital).

Examples of assets that are measured by GPI include: time committed to voluntary work, housework and childcare, financial security, income distribution, air and water quality, ecological footprint, carbon emissions, population health, and education attainment. Using such indices it is possible to rethink our view of how well an area is doing, and moves us usefully away from simply measuring economic growth. Although such calculations are for economists to do, not community organisations, the indices used could provide priority areas for community organisations to focus on.

One country that has taken GPI thinking and turned it into a policy framework is Bhutan. Here the national government introduced the concept of Gross National Happiness (GNH). Public policy is tested against GNH in the same way that Western countries use the effects on GDP as a policy determinant. Writing on the application of GNH in Bhutan, Tshoki Zangmo (2008) makes three critical points. First, as discussed above, ever-increasing economic growth does not necessarily lead to an increased sense of personal wellbeing – the use of GNH helps to correct the over-reliance on GDP as it includes the social, economic and spiritual needs of the people. Second, GNH forces policy makers to understand and acknowledge the impact of their proposals on the psychological wellbeing of the population. Third, to operationalise the GNH approach, four broad wellbeing indicators have been identified: life satisfaction, emotional wellbeing, spirituality and stress.

To follow up the GNH policy, population surveys have been undertaken in Bhutan to identify the subjective criteria for a happy life. The top five criteria are:

- Financial security
- Transportation
- Education
- Good health
- Family relationships.

The ranking of criteria is obviously location and culturally dependent, although it is reasonable to expect that financial security, health and relationships will always factor highly. In a mountainous country with few roads like Bhutan, transport will be important. In the Dharavi slum in Mumbai it might be access to drinking water and sanitation. In Bhutan the environment is still largely pristine so this does not rate a mention as it is taken as a given; in other locations it may be a major issue. The important point here is to ask the question and use the results to inform public policy. Community organisations could usefully ask what makes people happy and how this might be achieved in the areas where they work.

Rights, power and asset development

Rights

For Alinsky community organising was in many ways a rights issue. He wanted disadvantaged US citizens to access and implement their rights that were inherent within a democratic society. He believed that unless every citizen had full access to their rights, democracy could fail and be replaced by authoritarianism. This is an important issue for community organising – without an emphasis on human rights, community organising is simply about improving service delivery to poor people.

This view was reflected in the 1998 Oslo report on human development and human rights that concluded,

> ... human development can be seen as practically synonymous with human rights ... the two perspectives focus on the same ends (human life and human dignity) ... on the same processes and key characteristics (people-centred, participatory, equitable, non-discriminatory and empowering). (UNDP, 1998)

Statements of rights come in many forms, and for consistency it is usual to default to the UN for definitions, although even here there is a multiplicity of approaches. These include separate conventions on civil and political rights, economic, social and cultural rights, the rights of the child, against the discrimination of women, against torture and on the status of refugees.

It is sometimes argued that these definitions of rights are based on Western cultural norms that are inappropriate for non-Western societies. This argument is usually promoted by dictatorships and single party states. For example, the former President of China, Jiang Zemin, said, in comparing rights in the US to China, 'the two countries differ in social system, ideology, historical tradition and cultural background, the two countries have different means and ways in realising human rights and fundamental freedoms' (reported in *China Daily*, 28 December 1995). It can also be argued that China has a cultural tradition of obedience to authority, collectivism and family, which, it is claimed in Chinese government circles, is opposed to the 'Western' ideals of individual freedom and tolerance of political dissent.

Are rights therefore variable according to local culture, a Western conspiracy to impose liberal capitalist norms on developing nations, or a universal safeguard? It is true that the concept of rights is a product of Western thought. Xiaorong Li (1999) argued that the relativist cultural argument failed because the fundamentals of human rights protected rather than restrained cultural expression. Ayton-Shenker, writing for the UN (1995), commented that,

> Human Rights are the birth right of every person. If a state dismisses universal human rights on the basis of cultural relativism, then rights would be denied to the persons living under that state's authority. The denial or abuse of human rights is wrong, regardless of the violator's culture.

Reduced to the core principles, universal human rights are based on:

- individual and collective security under the law
- common access to essential conditions for physical and mental development
- the right and duty to work – freely chosen
- participation in the planning and working of political institutions
- freedom of association and contract
- freedom of expression, conscience, belief, assembly and for legally acceptable self-development.

It is in this sense that community organisations should take forward a rights–based agenda and ensure that these principles are embedded in their operation, policy and structure.

Power, empowerment and participation

Alinsky was very clear that in the early stages of activity the goal of organising was to create momentum, a feeling of success and the belief in the possibility of change. The main purpose was not for the gains that the initial action achieved (valuable as they may be), but to further build the organisation. The larger and more effective the community organisation, the more power it could acquire, and by extension, through the changes this made to the lives of local people; they, in turn, would be more empowered.

However, Alinsky understood that power was not, as was commonly thought, simply the ability to make people do things through authority or coercion. He realised, as Foucault pointed out, that power was the dynamic that determined the relationship between people. This power was often hegemonic and accepted as the norm. The task for community organisations was to challenge the legitimacy of existing power relationships, and such a battle could be won through the media, using large-scale events and by the threat of what the community organisation might do if its demands were not met.

The discourse and policy relating to development often talks less about power and more about participation, although it could be argued that the term 'participation' simply masks the issue of who is actually making the decisions. Writers on participation, for example, Arnstein (1969) and Wilcox (1995), are clear that the key issue is the distribution of power, which is often different from the nominal process outlined in many participative and partnership arrangements. They point out that many of the activities labelled as participation are at best token gestures to communities by the local state, or at worst outright acts of manipulation.

Arnstein believed that the goal within participation was what she defined as citizen participation. As discussed later, this is something close to the position of mature community organisations such as Woodlawn in Chicago. Arnstein defined citizen participation as,

> … the redistribution of power that enables the have-not citizens, presently excluded from the political and economic processes, to be deliberately included in the future. It is the strategy by which the have-nots join in determining how information is shared, goals and policies are set, tax resources are allocated, programmes are operated, and benefits like contracts and patronage are parcelled out. In short it is the means by which they can induce significant reform which enables them to share in the benefits of an affluent society. (Arnstein, 1969, p 216)

Social capital

Social capital is essentially about the nature of relationships between people, whether they interact with others, trust their neighbours and engage in reciprocal social relationships. It would appear at face value that community organisations are operating in areas where not much of this happens, and believe that both the process and objective of organising is to turn this around. However, some writers dislike the arguments in favour of social capital as they see them as inherently apolitical and over-generalised (see, for example, Navarro, 2002), or failing to recognise gender differences in how men and women interact (Skocpol, 2003).

It should be noted that high social capital is also not inevitably a good thing. Terrorist cells have very highly bonded social capital and this is what enables them to function.

What social capital means in practice and how ideas of social capital are constructed differs across the key writers on the subject. The idea of something like social capital can be traced back to Hanifan (1916) commenting on rural life, and writers on urban and suburban life (see, for example, Jacobs, 1961). Pierre Bourdieu (1986) coming from a European Marxist background, focused more on cultural capital, the possession of which enabled elites to hold on to their position. In this sense cultural and social capital is used by the privileged against the disadvantaged. Seen this way it is less a means of social development and more of a barrier to challenges to the status quo. In contrast, James Coleman (1988) took a different starting point and explored the relationship between social capital and marginalised groups in the US. In particular Coleman looked at the workings of family and peer groups and how they functioned to bring people together (or not) and the various social outcomes they reinforced.

Robert Putnam is the main proponent of the importance of social capital, and in his seminal *Bowling alone* (2000) he made three claims for it. First, high social capital allowed residents to solve local disputes. Second, it enabled communities to function more effectively. And third, it enabled people to see the diversity and interconnectedness of society that promoted goodwill, tolerance, and so on. Putnam argued that social capital was in decline in the US and this led to people having fewer friends and less social interaction, being less involved in community and volunteering activity, voting less and generally distrusting others. Some of the causes of this, according to Putnam, were that people were staying at home watching television, living in smaller social units or alone, with the decline of geographically tight-knit communities and increasingly dispersed patterns of work and leisure (although some of this could be an outcome of low social capital rather than the cause).

The extension of this argument in the age of the internet and growth of computer gaming has not been lost on politicians, and increasing social capital has become a policy goal in most Western countries. Do the new forms of interaction between people help build social capital or act to undermine it? Does constant texting, tweeting, posting to Facebook and chatting in online fora sustain or undermine local social relationships?

Perhaps the majority view is that in areas where there is high social capital the environment is better kept and is safer, child development is enhanced through increased positive social relationships, pupils do better at school, and people are generally healthier, happier and live longer (for a longer discussion, see Smith, 2000-09).

In operational terms, Michael Woolcock (2001) added to this debate by helpfully defining three types of social capital:

Bonding social capital based on building links between people who have a close connection, for example family, school friends, members of a sports club and so on.

Bridging social capital where ties are looser, such as distant relatives, work colleagues.

Linking social capital to people who initially appeared distant. This can be through horizontal links to, say, members of a different ethnic group, or vertical links to different levels of power and status.

It is reasonable to suggest that for community organisations, building bonding social capital brings people together, strengthens the ideal of community and creates solidarity of identity and purpose within the organisation. The bridging that social capital creates links to potential allies and assets for community use, whereas linking social capital puts the organisation in touch with power holders. We need to examine how consciously and how effectively community organisations reviewed in this book achieved this.

Leadership

For North American community organisations the development of local leadership is an essential part of building an organisation. Alinsky is supposedly quoted as saying that an organisation without effective leadership was 'a rabble'. Indeed, one of the core elements in community organisation training is on how to identify actual and potential leaders, and how to develop their skills and confidence.

Leadership can take many forms, and in some cases may be virtually ignored. In the UK, for example, there is relatively little importance given to leadership development. There is an emphasis on building capacity, for including community representatives on partnerships, for supporting social entrepreneurs and most recently, for identifying what is strangely called 'community connectors'. Some of these roles include leadership activities, but leadership as a distinctive activity is mostly ignored. It is almost as if the local state in the UK is trying to avoid the development of autonomous community leadership.

Leadership can be defined in many ways. Bass (1999) has suggested that leadership is about enabling a process of group change. To do this successfully the leader needs to have a range of personal skills that can be learned, and ideally personality traits that can be developed to some degree, depending on the character of the person concerned. Also important are how the leader deals with positional and personal power relationships.

What might community leadership look like? Hope and Timmel (1995), reflecting on their practice work in Africa, have suggested that leadership falls into three categories. First, there is authoritarian leadership where the leader makes the decision and presents it to the group. Discussion may be invited but only in the knowledge that the decision will be implemented regardless of what was said. While this appears to be contradictory to the values and purposes of development, it certainly manifests itself in many community groups. Second, they identified consultative leadership, based on the group discussing options and recommending courses of action. However, the leadership still had the final say on what was to be done. In community development only the third category of enabling leadership was acceptable, which was where the group had the power to make the final decision. Here the role of the leadership is to facilitate the discussion and ensure that an informed decision is reached. For this approach to work it was important that the organisation had policy and procedures in place to ensure that decision making was indeed a democratic process.

To take the radical end of the spectrum as an example of enabling leadership, Amilcar Cabral, the African revolutionary leader, commented: 'to lead collectively is not and cannot be, as some suppose, to give all and everyone the right to uncontrolled views and initiatives, to create disorders, empty arguments, a passion for meetings without results' (quoted in Hope and Timmel, 1995, p 50). He went on to suggest,

> ... collective leadership must strengthen the leadership capability of all and create specific circumstances where full use is made of all members.... To lead collectively, in a group, is to,
>
> • Study questions jointly
> • Find their best solutions
> • Take decisions jointly
> • Benefit from the experience and intelligence of each person
>
> To lead collectively is to:
>
> • Give the opportunity of thinking and acting
> • Demand that people take responsibility within their competence
> • Require that people take initiative
> • Co-ordinate the thought and action of those who form the group.

All community organisations need to deal with leadership questions, and examples of how this can be approached are explored in the the chapters that follow.

Assets

Approaching community development activity from an asset-based perspective has a relatively long history, albeit with a drifting in and out of fashion among practitioners and agencies. It is currently having something of a revival, as development practice is becoming ever more dependent on bottom-up community-led approaches and less on top-down government intervention. (See, for example, the work of the Asset-based Community Development Institute at Northwestern University and the writing of Kreztmann and McKnight, 1995 and O'Leary, 2011.)

Sometimes the asset approach is also called a capital approach based on exploring what has become known as the 'seven capitals', as described in Table 2.5.

Table 2.5: Seven **capitals**

Capital	Definition
Financial	Plays an important role in the economy, enabling other types of capital to be owned and traded
Built	Fixed assets that facilitate the livelihood or wellbeing of the community
Social	Features of social organisations such as networks and norms of trust that facilitate cooperation for mutual benefit, include a sub-set of spiritual capital (the form of social capital that links to religion/spirituality); bonding, bridging social capital
Human	People's health, knowledge, skills and motivation; enhancing human capital can be achieved through education and training
Natural	Landscape and any stock or flow of energy and material that produces goods and services; renewable and non-renewable materials
Cultural	Shaping how we see the world, what we take for granted and what we value
Political	Ability of a community to influence the distribution and use of resources

Source: O'Leary (2011, p 7)

Asset-based practice attempts to build a development strategy linking up tangible assets (for example, buildings) and intangible assets. Tangible assets are obvious – you can see them as you walk around the community. Intangible assets are easy to miss or to simply dismiss. Like social capital, it can take a lot of work to identify existing local intangible assets and to explore with local people how they might be used. In practice it is the strength of the intangible assets that underpin successful development activity.

Intangible assets can be divided into three categories (O'Leary, 2011, p12):

Individual assets: skills, knowledge, leadership capacities, experiences, personalities, what we have, what we can bring to the group

Relational assets: networks, relationships, partnerships, friendships, kinships, group ties, associations

Collective assets: stories, traditions, cultures, institutions, norms, collective experiences.

Generally, asset-based approaches attempt to integrate three operation themes, which are: the knowledge and skill development of local people, the understanding and use of local political and power structures and relationships, and the transfer of ownership and control of local assets (for example, building and land) to local community control.

One of the strengths of this approach is that it produces a more rounded, perhaps holistic, practice. This is in contrast to a more socially focused approach that responds to the effects on people from poverty and underdevelopment, but which does not attempt to deal with the causes of the problems.

Although it has seldom been described in terms of asset-based development, the activities of traditional North American community organisations have been based on gaining community control of services and resources, and building the capability of local people, underpinned by a conscious political strategy (see, for example, the case studies on Woodland and Back of the Yards in Chapter Three. One of the questions we need to explore is how far asset-based approaches are incorporated into the work of other community organisations.

Autonomous organisations

Finally, it is important to revisit the basic core of Alinsky's ideals that people must take responsibility for their own lives, and that change for the poor and the dispossessed can only come through building autonomous power organisations. Without power and independence, Alinsky believed that people would simply remain incorporated into existing power systems, and that nothing would really change.

In his book, *Crisis in black and white*, Silberman suggested that,

> … the essential difference between Alinsky and his enemies is that Alinsky really believes in democracy; he really believes that the helpless, the poor, the badly-educated can solve their own problems if given the chance and the means; he really believes that the poor and uneducated, no less that the rich and educated, have the right to decide how their lives should be run and what services should be offered to them instead of being ministered to like children. (1968, p 333)

It is possible, of course, to apply many of the above perspectives and approaches and to build organisations that are dependent on local or national government funding support. However, undertaking serious change-orientated work in collaboration with the state does, as Hoggert (2009) points out, involve the worker and the organisation in a complex set of dilemmas, complexities and split allegiances in trying to navigate a way through a contested political space. How far is it possible to be responding democratically to the needs of local dispossessed communities, while at the same time implementing government-funded programmes that are likely to incorporate people into the existing power structure?

Alinsky was very clear that effective change was only possible if these dilemmas were avoided and the community organisation positioned itself outside of the existing power structure to give itself maximum freedom of manoeuvre. One of the key questions to be explored, therefore, is how far new community organisations are keeping true to the ideal of autonomy, or whether they have, through convenience or necessity, developed closer ties with the state.

Conclusion

We now have a framework to help us analyse and understand what contemporary community organisations contribute to their localities. The areas discussed come from various and sometimes competing perspectives, which is okay, as taken together they enable us to see community organisations holistically. There is, of course, no expectation that any community organisation, or all community organisations taken together, will cover all of the categories listed below, but where do they, and where might they, make a contribution?

In the chapters that follow we explore the individual and collective contribution of the community organisations studied using the following criteria:

- Development of the MDGs
- Promoting organisational development within urban slum and other marginal areas
- Promoting sustainability
- Developing capability and capacity development
- Promoting quality of life, wellbeing and happiness as an explicit goal
- Rights
- Empowering people
- Building social capital
- Building local leadership
- Creating local assets
- Building autonomous organisations

THREE

Community organising revisited: the Industrial Areas Foundation model

> Never do something for someone that they can do for themselves.
> (Ernesto Cortes)

This chapter builds on the earlier discussion of the principles of community organising and the IAF model. We look at two of the classic Chicago-based community organisations from the early years of Alinsky and the IAF, that of the Back of the Yards Neighborhood Council (BYNC) and The Woodlawn Organization (TWO). In these two case studies we give a brief overview of the organisations, a summary of their current activity and an analysis of their development and contribution to the current community.

The nature of community organising is changing, partly as a reflection of different economic and social contexts, but also due to lessons learned from over 70 years of organising. In the final part of this chapter we explore where these revisions of the model have got to, and where they may be going.

Case study: Back of the Yards Neighborhood Council

Overview

The background to the development of BYNC begins with the building of the Union Stockyards in 1865. A consortium of railroad companies shipped cattle into the Stockyards, slaughtered and processed them, and then distributed the resulting meat products out across the US. By 1900 25,000 people were employed by the Stockyards, nine million animals a year were processed, which accounted for 82 per cent of US meat production. By 1925 employment had reached 40,000. From the 1950s, however, the Stockyards went into decline due to the development of the new interstate roads and the increasing movement of livestock by trucks. The Stockyards closed in 1971 having processed over one billion animals, to be replaced by a rather low-key industrial park. The Union Stockyards was an iconic place, the subject of Upton Sinclair's novel *The jungle* and Bertolt Brecht's play 'Saint Joan of the Stockyards'.

The Back of the Yards neighbourhood provided the cheap local housing for Stockyard workers, mainly Eastern European immigrants. By 1900 clearly defined sub-neighbourhoods had been established by Polish, Czech, Slovak, Lithuanian and Irish immigrants. These communities tended to be self-sufficient with their own churches, schools, men's social clubs, women's leagues and sports clubs.

Mexican immigrants began to arrive in the area in the 1920s and this expanded rapidly from the 1970s. At that time the Stockyards had closed, and many long-term residents had moved to other areas in Chicago seeking new employment, leaving behind cheap housing for the next wave of immigration. The 2000 census indicates that the BYNC area was predominately Hispanic (just over 50 per cent) with a significant African-American minority (35 per cent). The census also showed that 34.5 per cent of the population were living below the poverty line, with 12 per cent of households receiving public assistance, and 29.5 per cent recent immigrants.

Although poor, the immigrant communities were, in many ways, self-sufficient, until they were hit by the Depression years in the 1920s and 1930s. That said, the social and housing conditions in the area were appalling. Alinsky reportedly described the area as 'the nadir of American slums, worse than Harlem.' Responding to unemployment, poor working conditions and a reduction in wages, workers in the area formed the United Packinghouse Workers of America (later to become the UPWA-CIO, the United Packinghouse Workers of America-Congress of Industrial Organizations). Alinsky managed to link these trade union initiatives and organising methods to the leadership and membership of the Catholic Church to form the BYNC. In doing so he created the organisational model that he and the IAF would roll out in other communities in the coming years.

The story around the formation of BYNC is well known and recounted by both Slayton (1986) and Horwitt (1989), who both give a similar analysis. They argued that a number of factors had to be in place to have enabled the creation of BYNC. First, the experience of trade union organising, and that locally it was the CIO with a broad and quasi-socialist view that was amenable to responding to social issues rather than the more conservative and traditional trade union approach that was present elsewhere in the US. It was also significant that the experience of trade union activity had helped people to both think and organise across the ethnic sub-communities. Second, Alinsky, through his relationship with Joe Meegan, manager of Davis Square Park and its welfare services, was able to link into the local Catholic organisational structure. A number of younger and more progressive priests working in the area also assisted in developing the relationship with the church.

BYNC was established in 1939 to provide welfare services to the community and to promote union membership. This was a programme that had something for everyone, and enabled both Bishop Sheil and CIO founder John L. Lewis to appear on stage together for BYNC. To build the popular base, BYNC used federal money to extend the free lunch programme (the first time a community-based organisation had done this). This was extended into local schools and cheaper sources of milk were identified and supplied locally. Over the next few years BYNC developed anti-gang and anti-delinquency programmes, created local playgrounds and promoted youth employment and local clean-up activities. BYNC undertook a housing survey using schoolchildren to identify housing code violations. A local credit union was also established. In 1951 Adlai Stevenson wrote to Joe Meegan, commenting that 'if I were asked to choose in all America a single agency which I felt most admirably represented all that our democracy stands for … I would select the Back of the Yards Council' (quoted in Slayton, 1986, p 228).

With the closure of the Stockyards, alternative sources of employment were urgently required. BYNC was involved in the development of both the new industrial park on the Stockyard site and the building of Yards Plaza, a US$850 million development offering over 250,000 square feet of retail space. These developments and the holding together of the local community through traumatic economic change were, in Slayton's view, the greatest achievement of BYNC.

Today

BYNC currently organises the majority of its services in terms of youth, adults and senior provision, with extra support offered for local businesses. It also runs three community gardens and the annual Back of the Yards festival. BYNC operates a community technology centre that teaches basic computing skills to children, jobseekers, seniors and local businesses. In addition it is actively involved with the Chicago Police Department Community Alternative Policing Strategy. This strategy involves 'beat' officers meeting local community representatives promoted by BYNC. A notary public service is provided free to local residents.

Youth programmes include:

Ballet Folklorico: a major element of BYNC youth activity is centred on Hispanic culture. Ballet Folklorico teaches traditional folk dances from Mexico and includes pre-Hispanic and Mestizo dances as well as the main Hispanic dances. The classes include the history and meaning associated with the dances. Performances are given locally, but also include venues around the greater Chicago area and national US championships.

After-school tutoring: the tutoring programme supports around 32 students a day and focuses on developing ability in reading and essential skills. Homework completion is also a target.

Hoops in the Hood: a summer partnership programme between BYNC, youth agencies, the police and residents as a diversion from drug and gang activities. Around 95 young people between the ages of 11 to 15 are involved.

Adult services comprise:

GED (general educational development) classes: second-chance basic education classes offered free and taught in Spanish.

ESL (English as a second language) classes: conversational English classes to help native Spanish speakers improve their language skills.

Energy Assistance programme: this has been developed from the wider Chicago Climate Action Plan, which promotes energy efficiency and access to other programmes including home insulation, boiler replacement, assistance with energy bills and winter heating assistance.

Senior programmes include:

Circuit Breaker/Senior Freeze: benefits advice programmes including support for property taxes and medication costs.

Shuttle bus: Many local taxi companies will not pick up in the Back of the Yards area, so BYNC offers seniors a free, safe and door-to-door transport service. This is mainly to support access by seniors to essential services such as doctors and hospital services, pharmacies, shopping centres and local grocery stores, banks and a range of recreational activities.

Senior Club: BYNC has been delivering senior services for more than 50 years. The Senior Club is a regular meeting where topics such as healthcare, personal safety and social support are discussed. The club also provides an access point to the Circuit Breakers and shuttle bus services. Recreational trips are also organised through the club.

HRAIL (Home Repairs for Accessible and Independent Living): offers free repairs for those over 60 and those who are living on below median income. The funds are provided by the City of Chicago and enable seniors to remain living independently in their own homes.

It is apparent from the above range of activities that BYNC today is very much a local social welfare and cultural organisation. As such it provides important services that support a broad cross-section of the community. The area has, however, major problems in terms of housing quality and employment opportunities. These were the two main initial concerns of BYNC. Although definite achievements have been made on both fronts over the years, a current criticism of BYNC is that it has not, in recent years, managed to pull in significant investment to help address these issues. Would a more robust campaigning agenda be beneficial here?

Analysis

One of the best analyses of IAF activity during the key part of its history during the 1960s is from Hillary Clinton, then Hillary Rodham (1969), who wrote a university thesis on the organising process within BYNC, Woodlawn and

Rochester. Alinsky offered Rodham a community organiser job. She refused it as she was not convinced of the need to work outside the system to promote change, and decided instead to go to Law School. The thesis had restricted access while Hillary Clinton was First Lady, and has since become a controversial text. It appears on many right-wing websites, where it is used as evidence that Alinsky was a communist and that Hillary Clinton a fellow traveller. The fact that any objective reading of the thesis shows quite the opposite is simply ignored.

In her thesis Rodham showed that the basic organisation around BYNC was presented in terms of self-interest. For example, it was argued that if you were poor, it was obvious that no outside agency was coming to help and that you had no choice but to help yourself; for local businesses, any attempt to raise local income would be beneficial; and similarly it was suggested to the Catholic Church that improving the welfare of its parishioners was also in the interests of the church itself. The key to success, however, was convincing both the UPWA and the Catholic Church that it was in their individual interest to cooperate. BYNC's mission was stated as being, 'to promote the welfare of all residents of that community regardless of their race, color, or creed, so that they may all have the opportunity to find health, happiness and security through the democratic way of life.' This was a broad enough statement that everyone could buy into.

Alinsky developed a powerful relationship with Bishop Sheil that kept the Catholic Church firmly involved in BYNC. Sheil was impressed not only by the welfare benefits flowing from BYNC, but also that it promoted the workings of local democracy. It was Sheil who introduced Alinsky to investment banker and philanthropist Marshall Field III. Field suggested to Alinsky that he should create a tax-exempt foundation to export the BYNC model in other cities. From this suggestion the Industrial Areas Foundation was born, with Field both a funder and board member.

BYNC initially had two medium-term objectives: economic security for local people and improvements in housing and the local environment. In 1946 BYNC supported the Packinghouse strike. It worked with churches to run soup lines and to provide childcare. Local businesses supplied food, and (perhaps under pressure?) landlords ignored unpaid rents. Other actions at the time were against the Pennsylvania Railroad who were fined for the damage engine smoke had caused to local health, and the local meat factories that were forced to house their waste to reduce the stench that affected nearby houses. Rodham pointed out that these campaigns were successful because of the efforts to sustain BYNC as a broad-based democratic organisation. She quoted from the 1948 Annual Report of the Executive Secretary of the BYNC:

> While the achievements of the Council are great in themselves, underlying each individual achievement is the thread of the most important objective that we are working toward ... the most important element in democracy. By that I mean participation. I mean the recognition on the part of the people that democracy is a way of life

which can only be sustained through the part of the people. Only when the people recognise that theirs is the decision, the right, and the duty to shape their own life, only then will democracy expand and grow. That is why the cardinal keynote of the Back of the Yards Neighborhood Council is: "We, the people will work out our own destiny." It is for this reason that I am asking you to keep in mind clearly that every single achievement which I can report tonight has behind it a history of participation, of fighting and of awakening of a burning passion for justice and brotherhood of man by thousands of our people.

There is no doubt about Alinsky's commitment to making democracy work. However, it was a constant struggle to do so. Alinsky often spoke about his concern that dispossessed people were susceptible to fascism, and his experience of Chicago in the 1930s only reinforced this belief. Within BYNC in the 1960s, when the local economy was collapsing and the area was changing from a white to multi-racial community, white power and 'Vote Wallace' posters could be seen in windows and on car bumpers (Governor Wallace was a presidential candidate with strong segregationist views). Rodham quoted local opinion that this was due to inherent racial attitudes that had not been addressed, younger residents who did not have a history of involvement in BYNC and the values it propounded, and suggested that it was also the result of political frustration in that the all-embracing nature of BYNC hindered wider political organisation and debate.

Summary

The Back of the Yards neighbourhood is still a very poor area, with marginal housing and environmental conditions. The population has changed radically since the 1940s, with few of the original white residents remaining and an increasing Hispanic population. These new immigrants have little knowledge of the history of BYNC and consequently the organisation has less of a broad organisational base than in previous years. There is still an organisational history and memory that links back to Alinsky and Meegan, but in practical terms it is questionable how relevant this is for local people. For an organisation that is more than 70 years old, these changes are hardly surprising, but it does mean that BYNC today is a different kind of community organisation to that envisioned by Alinsky.

The current BYNC board includes a diverse range of representatives that link to business, the legal profession and wider political support, although one might question the success of the board in attracting the significant external funding the area requires. It is clear that the needs of the Back of the Yards area far outstrip BYNC's capacity to respond. The responsibility of this shortfall cannot be placed on BYNC, and is more a reflection of the apparent marginalisation of the area by the city and other agencies.

In terms of our criteria, BYNC offers services that contribute to meeting a range of basic needs across all age groups. Considerable emphasis is placed on valuing and promoting Hispanic cultural activity. BYNC appears to play an important role in trying to improve the basic quality of life and wellbeing for the local residents, and through this contributes to the maintenance of social capital and social cohesion. It is not clear how far BYNC attempts to develop local leadership and actively campaigns for the rights of disadvantaged people, and how it has perhaps settled into the role of local service provider.

Case study: The Woodlawn Organization

Overview

Woodlawn is a neighbourhood in Chicago South Side. Until the late 1940s it was largely a white middle-class area and home to many professional groups, including academics from the nearby University of Chicago. From the early 1950s changes in housing law made illegal the 'restricted covenants' that had been used to exclude African-Americans from living in the area. As a result landlords extensively sub-divided property into smaller lets more affordable to the poor. As an increasing number of African-Americans moved into Woodlawn, there was a corresponding white flight to the outer suburbs. By the 1960s Woodlawn's population had increased to around 90,000, with the majority being African-American. With the loss of the more wealthy white population the local economy declined, levels of poverty increased and housing conditions deteriorated. Local banks redlined the area and it was almost impossible to fund housing and other local investments, further leading to the process of decline.

The University of Chicago is located adjacent to Woodlawn and was expanding rapidly in the 1950s and 1960s. In the nearby Hyde Park area, the university instituted a renewal programme that led to the demolition of 20 per cent of the area and forced the removal of 20,000 residents, mainly African-American families. A second renewal area in Woodlawn, covering 60th and 61st Street, was planned.

The resistance to the university and the renewal scheme was organised by three local Protestant ministers and a Catholic priest operating under the name of the Woodlawn Pastors Association. Local meetings with Alinsky had taken place previous to this, but had not been followed through due to a local reluctance to commit to the confrontational strategies of the IAF. However, faced by an immediate threat, agreement was reached with Alinsky and The Woodlawn Organization (TWO) was formed in 1961, with Arthur M. Brazier of the Pentecostal Church, and advocate of black self-determination, the spokesperson (see Brazier, 1969). IAF appointed Nicholas von Hoffman as the lead organiser.

Using the standard IAF tactics of running winnable campaigns to build the organisation, TWO expanded during the 1960s. Campaign targets included slum landlords, the poor state of the segregated public schools, local store owners and, of course, the university. TWO was also locally involved in civil rights activities, the Freedom Rides and voter registration campaigns.

In 1967 the Office of Economic Opportunity funded TWO to develop a programme to train young unemployed residents. This was significant for two reasons. First, the funding indicated that TWO had achieved a level of respect within the system and that it was ready to move into the next phase of the IAF model, that of negotiating compromises with the system. Ultimately TWO had a seat on the City Planning Board, which enabled it to stop the university's plans for Woodlawn. Second, the training programme used the networks of the powerful local gangs, the Devil's Disciples and the Blackstone Rangers.

Particularly notorious, the Blackstone Rangers had become the dominant gang in Chicago South Side, running an overtly political activist front underpinned by a range of criminal activities. Increasingly politically active and influenced by the Civil Rights Movement and Black Nationalism, they changed their name to the Black P. Stone Nation, and at their peak, had around 50,000 members. Their leader, Jeff Fort, was subsequently convicted of fraud regarding the TWO training grant which led to collapse of the programme.

Arthur M. Brazier resigned his leadership role in TWO in 1965 and was replaced by Leon Finney. Under the new leadership TWO moved from its initial organisation building and confrontation stage to a more developmental and collaborative approach with city, state and federal agencies. The focus of this activity was rehabilitating low and middle-income houses and offering a range of support to small local businesses. In 1972 the Woodlawn Community Development Corporation (WCDC) was established. To date, more than US$300 million in housing funds has been attracted to Woodlawn, with further funds being invested by a range of private and commercial sources. Despite this investment the local population has continued to decline, from 81,279 in 1960 to 27,086 in 2000, although the quality of the housing in which the current population lives is significantly improved from that of the 1960s.

TWO currently describes its mission, 'to build community through advocacy, social service programs, and community development initiatives.' This is a long way from the building power organisation mission of the original IAF involvement.

TWO describes its current activities under nine initiatives :

WCDC: operates as the umbrella organisation for TWO's real estate development and management activities. More than 1,659 units of single family and senior housing in 14 different developments have been created. WCDC currently provides housing for more than 10,000 citizens.

Woodlawn Early Childhood Development Center: the current manifestation of TWO's involvement in childcare that reaches back to the 1960s. It has included Head Start programmes and cooperation with Chicago Public Schools. Since 2000 it has expanded to offer care for infants in addition to toddlers aged two to five. The operation is based on the south campus of the University of

Chicago in a 7,000 square foot facility. This is one of several activities with the university operating in contrast to the initial conflicts of the 1960s. It currently offers hands-on mathematics, reading, art and music activities; an early reading 3-5 literacy programme; computer education; nutritious breakfast, lunch and snacks; and educational field trips for two- to five-year-olds.

Woodlawn Neighborhood Recovery Institute: one of 23 initiatives established in 2010 in Chicago to reduce youth violence. The approach adopted is through job creation for young people and adults, promoting wellness and healthy lifestyles, developing youth and parental leadership, building community capacity and a healthier family and community environment.

TWO Baby Institute: under the slogan 'Giving your baby the care it deserves' the Baby Institute sets out to educate new parents on the proper pre- and postnatal care for infants. Its goals are to reduce infant mortality and to improve child safety and child development.

Hope4Youth Engagement Initiative: provides direct support to homeless young people aged 18 to 24. Around 1,500 young people annually, who are homeless or directly living on the street, receive crisis help. Such assistance includes food, clothing, assistance to obtain housing, re-entry to education and job finding. Services are delivered directly and through two drop-in centres.

TWO Digital Connection (After-school Matters): a pre-apprenticeship programme for 15 high school students from schools throughout the Chicago area. The students research the local nature of violence in their communities and make a violence impact documentary as an educational resource.

Circle of HOPE neighbourhood clean-up: provides paid employment to individuals who are considered hard to employ, under-employed or unemployed. There are 22 crew members performing duties such as pruning trees, landscaping and picking up rubbish. In addition to receiving life skills training they are also given academic support classes, case management and substance abuse counselling, if needed.

CeaseFire – Woodlawn: a violence reduction-focused initiative, CeaseFire uses an evidence-based public health approach to reducing shootings and killings. The approach is based on working at street level and involves outreach workers, community leaders, faith leaders and police officers.

Entry House/Power House: a substance abuse addiction counselling service delivered through TWO's residential detoxification and inpatient treatment facility. Over 1,500 people a year use this service. In addition there is a short-term detox programme and a 15-bed long-term residential treatment programme.

TWO delivers a wide range of services. Its housing portfolio is extensive, and significant in that it is both a major local property developer and landlord. While not criticising the quality of the housing services, it does ask the question of where residents could go to campaign for better housing. The other services attempt to tackle local issues around gang violence, addiction and homelessness, and offer a pre-emptive approach through improving childcare and parenting skills. Overall, it is an impressive range of activities.

Analysis

Like the Back of the Yards, Hillary Rodham Clinton provided a contemporary analysis of TWO in the 1960s. She suggested that organising in Woodlawn represented an evolution in Alinsky's theory. He still believed that Woodlawn was 'the sort of obsolescent, decaying, crowded neighborhood which social workers and city planners assume can never help itself' (quoted in Silberman, 1968, p 320). It was also an area where poverty and racial issues were embedded. Silberman suggested that the implications of such embedded oppression were that,

> Quite frequently, therefore, the apathy that characterizes the slum represents what in many ways is a realistic response to a hostile environment. But realistic or not, the adjustment that is reached is one of surrender to the existing conditions and abdication of any hope of change. The result is a community seething with inarticulate resentments and dormant hostilities repressed for safety's sake, but which break out every now and then in some explosion of deviant or irrational behavior. The slum dwellers are incapable of acting, or even joining, until these suppressed resentments and hostilities are brought to the surface where they can be seen as problems – ie as a condition you can do something about. (Silberman, 1968, p 344)

And if this was not enough, there was also the problem of opposing urban renewal that was generally seen as a good thing, as well as the power interests of the city and university.

However, one of the things that had changed was the increasing involvement of local churches in the battle for change. Along with the churches came actual and potential leaders, organisational structures and, potentially, money. Alinsky, however, refused to work with the initial group of churchmen who approached him, and told them to come back with a more representative group and sufficient finance to fund the development of a new organisation.

When the money was in place Alinsky sent in Nicholas von Hoffman as the lead organiser to listen to people and to get a feel for the area. Once local grievances were identified, the next task was to identify likely leaders and bring them together to plan actions designed to build the new organisation. Although identifying potential leaders was recognised as a problem due to the defeated and disorganised nature of the local African-American community, nevertheless, by the spring of 1960, the membership of TWO included 60 local businesses, 50 block clubs and 30 churches, representing at least 40,000 local residents.

The first 'target' was local businesses guilty of overcharging and short weighing goods. This was clearly an easily won and populist goal and fitted the IAF plan of creating early victories to build both the belief in change and support for the community organisation. The second target in the IAF model needed to be more substantial, and here the University of Chicago and their urban renewal plans fitted the bill. A total of 15,000 Woodlawn residents would potentially be affected by the renewal plans. TWO asked the university for more details; the university, not taking TWO seriously, refused. Local businesses would also be affected, and the university dismissed their concerns, thereby shifting the local business community further into the TWO camp.

To compound their difficulties the university attacked the Catholic Church in the city for its support of Alinsky and the IAF dating from their joint activities in the Back of the Yards. Monsignor Egan responded to these criticisms, saying,

> We felt the Church had to involve herself in helping people develop the tools which would enable them to come to grips with the serious economic, social, and moral problems which were affecting their lives, families, and communities. We also knew that there was needed a tool which would enable them to participate in a dignified way in the democratic process and which would give them the training necessary for achieving in action the meaning of the democratic way of life and of realizing their human and divine dignity. The Industrial Areas Foundation appeared to us to be the only organized force with the skill, experience, and integrity to supply these tools and organize in neighborhoods which had such a desperate need for them. (Egan, 1965)

The IAF strategy was to build a broad-based organisation with diverse constituencies. The university helped this along by bringing the business and Catholic communities firmly on side with TWO.

Rodham pointed out that a significant facet of the Woodlawn campaigns was that it directly confronted the legitimacy of bureaucratically controlled social planning, unless meaningful community participation was involved. This was a radical step for the time and brought onside such notable people as Jane Jacobs who worked with TWO in developing a more resident-friendly development plan. Faced with a threat to the legitimacy of the city government, Mayor Daley forced the university to negotiate with TWO on a plan that would build replacement homes for those lost through university expansion.

TWO went on to directly challenge the city in other ways, the most famous being the voter registration drive in 1961. Two thousand Woodlawn residents arrived en masse at City Hall to register. To do so they had to hire buses outside of the city as the usual sources of buses had suddenly become 'unavailable'. (It should be remembered that Woodlawn was essentially an African-American community and these activities were taking place alongside those of the Civil Rights Movement.) Rodham suggested that Alinsky felt the voter registration drive was one of his main achievements as it demonstrated that people had found their dignity and a belief that they could collectively shape their future.

Other initiatives by TWO at this time included the campaign for non-segregated schools, increased and fair police protection and housing improvements. With the organisational power of TWO, successful pickets were held on the School Board and the homes of slum landlords, suing the Board of Education for de facto segregation, and sit-ins at banks that funded slum landlords.

In 1967 the Office of Economic Opportunity made a grant of over US$900,000 to TWO to train several hundred unemployed school dropouts. Following the incorporatist strategy of IAF (and possible simple pragmatism), TWO recruited members of the main local gangs, the Blackstone Rangers and the Devil's Disciples, into the administration of the programme. The potential benefits from this were the possible reduction in hostilities between the two gangs, a greater reach into the gang membership and more effective delivery of services. As Rodham points out, it was also a high-risk strategy as it was essentially based on hiring what she called 'criminals', which, despite the political rhetoric, was the main activity of the gangs.

It appears that gang members were using money fraudulently, and this resulted in prosecutions. However, TWO's opponents in the city administration and the Republican Party used this as a broader opportunity to try and discredit them. Arthur M. Brazier called the subsequent hearing on the activities of TWO a 'political conspiracy to discredit a program conducted by a black community and controlled by black people' (Rodham, 1969, p 53).

TWO moved on from this scandal and, as outlined above, has in the past 40 years brought hundreds of millions of dollars into the community. The deployment of this money has transformed housing conditions, improved the local economy and job prospects of local people. However, it is one thing to attack poor landlords, but when you become the landlord, then for many you are the enemy, not the saviour. No service delivery organisation can be perfect, and TWO have been criticised for their housing management and financial control. Some of these criticisms may be justified, and some are certainly politically motivated, especially when the current Democratic President is a community organiser from Chicago and has personal links to some of the TWO leadership.

What is clear from the history of organising in Woodlawn is that it was originally about creating and deploying the standard IAF model and building a broad-based and financially independent power organisation external to the existing city services. From the late 1960s this changed to an organisation using its power to obtain significant external funds to deliver services. In doing so TWO moved back into the system, albeit with a degree of direct local democracy over its operations. Just like Back of the Yards, it is a two-part story.

—

Summary

How does TWO fare with our 11 criteria for development? In the first 10 years of activity the emphasis was on promoting organisational development as per the standard IAF model. In the 40 years since then, TWO projects and initiatives have worked on almost all of the criteria with varying degrees of success, the most significant being the promotion of community empowerment and political influence along with the extensive development of housing assets. Such a broad range of activity has been enabled and underpinned by the success in attracting several hundred million dollars of inward investment to the community for both capital development and project delivery costs.

The argument is, of course, whether these achievements could have been gained from just working within the system, or did this only happen because of the early conflict and power organisation building phase of TWO. It has to be concluded that it is very unlikely that anything like the activities of TWO could have been achieved without the creation of an effective power organisation in the early years.

A second, and troubling, question is that TWO is, on the surface at least, a far more successful organisation than the BYNC, although the two communities are only a few miles apart in the same city. Both communities were organised on the same IAF model, and both organisations moved from the initial power building phase to service delivery. Yet TWO has been far more successful in obtaining external funding that has enabled it to improve housing and to deliver a wider range of services. It is not at all clear why this is so, but it may be related to the effectiveness of TWO's organisational leadership and their connections, and their sustained ability to work the broader political system in their favour.

The Industrial Areas Foundation today

The IAF website currently describes its activities thus: 'IAF leaders and organisers first create independent organisations, made up of people from all races and all classes, focused on productive improvements in the public arena. IAF members then use those new political realities to invent and establish new social realities.' An integral part of this process is the national training event for professional religious leaders, people interested in public education, those interested in housing revitalisation, labour organisers and leaders. In addition, local three-day training sessions are delivered for advanced leaders and for congregational and organisational development.

Three reasons are presented why the IAF is committed to this work. First, because the IAF is *thankful*:

> IAF leaders and organisers deeply appreciate the democratic tradition
> that our fathers and mothers worked and fought and sometimes died
> for. We value the tradition of labor organising and worker rights that
> protected so many millions of Americans and helped make humane

and shared prosperity possible. We honor the many religious traditions (Christian, Jewish, Islamic, and others) that inform our public action and deepen our understanding. We know we are fortunate to live in a country shaped by these and other extraordinary forces.

Second, because the IAF is *angry* about the obstacles to happiness that people encounter in daily life, about poor schools, inadequate housing, criminality, poverty and poor wages.

Third, the IAF is *hopeful* that these obstacles can be overcome. This hope is based on the experience of the successes that the IAF has achieved over the years. As evidence of success they quote the living wage movement that grew out of an IAF affiliate campaign in Baltimore in 1994, the 3,000 Nehemiah Homes built in East Brooklyn, Alliance Schools in Southwest US and Blight Removal schemes in New York.

Underpinning the IAF is a commitment to what it calls 'revolutionary social change', and this is promoted through the IAF Training Institute, which is described as a 'school for professional radicals', where potential and current leaders are taught the core techniques of IAF organising. An objective of the training is to help leaders see the connection between their local issues and the broader national IAF objectives and associated progressive causes.

The terms 'revolutionary social change' and 'radical' are not defined, but can be assumed to come directly from Alinsky's book *Rules for Radicals*. Right-wing political commentators in the US take radical to mean communist and socialist, terms that many bloggers use interchangeably as if they were the same thing. Talking about revolution along with selective quotations are often used to back up this analysis, which is then used as a broad brush to tar a range of people, from Hillary Clinton to Barack Obama. In contrast, the socialist left in the US do not generally see Alinsky as a socialist, and describe him as being part of the non-socialist left.

One way to understand what the IAF mean by 'radical' is to look at what they actually do. A starting point is the clear statement by the IAF that it is not, contrary to many assumptions, a grassroots organisation. The Reverend Johnny Youngblood, an IAF leader, said, "We are not a grassroots organisation. Grassroots are shallow roots. Grassroots are fragile roots. Our roots are deep roots." The IAF still organises on the basis of being an organisation or organisations, not a recruiter of individuals, although individual members of the constituent organisations are counted, and the IAF claim that in this way it represents over 1.5 million people.

The IAF is clear that its mission, as it always has been, is the 'collection and exercise of political power and influence.' At the same time the IAF also claim it is a non-ideological and non-partisan organisation. Running through the IAF is a belief in pragmatism. According to Catholic Culture, everyone on IAF training events is still given a copy of an article by John H. Randall Jnr, titled 'The importance of being unprincipled'. This article is not quite what it appears to be from the title, and argues that in order to move forward, we need to compromise, and this involves letting go of some principles. Ernesto Cortes, who organises the IAF in Southwest US, suggested, 'One of the worst things you can be is overly principled. Everybody has got to compromise, adapt, change. So one of the hard things we've always had to learn in the world as it is, is that there are no permanent enemies and no permanent allies' (Cortes, 1986).

In a more poetic style, Barack Obama commented on community organising today,

> Organizing teaches as nothing else does the beauty and strength of everyday people. Through the songs of the church and the talk on the stoops, through the hundreds of individual stories of coming up from the South and finding any job that would pay, of raising families on threadbare budgets, of losing some children to drugs and watching others earn degrees and land jobs their parents could never aspire to – it is through these stories and songs of dashed hopes and powers of endurance, of ugliness and strife, subtlety and laughter, that organisers can shape a sense of community not only for others, but for themselves. (Obama, 1990, p 40)

Current IAF activities include:

Housing: as well as the Nehemiah Homes in East Brooklyn, there are similar schemes for 1,000 homes in the South Bronx, 900 homes in Baltimore, 135 homes in Philadelphia and 147 homes in Washington.

Schools: for example, the Alliance Schools Initiative developed in Texas to promote the restructuring of local schools. Recent research by Brown University suggests that schools in the programme show a 15 to 19 per cent increase in student achievement. In San Antonio a partnership between schools, districts, universities and businesses has been created to provide scholarships for B average students. To date US$20 million has been committed to support 2,900 students to complete college degrees. In New York a campaign to create new small and high quality public schools has led to the opening of five new schools with more in development.

Health: there is a range of initiatives covering health. The Affordable Health Insurance campaign was developed by the IAF affiliate in Boston. The campaign resulted in universal healthcare for all Massachusetts citizens. The main benefits of the programme are:
- expansion of the state Medicaid programme to cover 27,000 children and 58,000 adults
- reinstatement of dental and eyeglass benefits for Medicaid recipients

- enrolment of 65,000 low-income adults (below 100 per cent Federal Poverty Line [FPL]) in comprehensive private health insurance plans with no premiums or deductibles and with minimal co-payments
- sliding-scale subsidies for 150,000 low/moderate-income adults (100–300 per cent FPL) to purchase comprehensive private health insurance plans with no deductibles and with minimal co-payments
- insurance market reforms that make it easier and cheaper for moderate-income individuals and small businesses to purchase quality health insurance
- assessments totalling approximately US$100 million/year on businesses that do not provide health insurance
- US$125 million in additional new state spending on health insurance subsidies.

  The Children's Health Insurance programme in Texas enables an additional 127,000 children to receive free healthcare in the state. In Iowa a campaign forced local hospitals to offer the same discounts for medical treatment for uninsured lower-income patients as offered to those on medical insurance. The Illinois United Power Family Care campaign has resulted in extended healthcare for parents, children and young adults. Around 850,000 people have improved healthcare provision. The IAF affiliate in New Jersey has forced Honeywell Corporation to spend up to US$400 million to remove toxic chromium from abandoned industrial sites.

Reconstruction: in Philadelphia, Baltimore and Washington, affiliates are campaigning for large-scale urban Blight Removal programmes. Around US$390 million has been committed to these programmes so far. In Texas a group of IAF affiliates are campaigning for 'colonias' (unincorporated neighbourhoods) to gain infrastructure improvements including potable water and waste removal.

Employment: as well as the living wage campaign mentioned above, the Southwest IAF is developing a partnership between employers, community colleges and community leaders to create new workforce development and education programmes. Graduates of the programme will move into high-skill and high-wage employment in contrast to their only previous option of low-skill jobs with poverty wages. Similar initiatives are being developed in Arizona and Louisiana. So far 11,000 people have benefited from the scheme with an average annual income in excess of US$39,000.

Housing foreclosure: in recognition of the effect that the sub-prime housing market crash has caused in poor communities, IAF have developed work to mitigate the effects of foreclosure. The City of Los Angeles and the Society of St Vincent de Paul have invested US$2 million in a demonstration project that provides 'silent second loans' to prevent eviction. Work is also being undertaken with local lenders for modifications to existing home loans. In Milwaukee the

IAF affiliate is negotiating with local financial institutions to refinance and renovate hundreds of local homes.

Interest rates: in 2009 an international meeting took place with affiliates from London, North Carolina, Chicago, New York, Boston and Baltimore-Washington to launch the '10% is enough' campaign. The objective was to reinstate usury laws in both the UK and US and to limit interest rates to 10 per cent.

Immigration: activities around immigration issues are based in Southwest US and take several forms. Recent immigrants are offered educational programmes that include 'Know your rights' and financial information. In California affiliates have provided thousands of officially accepted ID cards and changed laws around the impounding of vehicles. In Arizona recent oppressive anti-immigrant laws have been blocked. In Iowa voter education programmes have been deployed to demonstrate the financial and economic benefits of immigration. Overall, the campaigns aim to promote more humane responses to immigration, and base the arguments in faith and democratic principles that seek to bring people together across ethnic, religious and language divisions.

Critiques of the Industrial Areas Foundation approach

The first community organisation to be created by Alinsky, the BYNC, took place in 1939, and the IAF was formed in 1940. There are currently 57 IAF affiliates operating in 21 states across the US, with further affiliates in the UK, Germany and Australia. Over these 70 years the broad understanding of community organising has changed, the IAF position has evolved and some long-term community organisations have transformed themselves from direct action campaigning operations into a broad range of service delivery organisations. Alongside the IAF and its affiliates alternative community organising models have developed, for example, ACORN, and a range of critiques have been deployed from all sides of the political spectrum. We now explore some of these critiques.

To place the IAF in context we need to understand that community organising is a broad concept. Even during the 1930s and 1940s community organising was not just the preserve of Alinsky. Wenocur and Reisch (1989) demonstrate that community organisation as a method of social work (alongside casework and groupwork) was under serious debate in welfare circles. In 1939 the Lane report from the National Council of Social Work identified community organising as a social work process, 'to bring about and maintain a progressively more effective adjustment between social welfare resources and social welfare needs' (Lane, 1939, p 499). As seen in the Back of the Yards and Woodlawn case studies above, mature community organisations became, in effect, successful social welfare agencies. In East Brooklyn the IAF affiliate built the Nehemiah Homes. In other places affiliates are concentrating on campaigning to make the city/state do the right thing. Important questions are therefore: how essential is the building of a power organisation and the conflict stage to reach the welfare delivery phase? How effective is the IAF model in delivering this? Is welfare delivery what this is really about, whether through an evolving community organisation or by public agencies?

As discussed, Alinsky was dismissive of established welfare organisations, which he often described as the enemy that simply sustained the status quo and inequality, a process Alinsky termed 'welfare colonialism'. This was, Alinsky believed, because people who had power never gave anything away so that poor people had to take the responsibility to organise and take power in their own self-interest. Therefore, the confrontational working outside of the system approach adopted by the IAF was a necessary (and temporary?) phase that provided the only way forward for poor and dispossessed people in a time of overt racial discrimination and political repression of progressive forces.

Rodham quoted Alinsky as saying,

> One thing we instil in all our organisers is that old Spanish Civil War slogan: "Better to die on your feet than to live on your knees." Social scientists don't like to think in those terms. They would rather talk about politics being a matter of accommodation, consensus – and not this conflict business. This is academic drivel. How do you have consensus before you have conflict? There has to be a rearrangement of power and then you get consensus. (1969, p 12)

An alternative view comes from Reissman (1967), who asked if the effect of the IAF model was to politicise an area, or whether it just directed 'people into a kind of dead end local activism?' (p 475). Rodham's critique of the IAF expanded this question. She pointed that out Nicholas von Hoffman, the lead community organiser in Woodlawn, recognised that at best only 2 per cent of a community would be active in any IAF organisational drive. So the claim that mass mobilisation and democracy are inherent in community organisation is perhaps mostly public relations. One of Alinsky's rules was that it was not what you had but what the enemy thought you had that was important. So it is understandable why the mass mobilisation claims were made. However, it is important that community organisations are directly accountable to the local community, so the degree of local involvement is a critical issue. Such involvement is likely to decline as the 'hot' issues are resolved and the community organisation moves into its welfare phase.

A more important criticism of community organisations is that they are built on the idea of self-interest. On the one hand, this is essential to get people on board, to build a collective sense of purpose and to sustain motivation. But simply promoting self-interest can easily lead to exclusion of others and take unfortunate directions. The white power activists in the Back of the Yards neighbourhood would say they were promoting their self-interest, as they perceived it. Just arguing in terms of self-interest is therefore not enough. Alinsky recognised this and located his arguments within a strong moral and philosophical framework, although it is hard to maintain such a discourse and to put these values into effect on the ground in poor communities.

Another side of self-interest is the position of the community organisations themselves. The IAF approach of creating an organisation of organisations means that once established, the organisation becomes, in effect, the dominant power holder in the community. But what are the checks and balances that prevent such a powerful local organisation from becoming corrupt and inefficient? How do you prevent a new radical organisation from becoming the power preserve of the controlling group? Not that this is inevitable, but the possibility is certainly there.

Hunter Gray, an organiser in the south of Chicago, has suggested that the BYNC degenerated over the years into an appendage of the local Democratic Party machine, and that a similar fate followed TWO (hunterbear.org). He believes that this is due to two factors. First, the Alinsky model relies on developing local people as the future leadership and this entails significant risk that they have the required moral outlook and personal values to do the job properly; and second, the failure to adequately instil a moral and political analysis into the organisation that has been developed through short-term pragmatic organising. Furthermore, Gray believes that under Ed Chambers the IAF has become very rigid in its model as they impose what the IAF believes is the only proven way to organise and, in effect, a top-down operation.

Rodman reported on an interview with Professor Shimony who believed that both Back of the Yards and Woodlawn were failures. Shimony contended that BYNC had not managed to effectively confront the white power elements within the community or to deal effectively with the local housing integration issues, and that Woodlawn had tried and failed to bring the local gangs under control. Anderson (1966) also believed that community organising had not led to fundamental change, and that it had just produced 'a better ghetto'. Rodman suggested that by the late 1960s Alinsky recognised the problem, and was considering sending IAF trainees into the Back of the Yards neighbourhood to organise against BYNC, which he is reported to have called a 'Frankenstein', and into Woodlawn to open up the organisation there to the white community. The two revitalised organisations could then potentially cooperate in future joint ventures.

By the mid-1960s Alinsky recognised a more fundamental problem to the standard IAF organising model, that of the viability of the neighbourhood as the focus for organisation. In his fight against Kodak in Rochester, Alinsky could not change the company employment policy simply through the efforts of the local community. He needed concerned middle-class people and in this case, stockholders, to join the campaign. From this experience he began to see the powerlessness of individualised middle-class people who had the potential to be collectively radicalised. If this could be done, the skills of the disaffected middle class could be deployed for social change.

This was not just an opportunity, but also a necessity. Rodham quoted Alinsky as saying the territorially defined community was no longer a viable societal unit. Alinsky believed there were a number of factors at play: first, the movement of middle-class people to the suburbs, a trend that included those within the ghetto who could develop the means to escape. Second, increased mobility and the 'car culture' meant that people could live, work and socialise over a considerable distance, with the resulting decline in the importance of the area surrounding their home. As a result people identified more with dispersed networks than a specific geographical area. Third, the IAF power and conflict model is based on having an enemy to attack. The enemy was no longer local, however, and was dispersed across a range of city, state and federal agencies. Alinsky saw this as a crisis of community power in which the basic Alinsky rules of engagement were difficult to apply.

This loss of local community is a continuing problem as the social trends identified by Alinsky in the 1960s continue to transform the nature of Western societies. No satisfactory responses on how to organise in this context have been made. For example, the Occupy Movement that started in Wall Street and spread across Western countries in 2011 is a current example. Diverse groups of people discontented with many facets of the modern world were motivated to protest, but without specific targets and defined achievable goals, the protests collapsed into short-term media events.

A different critique comes from Gary Delgado (1999), who, along with Wade Rathke, founded ACORN in 1970 and is the founder of the Center for Third World Organizing. Delgado argued that in the 1960s and 1970s, spurred on by the successes and glamour of Alinsky, a large number of people and organisations started to operate under the banner of community organising. By 1999 over 6,000 community organisations of various sizes and of one kind or another were operating in the US. Taken together these community organisations produced a significant list of achievements that Delgado identified as the development of sophisticated leadership, some redressing of power relationships and putting the dispossessed at the table with bankers, planners and politicians.

Delgado suggested that despite the successes, community organising had inbuilt flaws and had lost its way in recent decades. Organisers understood the importance of organising large numbers of people on specific issues, but they often missed the point that community organising was about building long-term power organisations, not simply winning campaigns. Delgado also believed that many of these so-called community organisations, as well as the IAF, had failed to understand the importance of 'race' and ethnicity in their work.

According to Delgado, the majority of organising in 'communities of colour' had been responses to discrimination rather than housing/employment issues per se. These actions were then separate from the work of mainstream community organisations. Delgado claimed this was because the IAF was interested in developing a pragmatic approach rather than an ideological one, and that the majority of lead organisers were white, male and middle class, who inadvertently replicated existing 'race', gender and sexual relationship in the new community organisations. This argument is rather generalised and tends to ignore that the actual leadership of the community organisation, once established, would often be from the Black community if they were the majority in the community (for example, Arthur M. Brazier and then Leon Finney in Woodlawn).

The solution proposed by Delgado was to move away from the neighbourhood as the focus of organising, something that Alinsky himself recognised, and to focus on issues of identity based on a new set of relationships between organisers, leaders and members. Miller (comm-org.wisc.edu) in his critique of Delgado's book, accepts that 'race', gender and sexuality are issues to be addressed, but questions whether these factors alleviate the need to respond to local issues such as crime, drugs, schools, slum landlords and so on. He suggests that successful organising is based not on geography or abstract concepts of identity, but on a commonality of issues that can be successfully organised around. 'Race', gender and sexuality are, of course, part of this, as are housing and employment, but what is required is a specific focus and achievable objectives for anything tangible to be achieved.

Conclusion

Despite some of the rhetoric coming from the IAF, it is unclear how far the organisation actually operates outside the mainstream of civil society. The range of current activities outlined above, while all very necessary to the people concerned, is hardly the stuff of revolution. Perhaps community organising through the IAF is just a practical way to build relationships with people and communities for the promotion of progressive social issues. Current activity is firmly focused on developing campaigns to persuade or force institutions to amend their programmes or to fund new initiatives to support poor individuals, families and communities.

The range of activities outlined above is both diverse and patchy in its application. Each region and affiliates pick up on what they are interested in and believe it is possible to deliver. In contrast, critics of the IAF say that it imposes its overall issues agenda on local groups. While the IAF certainly promotes particular issues, local democracy appears to be active in deciding what issues are promoted locally.

In terms of our criteria from Chapter Two, there are common activities across the IAF affiliates around leadership development, organisational development, capability, building autonomous organisations, empowerment of local people and in various ways, asset building. The specific issues being taken up by an affiliate are varied but all fall under the criteria of promoting rights, quality of life and developing wellbeing. A reasonable question is how these activities would have been addressed without IAF intervention. The gains for local people from involvement with the IAF are clearly visible.

FOUR

Industrial Areas Foundation in the UK and Australia

A small group of thoughtful people could change the world. Indeed, it's the only thing that ever has. (Margaret Mead)

In this chapter we look at how the IAF has developed its affiliate programme internationally. In the first part we look at the development of community work in the UK and the slow development of interest in community organising, and how the IAF model has managed to take a foothold. In the second part we consider a case study in Australia, that of the Sydney Alliance.

Industrial Areas Foundation and the UK

Until very recently the UK had not responded positively to the idea of community despite various attempts over the years to introduce the IAF model. There are a number of reasons for this. The UK is essentially a conservative country, albeit in different ways to conservatism in the US, and the IAF model is seen to be very un-British in its stress on power and conflict. Practice in the UK, described variously as community work, community development and latterly community learning and development, is underpinned by a restrictive policy approach based on small area and partnership working that is not conducive to broad area organising. There is a minority radical tradition in UK community work, but this has been in decline over the past few decades. There is also the social effect of broad-based welfare state provision and a history of municipal socialism, which, taken together, can be disempowering for attempts at community organising. In this chapter we summarise the background context to community work in the UK and explore the various attempts to introduce community organising.

Community work in the UK

One of the main underpinning features of community work practice in the UK is the legacy of colonial administration, especially in the post-1945 period. Community development as a practice was developed in the British colonies as a way of helping move countries towards self-rule and ultimately independence. Post-independence, many of these workers returned to the UK, bringing their model of practice with them. This approach became known as a non-directive model, described by Batten (1967), one of its main proponents, as,

> ... the community worker does not attempt to decide for people or to lead, guide or persuade them to accept any of his [!] own conclusions about what is good for them. He tries to get them to decide for themselves what their needs are, what if anything they are willing to do to meet them, and how they can best organise, plan and act to carry their project through. (p 11)

At the time, non-directive work was thought to be a radical position, although in retrospect, it is not what it appears to be as workers always exercise decision making over what they will or will not become involved in. Furthermore, we know from Paulo Freire that people need to go through a critical reflective process to work out what they want; if this process is absent, people tend to default to normative positions. The non-directive approach is, in effect, a very conservative form of practice.

In 1968 the Gulbenkian Foundation undertook a review of community work, concluding that it was 'concerned with affecting the course of social change through the two processes of analysing social situations and forming relationships with different groups to bring about desirable change.... In short community work is a means of giving life to local democracy' (Gulbenkian Committee 1968, p 3). Although the report talks about social change, it does so within a restrictive framework. Practice was defined as threefold: neighbourhood projects, interagency work and research linked to social planning. Current practice in the UK has mainly evolved from this position.

Also significant in 1968 was Enoch Powell's, an ex-Conservative minister, infamous 'Rivers of Blood' speech, predicting violence on the streets of English cities in response to continuing immigration. The government, in some panic over the public support for Powell, linked the discontent to new research evidence demonstrating continuing high levels of poverty in the UK. The response of the government was the establishment of the national Community Development Project (CDP), which was, like much of British social policy, built on policy experience in the US.

Anti-poverty programmes in the US in the 1960s were based on an area approach, for example, the Community Action Programmes for juvenile delinquency and the Model Cities programme that promoted community action and local participation. The underpinning ideological position behind these projects was that social and economic problems were not caused by fundamental structural problems in the economy, society or political system. Rather, they were products of local circumstances that could be solved through localised small-scale intervention. This view fitted comfortably with that of the UK government, which was not about to admit to any structural problems within British society. The Home Office described the CDP as 'a modest attempt at action and research into the better understanding and more comprehensive tackling of social need ... through closer co-ordination of central and local, official and unofficial effort, informed and stimulated by citizen initiative and involvement' (cited in Lees 1975, p 21).

Twelve CDPs were established in Coventry, Liverpool, Southwark, Glyncorrwg, Batley, Birmingham, Canning Town, Cumbria, Newcastle, Oldham, Paisley and North Shields. The projects were based on the assumption that the local research team would identify the nature and solution of the local problems and an action team would mobilise local people to solve them. The CDPs had rather mixed results, as might be expected, as they were trying, with very limited resources, to respond to fundamental problems around housing, unemployment and poverty. Green and Chapman (1992), in their review of the CDPs, showed that the projects had a number of other weaknesses in both practice and theory. They suggested that the CDPs had failed to take into account gender and 'race' issues, and that they had not managed to build broader political alliances or to develop a viable practice theory.

Purcell (2005) suggests that the CDPs did produce a number of influential documents that transformed the understanding of community problems and what intervention could potentially achieve. *The costs of industrial change* (CDP Inter-Project Editorial Team, 1977a) identified how the specific management decisions of multinational companies could have a profound effect on local communities. *Whatever happened to council housing* (CDP Inter-Project Editorial Team, 1976) identified that the conditions on many estates were due to government decisions concerning housing policy and the housing market, rather than the fault of tenants. *Gilding the ghetto* (CDP Inter-Project Editorial Team, 1977b) analysed the area-based social policy approaches and argued that it was simply a diversion from the class nature of economic and social change.

These documents were influential within the radical wing of community development practice, but had no noticeable effect on government policy. Some attempts were made by the more radical CDP workers to develop common grounds with trade unions over supporting unemployed workers and possible joint campaigns on housing issues affecting union members. The trade unions, however, had a limited industrial focus and refused to join in. This attempt to link community activity to trade union organising has a resonance with Alinsky, the CIO and Back of the Yards, but it is not clear if this was part of CDP thinking.

From the 1970s onwards practice in the UK became influenced by three new trends: the impact of feminism and 'race' relations, the co-option of community work by the state and a steady reduction in project funding. Purcell (2005) contends that feminism reshaped both the community work agenda and modes of practice. The increasing social confidence of women became reflected in the more active participation of women in community groups, the identification of local issues concerning women (for example, caring and reproduction), as well as recognising that women bore the brunt of dealing with housing and poverty issues. Feminist analysis also began to challenge male assumptions of practice. Gender relationships, the use of power within groups and the understanding that the personal was political confronted and eventually changed the patriarchal approach of many white male community workers.

During this period continuing immigration to the UK from East Africa and the Indian subcontinent changed the social nature of many English cities, bringing with it variations to existing social problems. At the time some community workers actively engaged with these issues while others saw the 'race' question as a subdivision of the class system, and still others simply ignored it entirely. In the years since then white community workers, faced by the critique of their practice from their Black and Asian colleagues, increasingly took on board 'race' issues and the importance of making themselves and community work appropriate and accessible to the new communities.

Purcell (2005) argues that at a policy level the 1970s brought other changes. The Comprehensive Community Programmes in 1974 and the Housing Action Areas led to the growth of social planning with community workers employed, in effect, as intermediaries between authorities and the local community. The economic crises of the decade and the arrival of the Conservative government in 1979 also set in train funding cuts for public services and community work employment, and crucially the closure of many community and resource centres from which community activity had been undertaken.

Waddington (1983) argued that the result of these trends was that community work in the UK lost it way. In his classic article commenting on the disorientation of many workers, he said, 'The plain fact is that many community activities, as we originally conceived them, have simply lost their point. Our current predicament is that we are no longer collectively quite sure of what we are trying to do or how to do it.' Barr's (1991) study of community workers identified that despite radical rhetoric espoused by many workers, practice was generally conservative and self-policed, with much confusion about the purpose and methods of community work.

In the last two decades practice in the UK has expanded through increased funding support by the previous New Labour government. The policy framework that underpinned the expansion continued the path outlined by Gulbenkian, that of small area approaches and increasing partnerships between community-based organisations and the local state. It has been argued (Beck and Purcell, 2010) that this approach excludes an overall structural analysis of social and economic problems, leaving these major issues un-dealt with. Community work practice has therefore continued with much the same confusion as described by Waddington. Purcell (2005) criticises current practice in the UK on five counts:

- poor application of basic concepts and techniques
- absence of a viable practice theory
- dominance of the social planning approach
- insularity and the failure to learn from the experience of others
- inadequate training in essential knowledge and key skills.

Purcell goes on to say that,

Many workers in the community are often unable to properly define and utilise a number of key concepts and processes. Community involvement and participation has become either a token policy requirement or a routine exercise without any real understanding of how or why it is important to do this. Key concepts such as empowerment, participation and sustainability are poorly defined. This has led many practitioners to reject the concepts entirely. In addition, practice often fails to apply basic techniques to properly identify community needs, effectively organize, plan or learn from experience. (2005, p 23)

Community organisations in the UK tend to be mostly small-scale and narrow in focus. Very little attention is paid to developing local leadership in the community, with the emphasis instead on identifying individuals who can sit on partnership committees as community representatives. To this end, capacity building programmes tend to be about training people to respond to the agenda of the local state and associated agencies. The ambition of most community organisations is defined by the policy objectives of the local state and the availability of grant funding.

The prevalence of grant support for community activity is a defining feature of community activity in the UK. These are often local authority grants paid ultimately from local or national taxation, via the UK National Lottery or in other cases from charitable trusts. For many community groups it is a given that they will work in partnership with the local state and associated agencies, and that funding will follow. Such an arrangement can have many advantages, of linking local organisations to public agencies and the provision of income to community-based services. It does, however, make the idea of building an organisation outside of these arrangements somewhat deviant. Few community-based organisations in the UK would see such an approach as a viable option.

Another key factor in the UK is what could be termed 'municipal socialism', where the local state is seen as the main provider of services to the community. One of the challenges therefore facing any attempt to build a broad-based community organisation to improve services is that the majority of people may simply say 'That's what the local council does.' Building a community organisation around broader issues of housing and employment may be more possible. However, asking people to pay subscriptions for a community organisation is culturally very difficult as the normal expectation is that services are provided free at the point of delivery, as they have been effectively prepaid through taxation. The idea that the way forward for a deprived community is through setting up an organisation outside the power structure is a hard sell when most people actually want core local authority services delivered more effectively. The aggressive tactics that can come with the IAF will feel very uncomfortable for most people and have been described several times as unfair, unnecessary and un-British.

Community organising in the UK

This section looks at various attempts to bring the idea of community organising, essentially the IAF model, to the UK and its relationship to what was seen as radical practice. We do this through exploring a number of key publications, and also discuss the work of Citizens UK, an IAF affiliate, and the present Coalition government's 'Big Society' programme.

As noted above there is a radical tradition within many UK communities and supported by a significant minority of community workers. Jan O'Malley (1977) wrote a very influential book that illustrates the nature of the radical tradition through a case study in Notting Hill in London. O'Malley focused on the struggles around housing, local planning, public space and children's play. Notting Hill is a multi-racial area, and in the late 1960s and early 1970s, was the site of much racial conflict, but these were seen as separate reactive issues rather than the main focus of organising at the time.

O'Malley opened the book by saying that it was about 'the struggles of the working class for survival ... and for control over the resources and decisions which determine their living conditions (1977, p 7). The first chapter explores the political economy of the area, looking at the process of capital accumulation, land and housing ownership, the housing conditions of working people and political powerlessness. This is an analysis few community workers would make today as questions like these are now seldom asked, such is the depoliticisation of contemporary practice.

The main point from O'Malley is that radical practice is about politics. The book quoted a statement issued by a 'conference of neighbourhood agitators' in 1972. It proclaimed, 'we, as groups involved in community organizing, are opposed to the capitalist system and the inevitable exploitation this brings' (1977, p 166). The statement talked about intensifying the class struggle, developing collective forms of power and political consciousness, and making alliances with 'women, claimants, blacks, new left groups and left political parties.' This is community organising but underpinned by a Marxist perspective and focused on challenging capitalism. In contrast, the IAF model of community organising (and it is unclear if anyone in Notting Hill was aware of its existence) looks rather moderate and non-political and therefore would have had little appeal (the right wing in the US who brand Alinsky and the IAF as communist would do well to reflect on this).

The first serious attempt to promote the IAF model in the UK came in 1984 with the publication by James Pitt and Maurice Keane of *Community organizing – You've never really tried it: The challenge to Britain from the USA*. The book, based on the authors' experience in the US, critiqued practice in the UK and argued for broad-based community organising to redress the political balance in favour of poor communities. This publication caused much controversy with intense opposition on the one hand, and lots of interest by a minority. Photocopied versions of the book were passed around various community work networks in samizdat fashion. For those who were interested in taking this further, the question was simply how to fund it.

In 1988 a major step forward was made with the establishing by Neil Jameson of the Citizen Organising Foundation (COF). The COF has developed a pivotal role in promoting community organising in the UK, and its current website describes its mission thus,

> COF acts as the national umbrella organisation of the broad-based organising movement in Britain and Ireland…. It is the focal point for an increasingly diverse alliance of congregations, community groups and labour organisations. (see www.cof.org.uk/)

It goes on to say that it works through broad-based organisations, which it describes as being:

> … made up of smaller local civil society organisations, such as congregations, union branches, schools, local associations – which affiliate to COF on payment of dues…. These BBOs [broad-based organisations] engage in a series of campaigns at local, regional and occasionally national level on issues which their members have identified as being important to their communities.

In 1996 Alan Twelvetrees published an interesting book based on his study in the US called *Organizing for neighbourhood development: A comparative study of community development corporations and citizen action organizations*. This was followed in 1991 by Barry Knight's study of the first two years of the COF. To coincide with this publication the Research and Training Initiative in Newcastle ran two seminars on community organising that brought together Barry Knight, Gary Delgado from ACORN, and a group of interested community workers (including Rod Purcell, co-author of this book) to explore the potential for community organising in the UK.

The momentum for promoting community organising in the UK was increasing, but it was still very much a minority interest. In contrast, the opposition to the idea was also growing. In 1995 the Churches Community Work Alliance published a short booklet titled *Community organizing: The UK context*. In the booklet, the authors Paul Henderson and Harry Salmon, although sympathetic to community organising in principle, identified a number of problems. The authors said that generally community work practice in the UK failed to achieve very much and that community organising was seen by some as the solution. However, they argued that the IAF, 'over its long history has failed to change or modify the structures of the USA which are increasing the level of poverty' (1995, p 33). They quoted Gary Delgado who suggested that community organising was effectively a zero-sum game in that organised communities simply drew resources away from less organised communities. In this process it was the more developed and less poor communities that would win as they had a stronger leadership base. And it drew on Delgado's critique (discussed above) that the IAF model failed to deal adequately with 'race' and gender issues and the broader problems of identity.

There were further criticisms of applying the IAF approach in a UK context, for example, the difficulty of creating an independent funding stream, a general 'the US is not like the UK' argument, that the 'macho' approach of working through conflict was unlikely to attract support in the UK, a dislike of working on the basis of self-interest, and that working through Christian churches in the UK was to exclude other religions and the non-religious from participating. Henderson and Salmon went on to suggest that a better way forward might be through the work of intermediary bodies, and gave the Standing Conference for Community Development (SCCD, later the Community Development Exchange, CDX) as an example. With due respect to the SCCD, it could be argued this was something of a 'clutching at straws' idea.

By the mid-1990s radical practice in community work was definitely a minority, and declining preoccupation with community organising itself a minor interest with radical workers. This can be illustrated through the 1996 publication *Radical community work: Perspectives from practice in Scotland* by Ian Cooke and Mae Shaw. It came at a time when community development was coming back into political favour, with both the soon-to-end Conservative government and future incoming New Labour administration. The book presents 11 case studies of practice covering: partnership, campaigning, housing, community care, disability, women, lone parents, anti-racism and community arts. While we do not wish to criticise the work undertaken in these case studies, what is interesting is how practice was conceptualised into what could be described as client groups. The overview chapter reasserts 'the primacy of class as a way of locating explanations of social inequalities' (1996, p 6). Alinsky gets a passing mention for his view on the importance of recognising the world as it was. The CDPs, the trade union movement and the Labour Party leadership get a lot of attention. There was a call for mutual solidarity, with the example of the Anti-Poll Tax campaign highlighted. All this is not that far removed from Jan O'Malley in the 1970s – the politics are much the same, but with the overt stress on Marxism toned down.

The overview chapter ends with a 'mission statement' for community work in the 1990s, with Sivanandan (1990, p 22) quoted as the way forward:

> ... to open one's sensibilities out to the oppression of others, the exploitation of others, the injustices and inequalities melted out to others – and to act upon them, making an individual/local case into an issue, turning issues into causes and causes into movements and building in the process a new political culture, new communities of resistance that will take on power and capital and class.

Quite so; the unanswered question is how to organise to do achieve this.

On 1 January 1997 *The Independent* newspaper ran an article by Peter Stokes and Barry Knight from the Foundation for Civil Society promoting 'broad-based organising'. This may be the first time such a discussion was aired in the mainstream UK media. The article asserted, 'We must tackle the structural causes of civic decline and fragmentation in urban communities. Just as workforces organised to advance their interests a hundred years ago, citizens must organise in new ways today to reverse the slide into powerlessness' (Stokes and Knight, 1997a). The article went on to report that the first community organisation in the UK was established in Bristol in 1990, and since then others had been set up in Merseyside, Sheffield and the West Midlands. The report noted that the latest, and which would turn out to be the most significant, was the East London Communities Organisation (TELCO). TELCO represented a coalition of 40 congregations and community associations, organising around local jobs and improvements to education, while campaigning against poverty and discrimination. These independent citizen coalitions were linked to the COF and through them, to the IAF.

In the article Stokes and Knight commented that the community organisations had worked on issues relating to local government and public bodies, but that their actions were 'increasingly targeting where the real power lies, in company boardrooms. The prime task is to hold arrogant, irresponsible, corporate power accountable.' How was this to be done? By creating big organisations that could 'mobilise many hundreds of people. At any time, each organisation may have a dozen action teams working on different issues, from high-street litter to malnutrition and the policies of the big food retailers.' The authors also pointed out that these new community organisations 'are diverse, and bring together schools and tenants groups, Christians and Muslims, Sikhs and Hindus, black and white, young and old, working class and middle class. They build an agenda for action around shared interests.' They noted that with their size, such organisations never went away and would become a permanent force in civic society.

So where has this got to by 2102? The overarching organisation is Citizens UK, with affiliates in London (with local chapters in East, North, South and West London as well as Shoreditch), Milton Keynes, Nottingham and Birmingham. Attempts are underway to organise in Cardiff and Glasgow. These organisations are based on dues-paying members, and around 250 institutions representing faith organisations, trade unions, community groups, universities and colleges. Formal training courses are offered that aim to help people build on their faith and value positions, and to understand how power and self-interest work in the world and how this can be used positively. Attending these courses is essential for anyone wanting to progress in the citizen organisations, and they provide a common model of organising developed from the IAF that appears non-negotiable.

Current campaigns include:

- For both the 2010 UK parliamentary election and the 2012 London mayoral election candidates presented their response to current issues and responded to questions from an assembly of citizen organisation representatives.

- The living wage campaign. This is calculated at the rate every worker needs to provide their family with the essentials in life. Citizens UK estimate 10,000 families have moved out of poverty due to this campaign.
- The Independent Asylum Commission produced 180 recommendations to safeguard asylum seekers in the UK, while promoting public confidence in the validity of the UK being a place of sanctuary. Campaigns are continuing on these recommendations.
- The CitySafe campaign encourages local businesses to offer their premises as a safe haven and to report local crime, to build effective working relationships with the police, and to promote dialogue between the police and young people.
- Promoting community-led housing.
- London 2012 Olympics. In 2004 an agreement was signed with the London 2012 bid team agreeing the benefits to the local communities from the games, and outlined six 'people promises':
  - affordable homes for local people through a Community Land Trust and mutual home ownership
  - funding to be set aside to improve local schools and health services
  - the University of East London to be the main higher education beneficiary of the sports legacy
  - £2 million to be committed for a construction academy to train local people for the coming construction jobs
  - that at least 30 per cent of the jobs created by the Olympics would be set aside for local people
  - that the Lower Lea Valley Area would be designated a 'Living Wage Zone' and all jobs guaranteed to be paid at least at that level.

What is interesting here is the sustained focus on campaigning and making existing power holders 'do the right thing'. Citizens UK has not taken the route of early IAF projects and become a service delivery or welfare organisation. For example, it campaigns for increased social housing but has deliberately not taken the East Brooklyn Nehemiah Homes route of building its own houses. It is not clear if this strategic decision is a reflection on what may have gone wrong in some IAF community organisations in the past, or recognition of organisational weakness that prevents it from delivering its own services. Either way, Citizens UK is, as it says, here to stay, and demonstrates what community organisations can achieve in the UK. It is an open question, however, how far it can expand across the UK.

The Big Society

With the coming to power of the new Coalition government in 2010 a new approach to community organising has taken the stage in the form of the 'Big Society'. Jesse Norman (2010), in his book on the Big Society, quotes Prime Minister David Cameron as saying, 'You can call it liberalism. You can call it freedom. You can call it responsibility. I call it the Big Society' (p 195).

In explaining what the Big Society is, Norman goes on to say that it is more than a political programme; it is about unlocking the latent talent and energy in Britain to redress economic and social decline, the sub-text being that the welfare state and municipal socialism has disempowered and de-energised people away from the entrepreneurial spirit that made Britain great. This spirit can be captured again for social benefit as well as economic growth. Detractors of the idea suggest this is simply rhetoric to cover the coming cuts in welfare expenditure, and what it is really about is getting volunteers to do for free what paid council staff used to do. Cameron would say getting people to do more things for themselves is exactly the point. For a community worker this is a challenging issue – is not people taking more control over their own lives and reducing dependency one of the main practice goals? Some factions within the Labour Party also see this as an approach they should adopt to promote social change.

To the astonishment of many on both the UK political left and right, the Conservative Party's (2010) description of the Big Society said that,

> This plan is directly based on the successful community organising movement established by Saul Alinsky in the United States and has successfully trained generations of community organisers, including President Obama.

It goes on to say that 'community organisers identify, recruit and develop community leaders, and help them to develop new relationships within and between communities. They develop local campaigns, based on local concerns and priorities, to encourage people to come together and make a difference in their area.'

Under the plan 5,000 new community organisers will be trained and employed independent of government. Is this recognition of the successful civic function demonstrated by Citizens UK? Is it a fundamental misunderstanding of community organising? Or is it a genuine experiment to loosen up civic life in the UK? The answers will be in what actually happens on the ground.

The recruitment of the 'neighbourhood army' of 5,000 community organisers is currently underway, with the management and training being organised by Locality, which describes itself as 'the UK's leading network for community-led organisations'. The training for the community organisers will be a mix of traditional community organising methods (but not the pure IAF version), a practice method based on the ideas of Paulo Freire and other community-related input. Specifically mentioned by Locality is the Brazilian sociologist Clodomir Santos de Morais' work on entrepreneurial awareness and wealth creation by the poor (see Raff and Sobrado, 2000). Freirean language has also crept in, with suggestions that the community organisers will be trained to listen and encourage dialogue rather than bring any message or seek any specific outcome. Locality say the 'programme will be based around consciousness-raising rather than capacity-building. This will involve finding the "generative themes" that motivate people to act, either to change the power structure or support "Do-It-Yourself" responses in communities.' It will be interesting to see what comes from this 'Alinsky meets Freire' hybrid.

It appears that so far the majority of the people recruited to the programme have limited relevant experience, and appear to be a long way from the profile that Alinsky expected of his organisers. But then they are to organise locally, not to build large-scale power organisations. Is all this just a case of taking the labels and the methods of something radical and then deploying them to largely normative ends?

Once trained, the community organisers will, according to the Office for Civil Society:

- identify gaps or failings in services provided by the state
- mobilise community support to tackle these gaps or failings locally
- help people to start groups and charities
- enhance social capital and strengthen interactions between all parts of the community
- liaise with civil society organisations, the state and the community
- help to secure funding for local activities and their own work.

Alongside the recruitment of the community organisers, an investment fund, known as Big Society Capital, has been created using up to £400 million from dormant UK bank accounts. This fund will support Social Investment Finance Intermediaries (SIFIs), who in turn will invest in social organisations tackling major social projects. The aim is to provide funds to allow organisations to develop their capacity and to improve their contribution to social outputs in areas of need.

It is reasonable to argue that it is not really community organising as we understand it from the US, and sounds more like a description of mainstream UK community development work. At a time when cuts in government expenditure are leading to the closure of CDPs and paid experienced community development workers are losing their jobs, is this not simply a transfer of activity to a lower skill and lower cost operation? Maybe, maybe not, but at the time of writing (mid-2012) it is simply too early to know.

What is clear, however, is that in the UK we now have two competing models of community organising: the IAF/Citizens UK model and the Big Society model. The former follows the current IAF practice of focusing on campaigning to make agencies and institutions respond more positively to the poor. The latter most likely will operate through local and small-scale initiatives and perhaps establish service delivery and welfare operations along with broader campaigning activities.

Case study: Sydney Alliance

We now explore the thinking and practice of the Sydney Alliance. This discussion is based partly on interviews held in February 2011 with Amanda Tattersall, Director of the Alliance, and Glenn Powell, one of its full-time organisers.

The Alliance was set up in 2007, initially funded by the New South Wales Trades and Labor Council (the peak body for unions in the state of New South Wales). It was inspired by and is an associate of the IAF in the US, and a sister organisation of London Citizens in the UK. Its explicit hope is that the shared desire for a 'fair and just Sydney' might serve as a 'glue that binds' a heterogeneous coalition of unions with other groups in civil society (Iveson, 2010, p 610).

Development process

Since its inception in 2007, the Sydney Alliance has moved through a variety of stages: a canvassing stage, a building stage and a founding assembly that took place on the evening of 15 September 2011 in Sydney Town Hall. This was the public launch of a process that began in 2007 with 13 organisations financially committed to building the Alliance. After about a year, 22 organisations committed AUD$1 million to funding a three-year organising drive. There are currently around 50 organisations working together in the Sydney Alliance.

A clear key framework that is also the organising cycle informs its practice. It starts with a listening process, moves on to a research phase, an action planning phase, the action itself and back to listening. All this happens within the context of the second key framework, which are the goals of the Alliance. These are building community leaders within partner organisations, strengthening community relations between partner organisations and taking action for the common good. Amanda Tattersall says the Alliance has a motto – 'Don't do for others what they can do for themselves.' This indicates an approach to practice that demands high levels of participation and an active relationship with policy makers and service providers.

Thinking about coalitions

The work of the Alliance is informed by clear thinking and a sharp strategy; it is an intentional long-term process that both recognises the capacity of organisations and also how their collective self-interest can be harnessed. In her keynote address to the Canadian Union of Public Employees, Amanda Tattersall (2011) outlined five principles for successful coalitions that would underpin practice within the Sydney Alliance.

The first principle for the successful development of a coalition is *less is more*. Restricting membership to organisations that have a high level of self-interest in the issues and demanding higher levels of commitment from those organisations is a more effective strategy than simply trying to gather as many organisations as you can. Organisation building is a strategic process based on a clear power analysis – if you identify the organisations with high levels of self-interest and power to do something about the issue, then the partners in the coalition become obvious. These partners then collaboratively establish goals, strategies and tactics that deal with the issue in a way that addresses their own particular needs.

The second principle is that *individuals matter*. There must be commitment from key leaders who can prioritise time and resources. Champions within individual organisations keep the issue on the agenda and develop participation within their organisation and strong participation of individuals at grassroots level. It is also important to have a coalition coordinator who can manage the relationships and help the coalition work through the inevitable tensions that will arise in the midst of campaigning.

The third principle is that *successful coalitions build an agenda*. It is not enough for a coalition to be clear about what it is against: globalisation, privatisation or cuts to services. It has to have an agenda of specific reforms that it is advocating for. Starting from their own issues, organisations collaborate in this wider sphere and develop themes of social justice that resonate more with the wider society and the power holders. Other than that, claims of narrow self-interest can undermine the power of an organisation to advocate for change. From that, campaigns that are clear and positive emerge. Within a broad framework for change, for example, the improvement of education, specific, winnable goals are established and communicated, such as reduced class sizes.

The fourth principle is *having a good plan*! Successful coalitions have a long-term plan that takes account of political developments, such as elections, that present a particular opportunity to have influence. Therefore the organisation building, research and action phases are all sequenced to take advantage of these moments.

The fifth principle is to take *multiscaled action*. Political power operates at different levels, which means that coalitions need to organise and operate at those levels too. The blending of international, national, regional and community-level organisation and action will maximise the coalition's ability to affect change. This calls for a level of sophistication in terms of organising and communication. A dialogue between all levels and a respect for autonomy of organisations and areas will ensure that the coalition has the flexibility to respond to particular needs in particular places, and that central agendas do not dictate and stifle creativity at other levels.

Finance

The Alliance has a budget of AUD$425,000 which comes from member organisations, making it financially independent of the state and other funders who might seek to control it. Small organisations pay as little as AUD$1,000 per year and the largest pay AUD$50,000 a year. This approach to funding was seen as very countercultural in that context. In the early stages of starting this approach, some people and organisations were shocked that the Alliance would collect money even from the poorest organisations. However, the development of both financial independence and a sense of ownership within all of the membership is a key foundation for the sustainable development of the coalition.

Without this financial self-sufficiency, its ability to advocate and challenge would be severely curtailed. Glenn Powell explains that in terms of funding for community projects in Sydney there has been a move towards competitive tendering, the upshot of which is community groups fighting each other for little pots of money. It became obvious that organisations that agitate for change don't get funded. From this it can be seen that reliance on regular funding from the state, in whatever form, severely limits the ability of the voluntary sector to advocate for change. Since the Alliance has independent funding it is able to take on power holders without fear that they can be manipulated by threats to withdraw funding. It is also useful provides a public focus for campaigning work and the conflict which it inevitably produces; this member organisations which are perceived as being one step removed from the action are to some extent protected from backlash, thereby making their funding more secure.

Make-up of the Sydney Alliance

As discussed above, this coalition building has focused on 'less is more' as a guiding principle. Amanda Tattersall draws a parallel between community organising and advertising. Advertising can have three dimensions, cheap, fast and good, but you can only have two of three. So in advertising you can have a campaign that is cheap and fast but that can't be good, or it can be cheap and good, but it won't be fast. In community organising the dimensions are broad, deep and fast: you can have broad and deep, but not fast, or fast and broad, but not deep. The Alliance has opted for broad and deep, and over the past five years it has strategically identified key power holders and influencers within the city.

And so it has strategically developed a broad and unusual set of partners that are able to act together, while respecting their diverse and individual traditions. It has formed a coalition of more than 50 organisations, comprising of thousands of citizens who are organised to actively participate in the running of their city. Its make-up spans a wide spectrum of civil society organisations, ranging from the Western Sydney Community Forum to the Archdiocese of the Catholic Church, the Unions NSW and the NSW Jewish Board of Deputies, the Cancer Council and the Construction, Forestry, Mining and Energy Union (CFMEU). Despite the diversity, it works because organisations are not asked to sort out their differences but to engage with their commonalities.

Churches and trade unions

The Alliance's success in being able to draw in both trade unions and churches is in part due to the staff it has in place. To exemplify this, we briefly consider the background and contributions of Glen Powell and Amanda Tattersall.

Glen Powell has been an organiser with the Alliance for about two years. Before that he worked for the Uniting Church in Australia, one of the major denominations at work in Sydney. He initially got involved in the work of the Alliance as a local leader within the the church. After undergoing their six-day training, he campaigned within the church for them as an organisation to become a member of the Alliance. He reports that within his work, churches are seeing the Alliance as an opportunity to shift their focus from individual and spiritual concerns to a broader operation, which embraces effecting social change within the city. Although this has, to some extent, always been recognised as the church's mission, he perceives a shift from a situation whereby the church's primary response to social issues within communities was concern being expressed by church leaders at a senior level to one where there are increasing levels of active involvement of individuals within the congregations on those issues.

His analysis is that about half of the church within Australia is Catholic, with a range of Protestant dominations making up the rest. Traditionally the Catholic community has aligned itself with issues of social justice, springing from a large proportion of immigrants within their ranks, while a Protestant church has aligned itself more with the business community. Although that picture is largely now a thing of the past, he still sees a Catholic influence within the union movement. This understanding of the church's historical and current involvement in social issues, coupled with his credibility gained through working in a church context, has enabled him to build relationships with the community and to support ongoing participation in the Alliance.

Amanda Tattersall's background includes several years working as a trade union organiser. That history has developed both credibility within the union movement and an understanding of the unions' concerns and aspirations. Because of this she was able to speak their language and has built very effective bridges between the Alliance and a range of trade unions. Developing these productive relationships has taken time; unions have a clear but fairly narrow sense of what their issues are, what they want to achieve and even particular ways of working which they are comfortable with. Widening out from these positions requires the development of trust and ongoing dialogue. Amanda notes, however, that trade unions in Australia do have a tradition of being involved politically, for example, through the Accord in the 1980s (Dow and Lafferty, 2007), which resulted in universal healthcare and universal pensions through their superannuation scheme. And so the Alliance offers community organising to trade unions as an additional tool with which to effect change with and on behalf of its members.

There have been a variety of reactions to this within the trade union movement. While some have enthusiastically welcomed it, others see it as a distraction from or competition to their political activity with the Labour Party. Amanda maintains that coalition approaches, such as the Alliance, have the potential to be not simply a tool for advancing union goals but, more than that, a means of achieving new kinds of social change that could also contribute to the reinvention of unions (2010, p 2). And so this pragmatic intersection of self-interest is explored and developed in the Alliance/union dialogue. Even when part of the Alliance, the Alliance/union dynamic is not always an easy one to manage. Issues of power, process and accountability are being worked through as that relationship matures.

Organisationally, the fact that the Sydney Alliance operates at a city level rather than just a suburban level also helps to develop the productive participation of the unions in the work of the Alliance, since the main power brokers within unions also operate at city level, not at branch level. This city-wide focus is reflected in many contemporary alliances that have tended to comprise a metropolitan-wide network of institutions that are then also connected to those working in other cities, and increasingly, to those in international networks of similar organisations (Willis, 2012).

There have been claims from outside that the inclusion of unions makes the Alliance look like a left-wing organisation that then makes it unattractive to conservative organisations and politicians. Amanda's long-term ambition for the Alliance, however, is to transform the way the economy works, which she sees as an impossible task without full involvement from the trade union movement, and so management of these perceptions and tensions is a crucial part of the ongoing process of social change.

There are clearly some issues that have the potential to create a degree of tension between the unions and churches. For example, some of the more ideologically focused trade unions have expressed concerns that their relationship with churches may lessen their ability to campaign on issues such as gay marriage. Amanda says that those issues will probably never be taken up by the Alliance since it does not garner broad-based support. That is not to say that other organisations or coalitions won't raise these issues; she believes that the Alliance is not the only answer to the issues in Sydney.

Training

Training and a connection with sister organisations are seen as highly important within the Alliance, and in particular, the link with IAF Northwest, which describes itself as a regional network of broad-based community organisations in Washington, Oregon, Canada and Australia (see http://iafnw.org/). They hold two major training events per year and always have someone from overseas as the lead trainer at these major events. Locally, they organise two-day training events that they call Alliance building institutes; this is part of the overall leadership development process and introduces new participants to the core concepts of community organising and the vision and values of the Sydney Alliance. The content of this course is constantly reviewed and adjusted to be in line with the development of the Alliance. In the early days they spent time looking at why an alliance was needed and now spend more time looking at power analysis and planning. Currently the content of the traing programmes includes:

- Community organising: based on the history and tradition of religious, union and community organisations
- Relational organising: individual relational meetings, listening assemblies, research, negotiation and action
- Strengthening organisations: building a culture that is relational, action-oriented and reflective/learning
- Using relational power in the public sphere to take collaborative action on common issues.

More than 2,000 people have undergone this training in five years since the Alliance has been in existence. People who have undergone training have an opportunity to come back in a training role, developing from small group leaders to lead trainers. In this way, the training programme is effective not only as a means of training new participants, but also as a leadership development process in itself. Leaders with a more strategic role would also undergo a six-day version of the training programme. For this, participating organisations are encouraged to strategically select leaders to attend the courses that will:

- refine and shape their understanding of themselves and their role as leaders
- equip them with the understanding and skills necessary to implement strategies to strengthen their organisation to more effectively achieve its purpose
- develop leaders within their organisation and grow cooperative relationships within their organisation and with potential partners in other organisations
- put principles into practice at a Sydney Alliance action during the six days
- set strategic objectives, develop achievable plans and then mobilise the human and other resources necessary to carry out the plan.

Listening campaign

A listening campaign was carried out from October 2010 to May 2011. In that time 6,500 people from a wide range of organisations participated. In bus depots, school halls, union branches, parishes and community centres people confronted one question: 'If there was one thing that could improve your life and the life of your family, what would it be?' Methods for engaging in this ranged from small informal conversations through to more formalised group processes. As an example, one Catholic parish held listening events during all of their masses over one weekend. The intention of this process was not only to elicit information from the community, but also to encourage their involvement in doing something about the issues that they raised. To that end there was a broad but flexible shape to all of these encounters. Participants were encouraged to share their stories of everyday life and the issues that affected them and also to consider how things might be different.

Issues

Hundreds of issues arose from that process, and were considered by all of the partner organisations that identified their priority issues for action. The crucial difference between this process and simple community research was that these were not issues that somebody somewhere should take on, but issues which they, as an organisation, were concerned about and were prepared to do something about. These issues were then themed into nine broad areas. The Executive Council of the Alliance estimated that it had the capacity to take on three themes initially, which would balance the need for diversity in order to keep a broad range of people involved and to focus in order to ensure effectiveness and success. And so a group of 280 representatives of partner organisations then came together to work out which issues to action. They came with their organisation's priorities, an understanding of what resources their organisations would be prepared to commit to the campaign and their own personal priorities and commitments. This resulted in the identification of three issues that the Alliance would work on, which were: building community harmony: social inclusion, community care; health and support; and transport. From these, research action teams would connect people to the strategy and further develop the campaign plan that would lead to action. Part of their ongoing campaigning is to hold large assemblies to which politicians, such as the state president, are invited to respond to the requests that are being made by civil society. This provides an opportunity for the Alliance to demonstrate its collective power and also offers an opportunity to either develop alliances or to create enemies, drawing on the thinking of Lord Palmerston (*Hansard*, 1948): 'We have no eternal allies, and we have no perpetual enemies. Our interests are eternal and perpetual, and those interests it is our duty to follow.'

Action

One challenge facing the Alliance in terms of action comes out of Alinsky's understanding that you should never go outside the experience of the people. Given the wide diversity of groups and organisations within the Alliance, finding action within a common experience will be challenging. Since learning is embedded within all its processes, the initial actions will act as learning experiences for those new to community organising. Based on principles of power, action and reaction and only taking on issues that you can win, a range of localised actions have already begun at a suburban level. Amanda said that they do not have the capacity yet to win at a state level, and have no intention of punching above their weight. So issues around policing, transport safety and healthcare in the home are being taken on as starting points. It is imperative that these actions are successful, that there is a real demonstration of people power. This has the twin impacts of developing confidence within the membership of community organising work and in training members in community organising principles and techniques through experiential learning and reflected on in the Alliance's formal training programmes.

An example of possible action that may emerge from these processes is taking on the issue of accessibility to Redfern railway station, one of the busiest in Sydney. The overall demand that has been made by the Alliance in terms of transport is that if you live in Sydney you shouldn't be more than 400 metres away from a transport service, you shouldn't have to wait more than 15 minutes, and you should only have to buy one ticket to get you where you are going. It should also be safe, clean, affordable and accessible. This overall strategy is now being operationalised at a local level, starting with situations where these demands have not been met. And so, while most of the stations in Sydney had lifts installed where necessary at the time of the Olympics in 2000, Redfern did not. Local people have been campaigning on this issue since, but not building the power to make it come about. A local children's charity have said that they could organise 100 women with prams to turn up at a time when the decision makers and the media are present, employing the classic Alinsky tactics of personalising the issue and using ridicule as a potent weapon.

Victories

The year 2012 is wholly geared towards gaining a victory for the Alliance negotiated with the state government and celebrated at the October assembly. But it is not only the outcome that is important – that has to be built through a process that rebuilds participatory democracy. To that end they are establishing districts that are suburban-scale hubs of the Alliance, starting with five this year and building towards 15 over a three-year period. It is envisaged that each of these hubs will have a contact list of 50 people, most of whom will meet together on a monthly basis. All of this is planned with a 2015 state election in mind.

Going deeper

At the time of writing the Alliance is in a new phase that it calls 'going deeper' – going deep into the organisations, deep into the suburbs of Sydney and deep into the issues. Each of these dimensions relates back to the three goals. And so the Alliance is going deeper into organisations in order to develop new local leaders, going deeper into the suburbs of Sydney in order to develop and strengthen committee networks and going deeper into the issues in order to take action for the common good.

As an example of going deeper into organisations, Alliance organisers will work with trade unions to identify what they want to do for themselves, and then work out how to link them into the broader work of the Alliance in a way that activates self-interest.

Key issues

Leadership: We were struck by the energy, the confidence and clarity of thinking displayed by the staff of the Sydney Alliance, and particularly its Director, Amanda Tattersall. The role of leadership within community organisation is always a significant one, and perhaps more so in the formative years of its history, and perhaps the vibrancy of the organisation reflects that of its overall leader.

Power: the development of social capital, both bonding and bridging (Putnam, 2000) is evident in the work of the Alliance. The five-year process to develop this coalition of well-bonded organisations that represent a broad spectrum of civil society, thereby making the Alliance attractive to a potentially huge number of people before the organisation's public launch, demonstrates an understanding of developing and using power.

Strategic long view: the Alliance has both a long and a wide view of its work. It is not content with firefighting random local issues but is developing processes that build power and strengthen local democracy through dealing with local issues. Its aim is to have an impact on the city politically and economically, and it is patiently building the capacity of the membership and developing a carefully considered network of organisations in order to achieve that end. I am sure it is essential for the ongoing vitality and energy of the organisation to maintain these overarching aims and longer-term goals. The Alliance makes sense of the small victories, giving them a purpose and impact beyond itself.

Work–life balance: since there has been criticism of Alinsky-style organising that it does not allow organisers to balance work and family (Sen, 2003), it is perhaps important to mention that Amanda Tattersall combines the role of lead community organiser with that of raising a family. This may tie into the long-term nature of the Alliance's strategies and processes. Alinsky's approaches were based on communities raising a certain level of funding for a short, fixed-term intervention. With the Alliance's establishment of ongoing member subscription, not all issues have to be tackled straightaway. This allows for a more planned, strategic and reflective way of working that might result in a broader range of people participating in a more sustainable way.

FIVE

The **ACORN** alternative

> The only way ... for our community to be a better place to live is for the people of the community to understand and accept their personal responsibility for what happens. (W. Davis Merritt, Jr)

Background

ACORN (Arkansas Community Organizations for Reform Now) was established in 1970 by Wade Rathke, an organiser for the anti-war Students for Democratic Society (SDS), and Gary Delgado. Their objective was to 'unite welfare recipients with needy working people around issues such as school lunches, unemployment, Vietnam veterans' rights and emergency room care' (http://acorninternational. org/).

In creating an operational model for ACORN, Rathke was greatly influenced by George Wiley and the National Welfare Rights Organization (NWRO), which focused on four specific goals: adequate income, dignity, justice and democratic participation. These objectives were to be achieved through developing local affiliates, voter registration, local and national demonstrations and lobbying. The effectiveness of these tactics enabled NWRO to meet regularly with senior federal government officials. By 1971 NWRO had 540 linked organisations and claimed to represent 75,000 families. At its peak it had around 25,000 members, mainly African-American women.

By 1975 ACORN operations, modelled on NWRO, had spread to Texas and South Dakota, and the name had changed, with Arkansas being dropped for Association, reflecting the growth of the organisation. ACORN expanded at a rate of an average of three new states a year. In 1978 over 1,000 delegates met in Memphis and marched on the Democratic Party Convention with a nine-point 'People's Platform'.

In 1982, as a precurser to the current Occupy Movement, ACORN established 'Regan Ranches' in 35 cities to highlight the campaign for the rights of the homeless. To better use media opportunities, ACORN established radio stations, television and cable programming. Activities expanded across more states and ACORN developed active campaigns on housing, a living wage and educational issues. At its height it claimed over 1,200 neighbourhood chapters in more than 100 cities, with 500,000 members.

As we have seen, community organisations are something of a bête noir to the political right wing in the US. Often viewed as a communist front and inherently un-American, many campaigns, often based on little hard evidence, have been run over the years to discredit community organisations and their leadership. After the presidential election in 2008 these campaigns stepped up a gear as the new Democratic President, Barack Obama, had been both a community organiser and had used community organising methods to run his election campaign.

During the run-up to the 2008 election ACORN had registered around 1.3 million voters, although it appears that around 7 per cent of these registrations were invalid against an average of 5 per cent for other organisations. Part of the problem was that some ACORN staff were paid by the number of registrations they made, and for some staff the accuracy of the registrations was not always their main concern. After internal investigation ACORN dismissed several staff for misconduct. Some members of staff were also prosecuted for false registrations. The Republican Party used the media to accuse ACORN of widespread voter fraud, and it is claimed by ACORN that this was a political response by Karl Rove, George Bush's top political adviser, to undermine ACORN's successful voter registration drive.

In July 2008 Dale Rathke (brother of the founder, Wade) was named in *The New York Times* as having embezzled almost US$950,000 of ACORN money between 1999 and 2000. The financial irregularity had been discovered at the time, but a group of ACORN executives decided to keep the matter internal and did not notify either the ACORN board or the police. The money was repaid over the next few years. The argument for doing this was that it if the situation had been made public, ACORN's enemies would have taken the opportunity to discredit the organisation. When the details of the 'cover-up' became public, Wade Rathke stepped down as chief organiser.

In 2009 conservative activists James O'Keefe and Hannah Giles released videos (which were later proved to be both selectively edited and partly falsified) claiming that ACORN was engaging in criminal activity, including prostitution and tax avoidance. Although these claims were proved to be false in four subsequent investigations, the accusations were to be the final nail in the coffin for ACORN. The adverse publicity arising from the videos resulted in government and private funders cutting funding to ACORN. This was followed by amendments (supported by many Democrats) to spending bills in both the House of Representatives and the Senate banning government funding of ACORN. As a result, ACORN filed for liquidation in November 2010.

Although the national organisation has formally ceased to exist, many of the ACORN network organisations have continued under different names. In California the local ACORN organisation became the Alliance of Californians for Community Empowerment. Similarly, in New York the ACORN organisation changed its name to New York Communities for Change. ACORN Housing became the Affordable Housing Centres of America. Although much of ACORN's work continues, it may now not have the national focus and drive from the centre, and it is an open question how ACORN offshoots will develop over the coming years.

Main activities

Living wage: this campaign, similar to the one run by the IAF, focused on private business that provided goods and services to government to pay a living wage to their employees. ACORN campaigning on the issue led to 15 cities, including New York and Chicago, passing living wage legislation.

Predatory lending and affordable housing, the Home Defender Programme: ACORN targeted companies with dubious lending practices and campaigned against foreclosure and promoted loan counselling for those in debt. It brought a class action against Household International, a sub-prime lender. This suit was settled by a US$72 million foreclosure avoidance programme. ACORN also campaigned for housing trust funds and enforcement of affordable housing requirements on developers. The Home Defender Programme organised mass action to prevent evictions and to 'defend a family's right to stay in their homes.'

Education: just as with the IAF, education was a major activity for ACORN. It developed a model for schools that promoted small classes, parental involvement, a community-focused curriculum and qualified teachers in every classroom. In California ACORN campaigned for more textbooks to be available and for necessary building repairs to be carried out in schools. It promoted Charter Schools and campaigned against school privatisation in New York.

Voter registration: this has been a major activity within poor and minority communities since the 1980s, and also something undertaken extensively by the IAF. ACORN also campaigned to remove some of the bureaucratic obstacles that various administrations placed in the way of voter registration.

Katrina relief, New Orleans: ACORN organised several responses to Hurricane Katrina in 2005. Fundraising campaigns provided relief for those made homeless by the flooding. A volunteer programme rebuilt 1,850 homes and became one of the official planners working with the city to organise reconstruction. The ACORN Katrina Survivors Association promotes equitable treatment for Katrina survivors.

Analysis of ACORN's approach to community organising

Many of ACORN's campaigns, the living wage, voter registration, housing and education, are similar to that of the IAF. The operation model of ACORN was heavily based on that of the NWRO, which itself had influences of the IAF within it. What, therefore, is different about ACORN, and what can we learn from its experiences?

A broad view of organising

John Atlas (2010), in his book on the history of ACORN, identifies the significance of the 1973 campaign against the planned Arkansas Power & Light (APL) Company power station on the Arkansas River. The proposed power station was felt to be potentially damaging to the local environment. This was both a local threat and an ACORN opportunity. A local ACORN chapter was set up with a membership of mostly solid middle-class citizens and landowners. This represented a major departure from the traditional community organising strategy focusing on poor communities. The second innovation was in the strategy that ACORN chose to use against APL – local protests, of course – but the main approach would be through APL's stockholders, in particular universities, where ACORN had a base. The main target here was Harvard University that owned US$10 million of APL stock.

The idea of approaching stockholders is not new. Alinsky had used stockholder influence (particularly through the Unitarian church) in his fight against the employment policies of Kodak in Rochester during the late 1960s, and had plans for greater mobilisation of the middle class. Here ACORN picked up the idea and moved it forward, using middle-class university students.

Harvard proved resistant to becoming involved in the campaign, partly because it would have created a precedent for future campaigns against other companies. So Harvard itself became a campaigning target. Eventually, Harvard came onside, helped by the fact that 19 other colleges and universities (including Princeton and Cornell) had agreed to use their stock holding to influence APL.

In campaigning to shift Harvard's position, ACORN worked with student groups on campus and sympathetic faculty members, in effect, building a campaign that linked middle-class landowners in rural Arkansas to wealthy students, to institutional stock ownership. The focus of this work was environmental protection, something relatively new at the time and a shift from the focus on poverty. Consciously or not, ACORN had demonstrated what community organising could do outside of its usual confines of poor communities and the potential power of a mobilised middle class.

Nevertheless, ACORN's main focus was organising poor communities, and Rathke believed he had a model that could be dropped successfully into any community. Atlas calls this an 'assembly line' and talks about interviews with former ACORN staff members, commenting that they felt like 'interchangeable parts' and that 'ACORN basically uses people as fodder'. Rathke's view, however, was that community organising was an art form delivered by well-trained and skilled professionals.

There were also criticisms that the ACORN model ignored local conditions and adopted confrontational tactics when cooperation may have worked better. Atlas concludes, however, 'On balance, however, the deficits of the assembly-line model counted less than its benefits to a national organisation that depends on hiring numerous organisers, namely, replicability – it is a model that is easy to teach'(Atlas, location 6871).

So what is the ACORN organising model? Atlas suggests that the ACORN approach had similarities to that of the IAF. He describes it thus:

- The local organiser analyses local demographics, politics, issues and current leadership.
- The organiser meets with local leaders.
- The organiser identifies potential allies and enemies.
- The organiser drives around the local area (the 'windshield tour') to get a feel for the area.
- Door knocking to identify local issues that are important to residents and to sign up members. The objective would be to knock on every door over an eight-week period and sign up 10 per cent of households. Membership dues in the mid-1970s were US$1 per month. The money paid for the organisation, but it also created a sense of ownership and involvement among the members.
- Within two months local people should be standing up at local meetings and prepared to take action.
- In areas that had multiple chapters an executive committee should be established to coordinate campaigns.
- The objective was to empower local people to take action on issues fundamental to their lives, not to solve their problems for them.
- Once a local organisation was established local people, mostly through the new emerging leadership, would make the decisions.
- Unlike the IAF, local chapters were expected to support national ACORN campaigns. (Atlas, location 919 – 948)

The democratic process

Whereas the IAF took some pride in operating outside of the system (at least in its early days), Rathke had an alternative view. He said 'It makes no sense to spend an afternoon confronting an elected official who is not doing the job he is supposed to be doing and ignore the same official – or his job – come November.'(Atlas, location 988). Rathke recognised that simply organising protests, even large-scale protests, would often fail to change the local political machine. His strategy would be to win elected office, although he recognised a potential flaw in the strategy, that the ACORN candidates, even if elected, would be a minority voice and easily outvoted.

The election approach, sometimes called an inside-outside strategy, started with winning a seat on the Little Rock School Board in 1972, and moved on to promoting ACORN-related candidates independent of either the Republican or Democratic parties. Particular opposition came from the Democrats who saw ACORN infringing on their 'natural electorate'. In response, Rathke wanted ACORN to organise voters to influence the selection of future Democratic candidates. In the 1980 election ACORN succeeded in getting 42 delegates elected to the Democratic National Convention. As might have been expected, these delegates failed to significantly influence Democratic Party policies.

ACORN debated for many years what its approach to electoral politics should be. Atlas suggests they had three options: to stay outside of elections like the IAF, endorse specific candidates (a tried ACORN approach but with limited success), or to develop their own party. In collaboration with some trade union support, ACORN went down the latter road, with the Working Families Party (WFP). No one expected the WFP to win elections. The strategy was to campaign in those states that allowed fusion voting where multiple parties could name the same candidate on the ballot. So in the 2000 Senate election in New York the WFP named Hillary Clinton as their candidate.

In the 2001 New York mayoral election the risks involved in this policy became clear. In the Democratic primary election, a leaflet put out attacking the Hispanic opponent of the WFP-favoured candidate was highlighted in the press as racist. ACORN and WFP took the blame, and the divisions this caused in the Democratic ranks probably cost them the election. Despite this setback the WFP continues, and due to its voting support, automatically has a place on the New York ballots. It is also active in eight other states, but has not, as ACORN once hoped, become a national party. WFP sometimes runs its own candidates and cross-supports selected Democrats. WFP supports ACORN-like campaigns such as the living wage, affordable homes and equal rights.

Overall, the electoral route had been opened up as an option for community organisers, something Atlas points out, that was to influence Barack Obama. Even if you are not trying to get your own people elected, it is important to ensure poor people are registered to vote. On the one hand, as Alinsky had said, this was about making American democracy work; on the other, it would support candidates who were more favourable to the needs of poor and minority communities. Voter registration was therefore an important part of ACORN activity. As described above, it would also contribute to its demise.

Employment: trade unions and the living wage

The IAF sought alliances with trade unions as part of its organisation of organisations strategy. In contrast, ACORN was interested in creating its own trade union among unorganised and unemployed workers. The local ACORN organisers and resources could add this as a new focus and it would result in increased influence, membership and income streams. The broader context at the time was that trade unions were in decline and represented less than 25 per cent of employees in the US. Trade union organisation was highest in the large factory plants such as steel and car production. Low-wage jobs and the growing service industries such as fast food were largely ignored by the mainstream trade unions.

ACORN's attempt to create a trade union was piloted in Detroit in 1979 among fast food workers at a Burger King outlet. The organising slogan was 'Union rights are human rights … no more threats, no more lies, we want the right to organise.' By 25 to 23 the outlet agreed to union recognition. This success was followed by attempts to organise at McDonald's. The initial successes quickly went wrong as ACORN was accused of parachuting in with their own agenda and only focusing on Black-owned businesses. In a re-vote, the Burger King branch de-unionised on a 28-1 vote, and McDonald's staff voted against the union 104-46.

Over the next few years the United Labor Union (ULU), as ACORN's union arm was called, grew steadily by focusing on small workplaces. In 1984 the ULU affiliated with the Service Employees International Union (SEIU). It left the SEIU in October 2009 and continues with a base mainly in Arkansas, Louisiana and Texas. Never a huge success, the attempt at developing a union demonstrates lack of class consciousness among US workers. As workplace and neighbourhood issues can be understood as linked manifestations of capitalist inequality, if you have that ideological perspective, in the US this perhaps is not going to work.

According to Atlas, Rathke was impressed by the IAF's affiliate in Baltimore that had built a local coalition of churches and trade unions to push the city government to introduce a 'living wage' law that would apply to city employees and contractors. Rathke decided ACORN should become involved, and Chicago was to be the pilot. In 1995 ACORN put together a coalition that included local union branches, SEIU, faith networks and neighbourhood groups. Atlas says this was an innovative approach for ACORN, although it did look very much like an IAF-style operation.

The Chicago Jobs and Living Wage Campaign, as it was called, started to lobby the city. The Mayor was opposed, using the standard argument that increasing the minimum wage would lead to job losses in marginal businesses and put up the costs of services to the city. Using the classic community organising strategy of 'pick a target and polarise it', the campaign used the Farley's & Sathers Candy Company to illustrate an employer paying poverty wages. This was matched to a campaign to support the threatened Vienna Beef company that was paying employees over the minimum wage. This dual campaign approach enabled ACORN to argue it was pro-business as well as pro-worker. By 1997 the campaign had signed up 60 organisations, representing around 250,000 people. In July 1998 the city agreed to implement the living wage. In the 1999 city elections living wage supporters, including Ted Thomas, ACORN president, were elected. Over the next four years living wage campaigns were successful in 12 other US cities.

In 2003 a campaign that included 40 organisers and 60 canvassers was launched in Florida. The objective was to link a voter registration drive in the state with a referendum on increasing the local minimum wage. The referendum would be voted on at the same time as the 2004 presidential election. A side benefit would be that the prospect of increasing the minimum wage would get new voters to the polls, who would then vote for progressive candidates. The Democratic Party, fearing that this would alienate the business community, offered little support to the campaign. The referendum was won by a 72 to 28 per cent margin. The lesson from the campaign was that in the right conditions, middle-class people would vote for pro-poor policies.

Never short of ambition, Rathke turned his attention to Wal-Mart, the world's biggest employer, with over 2,000,000 employees. The campaign, again starting in Chicago, wanted Wal-Mart to increase the starting wage from US$7.25 to US$10 an hour, and to include health benefits. Opponents of the campaign argued that this wage increase would force Wal-Mart out of many inner-city locations and would lead to unemployment, especially among the Black community. A similar argument was used against ACORN's attempt to unionise McDonald's. Although unsuccessful in this campaign, Wal-Mart became a continuing target for ACORN that, as we see below, is still a priority for ACORN International.

ACORN continued with its Florida strategy of linking a living wage referendum with national votes. In the 2006 elections six states approved living wage reform and an increasing number of Democratic candidates were elected. With a majority in Congress, the federal minimum wage was increased from US$5.15 to US$7.25 in 2007.

Somewhere to live

Another campaign that would eventually get ACORN into trouble with the political right was challenging the 'redlining' that many banks imposed on poor and usually Black, neighbourhoods. If you lived in these neighbourhoods then you would automatically be refused loans. This practice was first challenged by ACORN in St Louis during 1976. The approach was to pressure the city government to only deposit funds with banks that did not discriminate in their lending policies. This action and the threat that other institutions would follow in a broader bank boycott forced the abandoning of redlining by several banks.

Following on from this initial success, a coalition of groups saw the US Congress pass the Community Reinvestment Act (CRA) in 1997. Under the Act federal penalties could be applied to banks excluding low-income neighbourhoods from loans. However, the law was seldom enforced until the late 1980s, and it could be argued that the Community Development Corporations had a bigger impact in responding to housing needs in poor areas. Many banks also signed up a range of non-profit organisations for joint housing initiatives in low-income areas as a way of meeting the demands of the CRA. ACORN itself set up the ACORN Housing Corporation (AHC) as a spin-off company to do similar deals with banks in several US cities.

Another housing initiative took place in North Philadelphia in 1977. This was an attempt to build an alliance between homeowners worried about vacant lots and potential redevelopment, and homeless families. ACORN supported a local squatting movement to take over and renovate abandoned houses. The city government was eventually sympathetic as the squats had public support, and made available cheap rehabilitation loans to the new property 'owners'. Although squatting was an illegal act, the successes in Philadelphia encouraged ACORN to develop it into a national campaign under a slogan 'Need a house? Call ACORN.'

The campaign was run in 13 cities with mixed results. In St Louis and Dallas squatters were met with legal action. In Detroit the city council eventually agreed to set up a Homesteading programme and formally gave clemency to the squatters themselves. In New York a bitter two-year confrontation with Mayor Koch eventually led to the setting up of the Mutual Housing Association of New York (MHANY). As a mutual association, local residents operated as a collective to rehabilitate buildings for their own use, but with limited ownership rights. This model is common in Western Europe but was unusual in the US as it frames housing as a social product rather than as an individual investment. In the mid-1990s Mayor Giuliani adopted an aggressive anti-squatter campaign that undermined some of ACORN's gains. In contrast, Guiliani supported the IAF Nehemiah Homes development in East Brooklyn.

To raise the issue of homelessness nationally, ACORN set up a tent city in Washington. In 1982 Congress passed the National Homesteading Act (NHA) which made it easier for lower-income people to purchase houses owned by the federal Housing and Urban Development agency (HUD), one of the largest owners of empty properties in the US. The Homesteading campaign linked into the other housing developments coming through AHC.

Atlas suggests that the success of the Homesteading programme was down to ACORN framing it in terms of traditional American values: home ownership, self-reliance, family life and, of course, increasing local property values. While successful in this context, Atlas argues that the ACORN rhetoric also fed into the Reaganite ideology of self-reliance and the irrelevance of big government programmes, and that people could and should solve their own problems.

AHC took ACORN in a collaborationist direction. For example, bastions of US capitalism, J.P. Morgan and Chase Manhattan Bank, both donated several hundred thousand dollars to ACORN. Right-wing commentators saw this as appeasement by the banks to buy off trouble, while left-wing commentators saw it as ACORN selling out. ACORN argued that AHC gave its tenants and local communities a better deal than they would get elsewhere. Critics suggested that ACORN moderated its actions so as not to alienate potential partners, although no hard evidence has been produced to back up this claim.

A current criticism from the right is that the sub-prime disaster was in fact ACORN's fault (see Thenextright.com, 2008). Their argument is that if ACORN had not forced banks to lend to poor people, then sub-prime mortgages would not have existed. This is disingenuous to say the least, but does show the fear (or hatred?) that ACORN engendered in the political right.

In fact ACORN campaigned extensively against foreclosure and ran a direct action campaign against HFC, one of the worst sellers of sub-prime mortgages. The usual tactics of attending the HFC Annual General Meeting and lobbying city governments to disinvest were adopted. In 2002 ACORN took out a class action for deceptive practices against HFC. This is the first time ACORN had taken such a route. *The New York Times* and *Forbes* magazine took up the case, and in 2003, HFC settled with a pay-out of US$483 million to its borrowers.

Brooklyn

In 2004 ACORN was at the centre of another controversy, the Atlantic Yards redevelopment in Brooklyn. The Atlantic Yards project proposed the demolition of a sizeable part of Brooklyn, the building of a sports stadium, extensive office space and housing units. It was expected that ACORN would oppose the development as gentrification of the area at the expense of the poor. ACORN, in supporting the development, argued that it was an opportunity to create significant local affordable housing in a mixed environment that would allow people to move on from the ghetto, and create jobs. Atlas points out that internal ACORN discussions at the time were also concerned with which option would be in the best interests of building the organisation. Alongside this, local organisers met with around 3,500 ACORN members to discuss the position the organisation should take.

In the 2004 New York elections WFP received over 168,000 votes, an indication of the pressure ACORN could mobilise if they did not get their way over Atlantic Yards. Seven other local organisations were now also supporting the ACORN proposals. Eventually a deal was made that 50 per cent of the housing would be made affordable. Significantly, this was a truly mixed housing scheme as affordable units would be in every building and every floor of the housing development. In addition minority ethnic and women-owned construction firms would get 20 per cent and 10 per cent respectively of the construction work. Local people would have priority for the new jobs. ACORN claimed this was a model development that showed the way forward for urban regeneration.

However, Brooklyn residents, the New York press and the political class remained deeply split on the Atlantic Yards plan. The Black community was largely in favour of the development, but its opponents argued that it was in the interests of wealthy white people. In this argument ACORN appeared to some in the liberal establishment to be on the side of the wealthy and, like the attempt to unionise in Chicago, anti-Black. This view was underpinned when it was revealed in 2008 that ACORN had received a US$1.5 million loan from the developer. What the Atlantic Yards experience shows is something Alinsky argued all along, that ultimately community organisations have to compromise to put improvements in place, and this means principles sometimes have to be shelved and deals made.

New Orleans

In 2005 Hurricane Katrina brought out what may be thought of as the best and worst of the US. Atlas quotes future ACORN organiser Dorothy Stukes, sheltering in the New Orleans Superdome, saying, "You have an earthquake in Pakistan and they're over there the next day. And we're here in the Superdome without air, no way to use the bathroom. They can send help over there, but they can't save their own people? We are taxpayers."(Atlas, location 3962) Many not only lost their homes in the flood, they also lost their jobs and along with it, their health insurance. Wade Rathke's family was also hit hard by the hurricane.

The New Orleans chapter of ACORN had 9,000 paying members and a track record of delivering on campaigns covering education, after-school care and the living wage. Along with other ACORN chapters, especially in Houston, ACORN offered initial support and advice to the evacuees. A particular campaign was against foreclosure – many sub-prime lenders were attempting to foreclose on a mortgage if not paid after a month, even in the post-Katrina emergency situation.

The main focus, however, was on the reconstruction efforts after the floodwaters had receded. The Bush administration chose not to introduce a publicly funded housing reconstruction plan that could also have created work for local people. Instead it suggested that many of the poor African-American communities would not be rebuilt, and that private charities should take the lead in rehousing the poor. The fear among the evacuees was that developers would move in, buy up the foreclosed and destroyed homes and regenerate the area at the expense of the previous residents. It was suggested by government sources that some long established communities, such as the Lower 9th ward, should revert to wetlands. Atlas quotes a resident saying "You want to turn black people's neighborhoods into white people's parks."

ACORN, with others, campaigned for a more comprehensive redevelopment, and assisted residents with house clearing and preventing demolitions. Strong political support was built with many city council members. However, six months after Katrina, over 90 per cent of public housing was still empty, less than 15 per cent of schools were open and only 12 per cent of the flood debris had been removed.

In early 2006, after public demonstrations in Washington, the federal government authorised US$4.2 billion to repair flood-damaged homes in Louisiana. ACORN, among a range of other organisations, was involved in volunteer cleaning, renovating and rebuilding schemes. However, mayoral elections were due in April and the choice of mayor would have a significant impact on how future redevelopment would take place. With so many residents dispersed around the country, the key to the election would be the absentee vote. ACORN and other organisations actively helped register voters, and in some cases they assisted with transport so that people could return and vote in person. The outcome of the election was the narrow return of Mayor Nagin. But this time his election was due to support from 80 per cent of the Black vote, a position that meant he had to be more sympathetic to African-American communities.

The eventual redevelopment plan allowed residents to pick their local redevelopment team. ACORN Housing was on the list and became the agent of choice in the lower 9th and New Orleans East wards, where ACORN had the strongest local organisation.

Summary

From the 1970s onwards ACORN and the IAF have been the two leading community organisations in the US. As such they have given us experiences and models to work on, both within the US where a variety of community organisations exist, and internationally. In the chapters that follow we discuss this legacy and where ACORN and the IAF sit alongside newer models of organising, especially the experiences coming from SDI.

Both the IAF and ACORN were engaged on many of the same issues, for example, the living wage campaigns, voter registration and housing. We now summarise what ACORN brought to community organising that built on and developed the original IAF model. Atlas comments that at its best ACORN's 'defining innovation is turning a local community organising group into a national association with dues paying members and the ability to cause substantial improvements for the poor and the powerless.' (Atlas, location 6392)

There are also cautionary notes from the ACORN story. An organisation the size and scope of ACORN needs robust systems to ensure financial probity and effective administration. Once ACORN began to seriously threaten powerful vested interests, from the finance sector to the Republican Party, then a sustained attempt to shut down or seriously damage the organisation was likely to happen. Was this predicted and planned for in ACORN's thinking?

The key features, developments and innovations of the ACORN model can be identified as:

- Organisers paid a low wage but expected to have high-level education and skills; this means that most organisers have middle-class backgrounds (mostly white?)
- Not organising through faith groups and pre-existing organisations
- All leaders come out from the local campaigns, and do not generally include existing leaders from other organisations
- Belief in the inclusive collective leadership model
- Organising national campaigns that local chapters are expected to support
- Campaigns to win elected office
- Established a state-based political party
- Organising local unions
- Difference in scale of operation (in 2007 ACORN had 300,000 members)
- Rapid growth and size of the organisation means less time for building internal social capital
- AHC makes deals with the banking sector
- Partner in an urban renewal scheme (Atlantic Yards)
- Changing federal laws – Community Reinvestment Act, National Homesteading Act
- Using referenda at federal elections.

These characteristics and how they compare to the IAF and SDI are discussed further in Chapter Eight.

ACORN International

ACORN International was established in 2004 as an offshoot of ACORN with the intention of spreading its activities, campaigns and organising model to other countries. Despite the closure of ACORN in the US, the international operation continues from bases in New Orleans and Toronto. There appears to be little organisational funding and much of the work is developed through the use of volunteers, known as the 'intern army'. Many of these volunteers come from particular universities that have a longstanding link to ACORN, for example, George Brown College in Toronto, Carleton University in Ottawa, Georgia State University in the US and the University of Edinburgh in Scotland.

Currently ACORN International has federated member organisations in Canada, Peru, Argentina, Mexico, India, Kenya, the Dominican Republic, Honduras, South Korea, the Czech Republic and Trinidad and Tobago. Much of ACORN International's focus is on the mega slums such as Dharavi in Mumbai, La Matanza in Buenos Aries and Korogocho in Nairobi. Activities highlighted by ACORN include campaigns for potable water and better roads and schools in Lima, working with rag pickers in India, an after-school programme in Buenos Aires and tenants campaigns in Canada. A significant recent campaign was centred on the 2010 Commonwealth Games in Delhi to support families displaced by the new infrastructure developments.

ACORN claims that through these member organisations it represents over 55,000 families. It could be argued that as it has a presence in 11 countries, this is not very much. For example, the focus of ACORN's work in Mumbai is the Dharavi slum, which has a population estimated to be between 600,000 and 1,000,000. In Dharavi the work is concentrated on music and arts projects with children and campaigns over housing demolition and housing rights. For the people concerned ACORN provides important support. However, given the scale of the slum, it has to be said that it is perhaps a marginal player.

Despite the limited resources, new projects are being developed. A current campaign is against micro-finance. ACORN argues that no new donor or government funding should be invested in micro-finance as it has, it claims, failed to reduce poverty. This is a controversial position. The World Bank, for example, accepts that the way that many micro-finance schemes are operated needs to be reformed, but argues that cutting all funding would make poverty worse. In another initiative ACORN is working in Kenya and Canada on how mobile phones can be used for poverty reduction, for example, to use mobile phones to find up-to-date prices for selling local produce, for remittance transfers and general information via crowd sourcing. This links to its broader Remittance Justice campaign that seeks to reduce the fees charged by banks, Western Union and Moneygram.

The following case studies focus on two aspects of community organising in India that are linked to ACORN International. Specifically, we discuss two case study interviews with community organisers, one in Mumbai and the other in New Delhi.

Case study: Vinod Shetty, Mumbai, India

This case study is based on an interview with Vinod Shetty, Director of ACORN Foundation India. He is based in Mumbai and works with the Dharavi slum community.

Vinod became politically active through student organising in the 1980s when he was a college student. His main interest was in developing campaigning via the arts (he was both an actor and a law student). He was particularly interested in the use of street theatre to explore and promote political issues. Vinod also produced a magazine to further develop these issues through writing. From these activities Vinod says that he began to see another world was possible. As he became more exposed to international ideas and media about history, politics and social movements, his motivation to continue campaigning increased.

Vinod continued with campaigns in the Indian student movement on civil liberties and with the Democratic Rights organisations. He completed his studies in 1983 and through his rights work had opportunities to travel through India on fact-finding teams. This included trips to Kashmir and Orissa, to explore issues around women's rights, the impact of dams and nuclear missiles. From this work, Vinod says he developed a broad perspective on national issues and the various linked stakeholder issues, as well as a firm commitment to the importance of the democratic process.

His work continued through Joint Action Committees, linking together specialist organisations (women, trade unions, peasants and anti-nuclear campaigners). He became involved with the Textile Workers Union and industrial action by 250,000 textile workers in Bombay. This was one of the largest and most iconic strikes in Indian history, although the outcome was the collapse of the local mills that had been subject to under-investment for decades. By the end of the strike over 80 mills had closed and around 150,000 workers had lost their jobs. The land owned by the mills has subsequently been sold to private developers for up-market housing and shopping malls. The story of the strike has taken on folklore status in India, and has been the subject of many films (including the 2010 'City of Gold' directed by Mahesh Manjrekar) and the book *Murder of the mills* (Shekhar, 2000). Vinod says that the lessons learned from this campaign and the effects of the International Monetary Fund structural adjustment loan to India helped him to develop an economic perspective to his work.

In 2000 Vinod started practising as a lawyer with a one-year internship with a textile union. This led him to become a union lawyer and then general secretary of a general workers union operating mainly in small engineering companies. He was also involved in organising workers in the local call centres (young professional collective). Building on his arts and media background, Vinod has supported the development of a documentary from the Indian People's Media Cooperative as a means of developing organisations and to help bring out people's stories. As Vinod commented, it is necessary to "stay within the people, bring out their stories and provide resources to the people."

Disillusioned with the main political process, Vinod was committed to working directly with the people through day-to-day organising around trade union and rights issues. He became involved with ACORN International to help form broader links to other like-minded organisers and organisations.

In 2005 an ACORN community organiser from the US visited India to promote the campaign against Wal-Mart. Originally, the US-based campaign against Wal-Mart was based around what was called the 'Six demands for change': a fair living wage, affordable healthcare, equal opportunities for women and people of colour, zero tolerance of child labour, buying American goods, and respecting local communities.

The Indian campaign against Wal-Mart had a different focus and was linked to the wider local campaign against foreign investment in India (India FDI Watch). This partly reflects an ideological position against multinational capitalism and globalisation. From a more trade union perspective, the entry of Wal-Mart and other multinational retailers such as Carrefour and Tesco into India would threaten employment in the retail sector and also undermine the Indian shopping culture based on a multiplicity of small-scale retailers. There would also be implications for the farming sector, as multinationals would attempt to capitalise and reorganise food supplies to their stores.

In the tradition of community organising the anti-foreign investment campaign was a broad-based partnership linking together diverse local and national organisations, for example, the Centre of Indian Trade Unions, All India Trade Union Congress, the Confederation of All India Traders, Federation of Associations of Maharashtra, Indian Merchants Chamber, National Consumer Cooperative Federation, Khadi and Village Industries Commission, National Hawkers Federation, National Alliance of People's Movements, Youth for Unity and Voluntary Action Consumer Cooperative Forum (Maharastra), Mumbai Hawkers Union, Super Bazaar and Vikas Adhyayan Kendra.

The Wal-Mart campaign gave Vinod a new perspective on organising. He liked the US system of systematically bringing in all supportive stakeholders into the organisation. The initial success of the campaign against Wal-Mart demonstrated the potential power of bringing together new collections of people who had never united before. Vinod commented, "big traders understood the need to draw on the support of workers and hawkers ... the enemy needs to be larger than you so you recognise that you need the support of others." This is classic Alinsky in that it taps into the motivational force from collective self-interest and creates significant momentum so that other partners want to join in.

Moving on, Vinod looked for new issues to develop. He linked the above experiences to Ghandi – find the poorest of the poor and give support to them.

He consequently saw the potential in linking informal workers, rickshaw drivers, domestic workers and recycling workers with Dalits, the Muslim minority, women and children on issues relating to income, health and rights in the context of urban growth and globalisation. Vinod saw the potential and need for organising in the slum area of Dharavi, with its population estimated to be somewhere between 600,000 and one million, crammed into an area of less than two square kilometres. Originally a mangrove swamp, Dharavi was initially settled by Tamil migrants. The majority of present-day residents are Dalits. Through its estimated 5,000 businesses and 15,000 single-room factories it is said to have the largest recycling industry in Asia as well as pottery and textile production. Dharavi has acute water supply and sanitation issues, extensive poverty and is 'threatened' by redevelopment that will lead to the majority of undocumented residents losing both their homes and employment.

Vinod noted that the culture in Dharavi was that people tended to operate as individuals living on the edge, so they did not necessarily want, or were unable, to go to meetings or to join organisations. He built the organisation The Dharavi Project through being on the street and directly developing relationships with local people. The organisation works with recycling workers and now has over 500 members, and focuses on health, education, children, revenue generating and school activities. The underlying approach is to link the local activities of the organisation to larger issues and where possible, to develop a national and global perspective.

The local office and community centre serves as the base for the organisation, with one paid member of staff. The core organisation is deliberately kept small due to uncertainty of funding, which is currently supported by friends and Vinod's family members. Acorn International supports the one paid member of staff. There is also some small-scale corporate sponsorship. Vinod's father financially supports the costs of the ACORN office.

Drawing again on his arts background, Vinod has brought in international artists to run workshops in Dharavi. This multimedia thread to organising creates space for artists, musicians and filmmakers to come into the community to give the opportunity for new voices to be heard and new ideas to be explored. Volunteers also come to work with the children, to bring out their potential for developing the organisation. Vinod comments that voluntarism is not in Indian culture other than through working for a political party or religion. The use of external volunteers is therefore important as it introduces new civic concepts based on valuing individuals and helping them see their contribution to a broader goal. In doing so the developing links between international artists, volunteers and local people creates a feeling of global connectedness and broadens out the self-image and worldview of young people in Dharavi.

The strategy for developing leadership is through the experiences gained from working on local committees. In the early days many women were involved in the committees, but some have been pulled back through the pressure of cultural norms and resistance from their husbands. Young people have their own committee and they will become the future leaders of the organisation. All functions and decisions are taken by the committees themselves, with ACORN in a supporting role. No formal training is offed to local leaders (unlike practice in the US). As Vinod comments, we "throw people into the sea", and they learn and develop the necessary skills from the experience of doing and reflecting. Vinod comments on the danger of people wanting external educated people to do things for them, and that this dependency must be avoided. He adds that perpetuating this dependency culture is a classic Indian strategy for the elite to keep control.

ACORN also has functioning links with the Seeds of Peace organisation (www. seedsofpeace.org) that works for conflict resolution. Annually 16 children (13 to 15 years old) from lower middle-class and upper working-class English-speaking backgrounds go to a camp in Maine in the US. The camp brings together young people from a variety of conflict zones. In 2010 the camp had representatives from Afghanistan, Egypt, India, Israel, Jordan, Pakistan, Palestine and the US. At the camp there are morning issue-based discussions, with mixed group play sessions in the afternoon. Local mentoring support is provided when the young people return home. The project also places local people in home stays in Pakistan to help counter the India/Pakistan and Hindu/Muslim divide that is embedded in much of Indian society. Some of the participants in the Seeds of Peace projects become volunteers for ACORN and work with children in Dharavi. In some cases these volunteers develop leadership roles.

Vinod comments that given the population of Dharavi, it is not possible to organise the entire community. What is more important is the quality and sustaining of work in the community. Successes can be disseminated through the use of multimedia, and this creates a multiplier effect for change. In doing so it is essential to keep an eye on the more powerful and affluent parts of society, as they are the people who can effect change. Poor communities are isolated from the wider society and this has to be challenged. It is clear that these international and external links are important to the nature of the organising in Dharavi. The significance of Vinod's background and networks in drawing in a wide variety of organisations to develop such links cannot be overstated.

Ideally, ACORN would like to build capacity and scale up the operation, perhaps tenfold. The constraint is the limitation on resources and expanding income is difficult, as in India corporations do not have a history of supporting such activities. Vinod's view is that to successfully expand it is necessary to have two- to three-year funding in a bank before starting a new organisation. Many Indians give money to their religious organisations, their own community and then their own families, so it is difficult to convince them to give to the poor. Muslims want to support Islamic organisations and Hindus don't want to support Muslims. Christians want to support their own organisations. Community organising is a secular activity and therefore sits outside this tradition of religious donation. Corporations see being involved in Dharavi as bad publicity and so do not want to be involved. Furthermore, ACORN is not seen as the usual non-governmental organisation

(NGO) operation and does not have links to the ruling party, so it is perceived by business that there is little to be gained from offering financial support.

Vinod comments on the complexity of his role. It is necessary to have a global perspective and to understand the common process of organising. However, the strategy and action is local and rooted in an understanding of local culture and processes. As Vinod puts it, you have to "swim with the fish and fly with the birds; hold two perspectives at the same time." He also notes that "people have to look at you as a leader ... and this is tested on a constant basis." There is suspicion, born out of previous bad experiences with some NGOs, that community organisers must be on the make – why else would they be working with the poor? Consequently, it is important not to live an extravagant lifestyle.

As a part of ACORN International there are strong links to ACORN Canada, and Vinod is also involved in some joint campaigns with them, for example, the campaign against the exorbitant fees charged to migrant workers to send money home.

Case study: Dharmendra Kumar, New Delhi, India

Dharmendra first became politically active as a teenager when Rajiv Ghandi, the then Prime Minister, came to his home city. He waved a black flag in protest against the Prime Minister, an action that led him to be assaulted by the police and to being hospitalised. The next day he was interviewed by the papers that asked him why he was taking political action at such a young age.

At university Dharmendra studied philosophy, sociology and journalism, and become very active in the student movement. He was particularly influenced by the Naxalbari peasant revolt and the people's movement in Bihar during the 1970s. He was one of the key players in developing the All India Students Association based on a Marxist analysis of society. To promote these ends he set up his own student organisation in Delhi.

Leaving university Dharmendra considered a political career but did not have the money necessary to successfully do this. Instead he committed himself to activism. Apart from five years in the Communist Party (Marxist-Leninist), he has no formal political affiliations.

Dharmendra worked for four years during the 1990s on trade union issues. This was with poorly organised construction workers during the early phase of the modernisation of Delhi. He also formed a new NGO to publish a magazine dedicated to supporting the radical transformation of the Hindu heartland in Northern India. The magazine generates significant monies, but Dharmendra feels that this is a diversion from what he considers to be real political work.

Like Vinod, Dharmendra met the ACORN organiser promoting the Wal-Mart campaign. He sees, and opposes, the penetration of the expanding markets of India, China and Brazil by multinational corporations. His support for the anti-Wal-Mart campaign is a practical action as part of the wider anti-foreign direct investment campaign (www.indiafdiwatch.org), and the opportunity it creates to bring together diverse stakeholders including farmers, small shopkeepers, street venders and so on on a wide organisational basis. Although considerable lobbying has succeeded in blocking international retail investment, the government has allowed international investment in the wholesale sector. This has offered Wal-Mart and Carrefour a foot in the door to operating in India. As a result, large Indian corporations now see the opportunities and have begun moving into retail.

Dharmendra questions whether to develop future campaigns about stopping the Indian corporations moving into the retail sector, as they will do the same damage to poor shopkeepers as foreign corporations. There is a need, he believes, to explore the sustainability issue around mass retail as opposed to local people's tradition. Food inflation is currently around 10 per cent, and this is increasingly a political issue – how can the small producers get some of this increase as increasing income goes to wholesaler sector?

The lesson that Dharmendra takes from this experience is the need to organise poor people to help them understand and respond to broad economic and social development issues. These issues can be linked to other concerns about undocumented status and the right to vote. To promote this work Dharmendra uses the ACORN model with a local variation, in that people are organised on an occupation basis, not by locality or community. An essential element of this work is the linking of national issues to local action.

The organisation works with small shopkeepers, rag pickers, street venders and female street workers, but they all relate to the same committee. Overall there are 2,000 members with two paid staff and volunteers. ACORN International provides US$500 for this work with the rest coming from the membership at a rate of 10 rupees per person a month. These subscriptions are significant in that they directly link people to the organisation, but contribute little income to the work. In addition there are collections and donations organised around specific campaigns. Overall, the organisation is independent and self-sustaining.

As Dharmendra is located in the Indian capital he sees the opportunity to influence the development of national policy. This is taken forward through various campaigns, for example, the right to food and the right to work. The **2011** Indian census is currently underway. This is problematic as many poor workers are both undocumented and homeless, and they need to be included in the census. Dharmendra stresses that organising is about joining up various local, national and international issues. For example, the right to food campaign is based on key organisations and their initiative in Rajasthan. This links to the ACORN work on the threat of supermarkets to small retailers and farmers.

Through working on homeless issues in Delhi, various organisations now provide a network of 84 temporary centres across the city to provide protection from winter weather. Each centre is run by a partner organisation with money provided by the state government. Often the homeless people themselves contribute to the operation of these centres. A recent government survey suggests that there are over 100,000 homeless people in the greater Delhi area, and this information is being used to support further campaigning on the issue.

Dharmendra comments that the overall aim of these campaigns is to raise the consciousness of members. This is to be achieved not through training but through political discussions around the issues. Members learn issues, tactics and organisational skills from the current leaders. New leaders are elected from the membership, but their skills still need to be developed. The organisation's membership has the potential to expand, but to do so it needs increased resources (even collecting more subscriptions is not financially viable). Dharmendra is currently exploring the potential of using mobile phones to promote organising, but most members don't know how to use SMS. Facebook has limited penetration – possibly only 300 members are online, due to limitations based on class and income. The main challenge to overcome is that for most members their experience in life is that things do not work and change does not happen. Trust needs to be built and successes have to be achieved so people believe that beneficial change is possible.

In 2008 Dharmendra was invited to Parliamentary Committee 4 of the House of Lords in the UK to discuss the free trade issue. He has also met with European Union (EU) officials in India to lobby against a free trade deal between the EU and India. Dharmendra suggests that he may have influence beyond the actual scale of the organisation: "what you appear to be and who you know is perhaps more important than the actualities."

However, Dharmendra says that he is not comfortable having dialogue with authorities, as he is not trained to do this. His expertise is in organising protests. In India the state does not have a history of engaging with local organisations. There is a need to develop new capacity to understand what might happen, the tactics of a more responsive state and how to respond to this. To this end campaigning organisations need to draw in other professional expertise, build alliances and develop political and media influence. This is a strategic rather than a numbers game. Consideration needs to be given to the role of leadership and the organisation in leveraging in this support.

Themes from the case studies

Although we are only considering two case studies here, there are many commonalities between them that may reflect the particular nature of practice in India and the interests of ACORN International. There are also some clear differences to community organising in the US. Readers may also wish to compare these case studies with that of SPARC (Society for the Promotion of Area Resource Centres), another Dharavi-based organisation, and part of SDI, as discussed in Chapter Six.

The two organisers themselves come from solid middle-class and higher education backgrounds. Both have high social and cultural capital, which they can draw on to support their activities. They are both motivated by a strong trade union and Marxist-influenced ideological position, and clearly understand the effects that globalisation and international capitalism have on the economy and the traditional culture of India.

The organisations they run are poorly financed. There are some subscriptions from members, but these are more of symbolic value. There is no foundation support other than a limited contribution from ACORN International. Families and friends contribute significantly to keep the organisations afloat. There are Indian cultural reasons why there is no wider institutional funding, but this seriously undermines the capacity of both organisations to develop their work. There is a member base to the organisations, but the impression is that it is led from the top in a social entrepreneurial fashion. This is in keeping with the NGO model in India, where many organisations are, in effect, an individual's social business.

Like community organisations elsewhere, the organisers seek to link local activities and concerns to wider global issues and campaigns, although the process that underpins this appears to be based on issues identified by ACORN International and then developed in an Indian context. Music and the arts are widely used to promote ideas and to develop campaigns. Interestingly, and unlike community organising in many other contexts, leadership training does not take place. The model is to throw people into activities and for them to learn through doing. Lessons are learned from experience and discussion but apparently with less formal structure to help with critical reflection than in the US.

In contrast to community organisations in the US, the Indian organisations are quite small and often organised by occupation. This difference reflects the nature of the campaigns and the trade union background of the organisers. Success, therefore, comes through creating an impact from the use of the media and political influence, rather than developing mass campaigns and large protests (although protests do take place).

In terms of our criteria from Chapter Two, the results of these two community organisations appear limited. This is not to criticise the effort, commitment and ability of those involved, but a consequence of limited financial resources. Both organisations make important links between poor communities and the wider world, and through ACORN International bring in outside workers, musicians and artists to broaden out the worldview of local people. Campaigns are won and the improvements made to the living of poor people. The lack of stress on leadership training and organisational development is interesting, however. Would the campaigns be more effective if more time and training was put into leadership development?

SIX

Slum Dwellers International and case studies

The federation believes that addressing shelter poverty requires a political solution. It recognizes that powerful interests are unlikely to give up power and control over resources and profits voluntarily, and are reluctant to countenance revolution. So it has to negotiate a path that offers the state both an opportunity and a threat. It needs to offer a practical solution to recognized problems, with a moral legitimacy to its activities that makes it hard for more powerful forces to organize against it. (Muller and Mitlin, 2007, p 438)

Introduction

This chapter explores another stream of community organising practice that we have observed in various parts of the world that is linked to Slum Dwellers International (SDI). Their network currently extends to Asia: Cambodia, India, Nepal, Philippines, Sri Lanka, Thailand; Africa: Ghana, Kenya, Malawi, Namibia, South Africa, Tanzania, Zambia, Zimbabwe, Uganda; and Latin America: Brazil. There are also emerging initiatives in Indonesia: East Timor; Mongolia; Africa: Lesotho, Swaziland, Madagascar, Angola; and Latin America: Colombia (Mitlin, 2008). Although SDI is the central thread that runs through this approach, as we demonstrate, this approach to community organising weaves together numbers of organisations that collaborate organically across different projects.

As previously discussed, community organising is a term that describes an approach to organisation building and social action developed in the US after the Second World War. In the absence of mutually acceptable agreements between community and state, organisers build alliances between community groups, churches, trade unions and others in order to develop 'people power'. These 'organisations of organisations' then enter into campaigns of non-violent disruption, public shaming and economic action, including strikes, corporate campaigns and boycotts, until the demands are met (Miller, 2010). In addition they develop mutual aid and alternative institutions such as co-ops, credit unions and support groups in order to develop services that are both more sensitive to and more relevant to the needs of their communities. Finally, at a national level they engage in mass lobbying for reform programmes and legislation (Miller, 2010). This action is based on an understanding that 'Change comes from power, and power comes from organisation. In order to act, people must get together' (Alinsky, **1971**, p 100). SDI's approach to community organising is in line with

Sen's observations of community organising practice (Sen, 2003) that starts with the most marginalised people rather than those occupying the middle, chooses issues that enable the organising of the worst-off, sometimes privileging those concerns over blander issues that might be more winnable, and incorporates political education within their organising practice (Sen, 2003).

Since the SDI approach incorporates all of these elements, it can therefore be seen as being part of the community organising tradition. However, where the more traditional model of community organising, as seen in the IAF-related organisations, has one clearly definable identity, and organisation of organisations, SDI seems more like an organic collaboration between organisations with complementary skills and resources.

> In each country where SDI has a presence, affiliate organizations come together at the community, city, and national level rooted in specific methodologies. SDI's mission is to link urban poor communities from cities across the South that have developed successful mobilization, advocacy, and problem solving strategies. Since SDI is focused on the localized needs of slum dwellers, it has developed the traction to advance the common agenda of creating "pro-poor" cities that address the pervasive exclusion of the poor from the economies and political structures of 21st century cities. Further, SDI uses its global reach to build a platform for slum dwellers to engage directly with governments and international organizations to try new strategies, change policies, and build understanding about the challenges of urban development. (www.sdinet.org)

Key features

Although there is diversity in the case studies that we later outline, there are a number of key features that remain constant across this approach. At the heart of the development process is the establishing of small, local savings groups that are linked up across cities and across nations. In addition to developing locally owned resources, these networks of savings groups develop relationships among people from which trust and confidence grows. This conscious building of both bonding social capital within the individual savings groups and bridging social capital across the much more diverse federations of groups (Putnam, 2000) lays the foundation for all of the other activities that SDI engages in; it prepares the ground for the development of linking social capital (Woolcock, 2001) and the relations of co-production (SDI, undated a) that it seeks to establish with policy and decision makers in the city and beyond.

Women are centrally involved in the development and leadership of these savings groups. This is an intentional part of the SDI strategy, which is not only based on pragmatics.

> For SDI, the central participation of women is not just an ideal but a critical component of a gender-sensitive mobilization strategy, which sees men and women re-negotiating their relationships within families, communities, and Federations. By prioritizing the leadership potential of women, SDI is attempting to change a social structure which is presently set up to exploit women's involvement and commitment to family and community. (www.sdinet.org)

This consciously inbuilt anti-oppressive approach indicates an aspiration within this approach not only to deal with localised issues of injustice but also to have an impact on more structural issues.

Learning is also an integral part of the SDI development process. This primarily happens through a process of local and international exchanges, which are described as horizontal learning exchanges, that is, not relying on experts' privileged knowledge but rather sharing experiential knowledge among peers. This approach attempts to break the hegemony of the professional expert and acknowledges that people are experts in their own lives. It also has the double impact of developing skills, knowledge and confidence among individual participants and strengthens the network at the local, national and international levels. Reeler (2005) makes the link between expert-led theoretical learning and the legacy left by colonialism that leads to the undermining of traditional and community-based horizontal learning. It is therefore clear why horizontal learning as a strategy is important within this development context. He also stresses, however, that there is a place for teachers and experts who can bring 'more conceptual clarity than is often available in the peer group' (2005, p 7), but great care must be exercised in when and how this approach is deployed.

SDI supports local communities to carry out local socioeconomic research that it calls 'enumerations'. These are described by Makau et al (2012) as processes that enable slum dwellers to gather baseline information on housing, population, infrastructure, basic service provision, livelihoods and governance, and to use this information to create a slum upgrading plan to guides the delivery of social services. Through this they engage local government in order to strengthen the working relationship between them and the urban poor communities. As communities develop and own their own information, they become more able to be involved in official planning and development processes. By working with local authorities they are able to feed in the community-collected information to city-wide planning processes.

The information gained through the community-based research can often act as a basis for the incremental and in-situ development approach advocated by SDI in contrast to normal top-down redevelopment processes that rely on clearance, relocation and rebuilding. In these more mainstream approaches people not only lose their housing but also their access to employment opportunities and existing networks of family and friends that offer childcare and other forms of support which enable them to access employment and other opportunities. By contrast, the approach advocated by SDI not only results in better housing solutions and more integrated opportunities for social and economic development, but also facilitates a shift in social power. This is exemplified in the ongoing work in Joe Slovo, Cape Town, South Africa, where it is reported that:

> Through this process of community organizing, blocking and enumerating, the upgrading of Joe Slovo has shifted from being the sole responsibility of the representatives of power to being a physical expression of the real power of the urban poor – the power to define, design and develop their own built environment. (Baptist and Bolnick, 2012, p 6)

This idea of co-production between local authorities and the local community is very important within the SDI model. In contrast to the more confrontational models advocated by Alinsky, SDI is actively seeking partnership right from the start of the process. 'Slum Dwellers International is a platform where governments and slum dwellers engage as partners in urban development. Together they co-produce cities that include the poor' (SDI, undated a).

By engaging governments, slum dwellers broker deals to leverage resources into the community in order to build a different kind of city, one that is inclusive of the poor. As previously mentioned, this is a manifestation of linking social capital that enables communities who have already developed strong bonds internally to leverage resources, ideas and information from formal institutions beyond the community (The World Bank, 2000). Although this process might begin by resisting eviction through protests and other forms of confrontational social action, it quickly moves to a situation where the community offers local government information gained through the enumeration process outlined above, and specific solutions to local issues that are developed by local people and strengthened by examples gained through international exchanges. In this way it is more difficult for local authorities to ignore the demands of the poor.

Guiding principles

In line with their practice of horizontal learning to national and international exchanges, members from South Africa and India gathered in 2010 to review the projects, to learn lessons together and to reaffirm their principles. These principles were restated as follows by Sokupa and Adlard (2010):

1. A "voice of the urban" and not a voice for the urban poor.
2. Daily saving by members is a mobilising & developmental tool, creating accountability, self-reliance and financial and human resource management skills.

3. The participation of women and of the most marginalised members of slum communities is central.
4. Community learning and solidarity through horizontal exchange programmes.
5. Incremental human settlement development.
6. Grassroots-driven gathering of information through surveys, enumerations and settlement profiles.
7. Solution-finding through negotiations and dialogue.
8. Community-based shelter training, including house modelling, community action planning and community design.
9. Small core groups of professionals to provide technical and financial support to federations.
10. Consistent engagement with local authorities through urban poor funds, enumeration data and citywide development strategies.
11. International advocacy in order to strengthen local city level initiatives.

Having outlined the key features of the SDI approach, we now go on to examine its local manifestations in South Africa, India and Cambodia.

Cape Town, South Africa

This section considers some examples of community organising in Cape Town, South Africa. It is in part a reflection on a study visit carried out in May 2011. The focus of the visit was to explore local manifestations of community organising within that cultural context. We briefly review some of the main themes of community organising and compare these to the approach found within Cape Town. We give an overview of three interlinked elements of provision which could be considered to be the key elements of a holistic organising process, namely, the developing of participation around basic services, the development of critical thinking and the development of processes and organisational structures that create a bloc of political power. We then go on to explore in more depth an example of practice relating to the redevelopment of an informal settlement, finally suggesting lessons and challenges for practice.

A network of provision

During our visit to Cape Town, we explored three interlinking and overlapping forms of provision that support communities in the process of social change and indicate a terrain of possibility for interlinked and organic approaches to community organising offered within that context. These were projects supported by the South African National Community Development Workers Programme, the Community Healing Network (CHN) (both of which I discuss briefly) and organisations connected to SDI, which I discuss in more depth.

Department of Local Government and Housing community development workers

This work is underpinned by an understanding that social transformation comes about largely through accelerated service delivery, public participation in government, capacity building of communities to educate them on local governance, living securely and an accountable government (Department of Local Government and Housing, 2009). In order to operationalise that, and in line with the Western Cape provincial master plan 2008–14, community development workers have been deployed at ward level throughout the Western Cape. It is envisaged that they will develop productive relationships with local committees and other local structures and are accountable not to them but to the local authority. In order to illustrate the work they do, we now highlight three examples of their practice.

First, a number of community centres are staffed by local authority community workers. We visited Sun City Community Centre that was staffed by a lone community development worker who also lived in the local community; this gave her a higher level of understanding of local issues and also high availability to the local community. Although this was a strength, it was also problematic in that the boundary between work time and personal time was often blurred. She ran a variety of programmes for young people in the area, and worked closely with groups and individuals on welfare issues, housing, sanitation and health. These services ranged from community development work – developing and supporting groups, linking with other service providers and signposting to other sources of information and support – to much more individualised caring and befriending roles to individuals experiencing difficulties in the community.

Although this provision could not be considered as taking a community organising approach, it does provide an invaluable network of support services which enable people to deal with very pressing issues which, when dealt with, give them more of an opportunity to think about some of the wider issues that affect their lives. And without some of these first steps in participation, it could be argued that people would be less likely to link up with each other and develop the capacity for collective action.

Second, the Department of Local Government and Housing support are a range of voluntary sector projects through worker time and the provision of some finances. One of the projects we visited was a voluntary youth project that worked with over a hundred young people from the age of seven to 22 from the districts of Samora and Kosovo in Cape Town. The project was run by volunteers and supported by local authority community development workers, the local council, a range of other council services, and was funded through the Breadline Africa fund. Their overall aim was to support young people to be motivated and productive members of society. Their methods to achieve this were to provide a range of sporting activities, run homework clubs and invite speakers to talk to the young people. Furthermore, they aimed to develop positive relationships with both the young people and their parents in order to provide positive role models.

Again, although this in itself is not a community organising approach, it does lay foundations within the young people of participation and learning, which provide foundations for future action.

Finally, they support a number of environmental projects which combine the development of community gardens, food production and recycling. The community workers and participants in the projects reported a variety of impacts from these ventures that included the redevelopment of derelict land, improvements in availability of fresh food and awareness of healthy eating. More broadly, the development of these environmental initiatives had resulted in the establishment of new local groups that were beginning to form local networks, all of which has greatly enhanced community participation in community activities and has led to an increased sense of community cohesion.

These projects, although still not using a community organising approach, represent a prefigurative stage in the process. Communities are responding to locally identified needs, collectivising them, coming up with locally devised and managed solutions and are beginning to share resources and learning. Although all of this action is focused broadly on community gardens and has not, as yet, begun to use the collective power they have developed as a tool for broader social change, it is clear that the opportunity for that to happen is there. Perhaps it is unlikely that the community development workers will ever get involved in broad-based organising as the focus they have been given seems to be to link individuals and local groups into state provision and allied services rather than linking them to one another, but the potential for more radical approaches is still there.

Community Healing Network

The Community Healing Network (CHN) is based in Vrygrond and works with a wide range of communities in Cape Town and beyond. Their analysis is that South Africa needs to deal with the individual and collective wounds from its history. They believe that:

> ... multiply-wounded societies run the risk of becoming societies with inter-generational traumas ... where large population groups are traumatized, the trauma is transferred to the next generation. Working with the multiple wound phenomenon means accepting that the wounds are collective as well as personal. (Hunter, 2010)

Using Popular Education techniques, inspired by the work of Paulo Freire (Beck and Purcell 2010), they develop programmes that foster the creation of informal networks of groups who develop safe spaces for dialogue. These in turn begin to deal with some of the conflicts and divisions that still exist in post-apartheid South Africa. Through the development of critical dialogue and participatory reflection, individuals and groups develop a new understanding of the world and their place within it. This process of sense-making and reimagining is an essential first step in a holistic process of creating a new world. Without this, even though the players may change, the patterns of exclusion and oppression will remain. As Freire (1972) indicates, without a process of critical reflection the powerless, when they come into a place of power, will recreate the experience of power that they have known, thereby becoming sub-oppressors.

This practice of grassroots democracy based on tolerance and diversity has led to the development of new partnerships between residents, with NGOs and with organs of the state, and has significantly reduced violence in the community, especially during periods of intense social and economic stress (Abrams, 2010, p 39).

When we met with Derek from CHN we visited a range of the many projects that he was involved with. These included a young man who was setting up a youth club in the local shebeen, a drinking establishment that is run as part of the informal economy. We also visited schools where working with the children, increasing parental involvement and developing environmental initiatives were woven together. Finally, we took part in a training event where local leaders used popular education techniques to explore social, economic, political and cultural issues; this was run in conjunction with the Department of Adult Continuing Education in the University of the Western Cape Adult Education Department.

Although there did not seem to be a formal organisation that coordinated all of the links and collaborations, there was clearly a highly developed relational, organic structure that facilitated the sharing of information, experiences and resources across a wide range of groups, and therefore offered a richer variety of opportunities and support to local people working to achieve change within their communities. Thus insights and approaches from popular education inform, to some extent, youth work, informal education, environmental and community-focused developments. And so while we could not claim that CHN is an example of community organising in itself, it does bring a degree of reflection and criticality, which is informed and in dialogue with theory, into the mix of approaches that support community organising in Cape Town. This is perhaps a very useful addition to the horizontal learning described below which does not always reflect on practice in the light of wider theoretical perspectives. We explore more fully the ways in which Freirean approaches to learning and community organising practices could be mutually enriching in Chapter Ten.

Slum Dwellers International

Post-apartheid South Africa still has many features of a divided society. The issue of inadequate housing remains a major concern within Cape Town, where 43 per cent of Black people live in informal settlements. This is in contrast to the white population where 0.3 per cent live in informal settlements (South African Census 2001). This split is also reflected in ownership of goods which allow access to the new digital world. For example, 2.8 per cent of Black South Africans in Cape Town own a computer as opposed to 52.2 per cent of computer ownership by white South Africans. These figures may have changed dramatically since, according to South Africa's Community Survey 2007, computer ownership in the home almost doubled between 2001 and 2007; 8.6 per cent of households owned computers in 2001 increasing to 15.7 per cent of households in 2007. However, large sections of the community remain socially excluded and it is within this context that the work of CORC (Community Organizations Resource Centre) and FEDUP (Federation of the Urban and Rural Poor) takes place.

We visited the offices of CORC and FEDUP, the successor to the South Africa Homeless People's Federation. FEDUP is active in all nine provinces of South Africa, developing community action and participation based on the foundation of locally managed (mainly by women) savings schemes. This work was initially supported by an NGO called People's Dialogue on Land and Shelter.

CORC and FEDUP are currently part of Shack Dwellers International, a network of community-based organisations of the urban poor in 33 countries in Africa, Asia and Latin America. It was launched in 1996 when 'federations' of the urban poor in countries such as India and South Africa agreed that a global platform could help their local initiatives develop alternatives to evictions while also having an impact on the global agenda for urban development (Slum Dwellers International, undated).

They refer to themselves as an alliance of a number of different organisations. Historically, this coalition emerged from the South African Homeless People's Federation that developed in the early 1990s. In 1991 they held an event called the People's Dialogue that involved a number of slum dwellers' leaders from South Africa as well as a range of international speakers. 'People's Dialogue helps empower informal settlements in the most profound way possible. Through exchange, through face-to-face sharing of experiences, southern African squatters can learn to measure, to harness and to exercise their enormous strengths and talents' (Bolnick, 1993, p 92).

Among the international speakers was Jockin Apurtham from National Slum Dwellers Federation in India. He shared his experience of developing organisations in India based on women in leadership, community-based savings projects and the development of productive relationships with local and national government. This approach resonated with the people's experience as there was already a strong tradition of savings and self-help projects within South Africa which had developed in the 1980s. He encouraged them in a process of federating these local schemes.

The first Minister of Housing, Joe Slovo, who had been one of the leaders in the struggle against apartheid, dedicated the first grant of 10 million rand from the government for the Federation to build houses for themselves based on a people-driven model even though there was already in place a state-run programme for housing development based on a subsidy model. In effect he said, here is some money, show me a new model. This approach was continued by subsequent administrations and exists today as the People's Housing Process. Along with the issue of providing housing has been the provision of basic services and challenging the spatial divides related to the apartheid city.

Joe Slovo settlement

In order to demonstrate the SDI approach within the South African context we now look in more depth at some of the organising processes carried out in Joe Slovo, an informal settlement in Langa, Cape Town. In contrast to the IAF approach discussed earlier, where there is an overarching organisation that coordinates the activities of other related organisations within the community, the approach to community organising adopted in South Africa seems to rely more on informal collaboration among a range of separate but complimentary groups and agencies. In Joe Slovo several organisations worked together on the in-situ redevelopment of the informal settlement. The organisations involved included:

- Fed-Up, a federation of local savings initiatives
- A community organisation resource centre, a group of professionals and grassroots activists providing support to urban and rural poor communities to mobilise around their own resources and capacities
- University of Cape Town's African Security and Justice programme, which supports poor entrepreneurs and the communities they work with on the environment, income generation, development and improvement to welfare
- iKhayalami, a not-for-profit organisation that designs and manufactures affordable housing solutions in order to upgrade informal settlements
- Joe Slovo leadership.

The context of this work is complicated. In 2004 the national government launched their flagship programme known as the 'N2 Gateway' (CORC, 2009). This pilot project was designed within the government's Human Settlement Plan and was approved by Cabinet in September 2004. According to the government this project was to demonstrate a new way of building human settlements with all basic social and economic amenities accompanying the houses. The upgrading of the Joe Slovo slum was identified as the first project within this development. However, from the outset this project had a range of problems. This top-down approach lacked proper consultation with the community that resulted in poor decision making within the project and a lack of ownership from the local people. This led to protests, demonstrations and burning of tyres as the local community resisted the government plan.

> The form of action was symbolic: just as the N2 Gateway project had targeted the settlements surrounding the highway due to their visibility in this main portal into the city centre, so did the Joe Slovo residents use this "strategic location" to make their protest seen and heard. (Jordhus-Lier, 2011, p 12)

Essentially the plan was to remove the residents and move them to an alternative settlement in Delft, some 20 kilometres away, and to build new housing on the site. This was inappropriate. First, because this new settlement was far from people's places of work, which would mean prohibitive transport costs. Poor households need different forms of land access and tenure security and might often primarily seek a right to stay and a location close to livelihood opportunities and amenities (Ley and Herrle, 2007). Second, the rents proposed were unaffordable to most residents. And third, the new houses were often too small for the families who were to be moved. And so while it was accepted that the living conditions in Joe Slovo were unacceptable, the solution suggested by the government was also unacceptable.

Despite all the protests, the government pressed ahead with its plans. To enable the start of phases 1 and 2 of the project, the first group of Joe Slovo residents was relocated to a transit camp in Delft. The remaining residents resisted relocation to Delft and this resulted in a long court battle with the National Department of Housing, which ended up in the Constitutional Court. While the community awaited the outcome of the Constitutional Court hearing, they decided to gather relevant information with regard to their settlement. The Joe Slovo Task Team then agreed to work with CORC, who have considerable experience in enumerations, to survey and map the entire settlement. This enumeration process was conducted in conjunction with a community-based blocking out and upgrading exercise in a section of the settlement that had been devastated by a fire in March 2009 (SDI, undated b).

CORC provides support to networks of urban and rural poor communities who mobilise themselves around their own resources and capacities. Its interventions are designed to enable rural and urban communities to learn from one another and to create solidarity and unity in order to be able to broker deals with formal institutions, especially the state. They linked Joe Slovo with community organisations, such as FEDUP and the Poor People's Movement (PPM), who were well versed in the practice of community research and enumeration. Muungano Wa Wanvijiji, the Kenyan federation affiliated to Shack Dwellers International, also provided support during this process and in particular in preparation for the data analysis and mapping of the community. The data collecting and management exercises also equipped the community with new skills and capacities. In the process it democratised and demystified vital planning methodologies that were traditionally the preserve of professionals, consultants and governments. During the enumeration process local people gathered the following data:

- household details
- employment
- nature of the house
- disaster history
- migration
- sanitation.

> The power of community-driven enumerations was highlighted in an account from Mzwanele Zulu, a community leader from Joe Slovo. He explained to the group how their particular enumeration proved that there were less people than originally thought within the settlement. This meant that upgrading could be done in situ without having to relocate people to the periphery. (Baptist and Bolnick, 2012, p 64)

This allowed the community to begin a process of redesign that started with 'blocking out'. Blocking out is a way of refining the planning of informal settlements. Put more simply, 'blocking out' or 'reblocking' refers to a rearrangement of shacks in an informal settlement. Reblocking is a way of addressing the larger concept of spatial reconfiguration versus the simple delineation of sites. The difference is between focusing on individual households or space that is used by whole communities. The space can be used for communal amenities, or to create lanes for installation of services such as water, sanitation and electricity.

Blocking out is also understood as a way to increase tenure. It demonstrates community capacity with regard to planning, and makes way for the installation of services, which can provide a greater level of security to residents in situ; reconfiguration of space within a settlement can make a large contribution to the building of social bonds and life within a settlement, as well as create a safer environment from both crime and natural calamities. It was emphasised that community mobilisation was the key to the sustainability of any upgrading project. As long as the NGO drives the process, the project fosters a growing sense of entitlement in the community and prevents residents from taking ownership (Bardlow, 2011).

Of course all community action brings with it some difficulties. During the redevelopment of Joe Slovo came the realisation that the federation model was not effective in reaching all sections of the community; not everyone wanted to save and not everyone wanted to be led by women. And so the challenge was to develop strategies that involved broader representation of the community. The enumeration process helped to widen participation since some people who had not been involved in savings projects were able to engage in the community–wide information gathering, thereby allowing them to be involved in the shaping of developmental priorities.

There was also a push to network with existing traditional leadership structures that existed within many of the informal settlements. These tended to be male-dominated and took the form of development or committees, often linked to the South African National Civic Organisation. These were then networked at a city-wide level into the informal settlement network that began to emerge in 2008 in order to engage the city authorities since they had primary responsibility for things such as the provision of basic services.

The federation has a range of social technologies that link in with existing leadership structures. These are savings, basic information collection and planning, experiencing negotiation with authorities at all levels of government and leadership by women. This has resulted in a number of partnerships with local authorities that see this network as facilitating a shift towards the incremental upgrading of the informal settlements rather than the top-down approaches that were previously practised, which resulted in pushing people towards the periphery of the city. This has particular significance in a post-apartheid context.

The federation has developed what it calls a community upgrading finance facility that enables informal communities to undertake local housing and development projects. The majority of the board of this fund are slum dwellers who have come through federation processes. One of the criteria for funding through this project is that the community must already be involved in savings projects and able to make a financial contribution. Even though this happens in a wider context where people can get housing free from the government, communities still buy into this scheme because they see how it builds their own ownership of the project.

Reflections on Joe Slovo

Although they did not win their legal challenge to the N2 Gateway project, there were many victories and improvements that flowed from the organising process. First, the in-situ development has made the settlement a safer and more secure place to live. Also, having to come together to fight a common enemy has moved a divided community towards one that functions more cohesively; this, in turn, has produced a more productive relationship with the local authority. In Baptist and Bolnick's estimation, it produced within the community 'empowered actors able to forge their own solutions, setting new precedents for housing and infrastructure provision in Cape Town' (2012, p 66).

It is important not to assume that a model that works in one community will work in all. The central role of women in organisation and leadership, which is generally a strength within a movement, was problematic in Joe Slovo. The fact that they were able to reflect on that situation and adapt the model for local cultural circumstances is encouraging for the future success of this approach.

There was clearly conflict within the community and at times between the various agencies and organisations that were working in the settlement. Although it may not have been possible at the time, a longer-term ambition might be to develop an umbrella organisation to synergise the strengths, resources and actions of the currently disparate groups.

The partnership and cooperation with the local authority, which is a central aim within this approach, has been developed through the organising process, but there is little doubt that a context where dialogue was preferable to those in power was developed in part by the civil and legal protests that were carried out by local people. Perhaps that is always the case.

Indian Alliance

This case study explores the work of the Indian Alliance, a collaboration of three interlinked organisations working with the urban poor:

- National Slum Dwellers Federation (NSDF) organises poor urban communities living in slums and informal settlements and mobilises them to articulate demands, to explore development strategies and to negotiate with city authorities.
- Mahila Milan (MM) (which means 'Women Together') consists of a network of poor women's collectives. Their work focuses on savings and credit activities, slum surveys and mapping, and housing and infrastructure projects. MM empowers women to become active leaders in community and urban development.
- SPARC (Society for the Promotion of Area Resource Centres) was established in 1984 to address the plight of pavement dwellers, who were overlooked by city planners and policy makers and faced routine demolitions. It provides professional support to its grassroots partners in order to build their capacity to play a proactive role in developing solutions to urban poverty, and creates links between the community-based organisations and formal institutions and resources (SPARC, 2009).

Today, NSDF and MM have a membership of close to two million and have been responsible for the construction of housing for over 8,500 families and toilets for 500,000 households (Goff, 2007). The Indian Alliance now works in 72 cities in nine states in India and is a founding member of SDI.

Given the contexts (for example, 48.9 per cent of the Mumbai population reside in slums; Government of India, 2001) and the groups they work with, their focus is generally on housing. However, the Indian Alliance is a broad-based organisation tackling a range of interconnected issues including housing, savings and credit issues, environment and sanitation and the resettlement of slum dwellers. Although the long-term aim may be security of tenure for informal settlement dwellers, in many cases a strategic decision is made to start with the demand for sanitation since government, civil society and the upwardly mobile middle class can easily see the relationship between the sanitation needs of the poor and their own heath and wellbeing. This less threatening demand for sanitation is more likely to produce a victory than any demand for land tenure (Burra et al, 2003). This practice is in line with traditional Alinsky organising tactics, developing as it does both the confidence and the capacity of the organisation and their ability to develop productive partnerships with municipal authorities.

Its overall aim is to:

> … organize the urban poor to form a critical mass so that they can seek their entitlements to social justice and as citizens in their city of

choice, to develop with them a wide spectrum of activities that can demonstrate what they aspire to and present these to government for wider application, policy formulation and policy change, and finally to delve deeper into creating models for development that accept urbanization and address poverty and developing innovative investments to make them happen. (SPARC, 2009)

They understand, however, that the ability of the urban poor to participate in decision making on city development and management is determined by a combination of factors, including having the collective financial, informational and organisational strength to have their demands taken seriously and to believe that they have the capacity to solve their own problems. In order to facilitate this process they establish networks of savings and credit groups that are federated at local and national levels, and carry out slum audits and other community-level research. This provides an organisational structure, the beginnings of financial security and an information base that is used to engage in city-level and national negotiations with policy and decision makers.

The approach adopted by the Alliance is to build internal consensus within the communities about critical non-negotiables – what it is, that when it is at stake, would motivate behaviour change (Bishop, 2007). This is achieved through dialogue and negotiations. Because they recognise that the state rarely does things that are good for the poor alone, they devise solutions that will be attractive for the city as a whole. They contrast their approach to many rights-based NGOs which adopt a 'shame and blame' approach, and see negotiations that produce solutions between local communities and the state with disdain, labelling this 'co-option'. Their approach, however, is in line with feminist organisers who have a more collective concept of power that stresses the development of the community through collaboration (McGaffey and Khalil, 2005). We discuss later how all the forms of community organising are on a continuum between conflict and consensus.

Guiding principles

The Alliance prioritises work with the poorest of the poor, considering that if solutions that are developed do not work for the bottom 30 per cent, they should be left out of its plans. Within that, a central plank of its approach is maximising the participation of women. This is based on the understanding that women have a primary role in holding together their homes and communities, and therefore any approaches to development that do not have women at the centre are not likely to be sustainable. Further, it recognises that the poor must be partners with the Alliance and not just the beneficiaries of its services. And so it draws on local knowledge to develop strategies that will work. It then helps organise poor communities to make demands on power and to sustain them in those processes over a long time; change is a long-term process. It aims to support communities for life, not project timelines.

In terms of its tactics, it has come to recognise that protests alone do not lead to sustainable change. Dialogue and building partnerships with authorities is crucial since all issues and their solutions are political, not just technical. For example, access to land and shelter is a systemic and political problem, so solutions cannot be primarily technical or managerial. Finally, it strives to achieve inclusive governance that honours the participation of poor people and women in development decisions and practices.

Development process

Core activities that establish the federation model within communities are:

- setting up area resource centres that serve as a meeting space and base for activities
- encouraging households to join a community-level savings and credit programme that builds financial assets and local capacity
- completing community-led slum surveys and maps to create a powerful informational base for strategising and negotiations
- facilitating peer exchanges among groups on local, regional and national levels so that communities can learn from each other
- organising housing exhibitions that showcase affordable solutions and act as a tool for mobilisation and dialogue with officials
- undertaking precedent-setting housing and infrastructure projects that not only provide much-needed improvements, but also demonstrate how such solutions can be scaled up and how the capacity of poor communities to deliver them is increased
- supporting dialogue and negotiation on win–win solutions with relevant authorities
- advocating for pro-poor policy changes on the basis of grassroots experience and demonstration of good governance practices.

Area resource centres

These are an essential building block in the organising process. They provide a space outside the home where women can discuss community issues with other women as well as being an official space and focal point for interacting with the wider world.

Daily savings

Community-managed savings and credit groups in which each member saves each day underpin the whole federation/MM structure. They are seen as the glue that holds the federation together. There is no minimum amount that the savers have to contribute each day. Women are particularly attracted to this, as these groups provide crisis credit and can develop into savings accounts that help fund housing improvements, new housing and start-up funds for income-generation initiatives. The daily contact between each saver and the community representative who collects the savings also acts as an important information channel; issues from the community can be fed into the organisation and information from the organisation can be disseminated to the wider community.

The effectiveness of the project is based on the stocks of social capital within the community. The relationships and trust established through daily contact ensures that loans are made safely and repayments are reliable. The savings scheme is run and managed from the local area resource centres; as discussed above, the centres serve as a key focus for community discussion, and for planning and managing community initiatives. It is therefore easy to see the connection between these savings groups and broader developmental issues.

Surveys and maps

Community-managed research at the level of household, settlement and city are important in helping communities to analyse themselves and their circumstances, to strengthen their organisation and to create an information base that increases their ability to interact effectively with government agencies and others who have influence on their lives. The Alliance supports a range of community research, including listing of all settlements, household enumeration and intra-household surveys. One of the techniques that it uses is the development of visual maps. These represent how the present physical situation relates to the experience of the community. These maps are also particularly useful in developing plans for improvements with external agencies.

Members of the Alliance work with local people to explore survey methodologies which, although based on the experience of other communities, is adapted and modified to fit the particular local situation. Local people then carry out detailed hut counts. This process not only delivers in-depth information on which to base further negotiations, but the regular interaction between people further enhances the sense of community. Community ownership of the production of knowledge is a powerful tool in the organising process, developing skill, confidence and a greater capacity to deal with powerful partners.

How they build capacity

Patel and Mitlin (2001) outline their thinking on the range of activities whereby the Alliance develops individual and organisational capacity. Communities initially identify needs and priorities and, through discussions within the Alliance, develop a strategy to address them. The strategy is then piloted by one or more community in order to assess its viability. There can be many failures in this experimental phase, but this is seen as valuable learning. Pilot projects are universally accepted as experimental learning tools that can be used to test possible solutions, strategies and management systems. Pilot projects start when a particular community wants to address one of its problems. Once completed, the experience can be reviewed, and the community and others (including government agencies) calculate what it would cost to scale it up. Pilot projects also help set precedents that are used to promote changes in policies, practices or standards.

Once a solution has been developed, community exchanges are organised which encourage other volunteers to try out the strategy and refine it to suit their local circumstances. Since 1988, there has been a constant process of exchange between communities. Community members, beginning with the pavement dwellers, travelled first to other settlements in their own city and later to other cities in India to visit other communities. They shared their knowledge, finding people interested in acquiring their skills and understanding. Although most exchanges are within cities or between cities, there have also been many international exchanges, with community organisers from India visiting many other countries (including South Africa, Thailand, Cambodia, Laos, Uganda, Zimbabwe and Kenya), and community organisers from these countries visiting India. The federation builds a core team from those who implemented the solution, they then visit other cities to demonstrate how it worked, and this encourages further innovation. They also use these examples of good practice to put pressure on local officials and politicians for change to support more community action.

There are many impacts of these community exchanges that build on the logic of 'doing is knowing' (Patel and Mitlin, 2002). They draw large numbers of people into the process of learning and teaching, and these are often women who have been previously marginalised. This process of sharing local experience, reflection and analysis enables the urban poor to own the process of knowledge creation and to develop collective vision and action. Additionally the process creates strong, personalised bonds between communities who share common problems, presenting them with a wide range of options through which they can address their problems. From this increased number of organisations who have increased in knowledge and confidence and the political force that they represent, the Alliance is able to apply greater pressure for policy change. Finally, these community exchanges are not limited by national boundaries. The international dimension of the work gives communities a global perspective and the possibility for negotiation on an international stage.

Cambodia

The recent history of Cambodia is well known (Tully, 2005; Chandler, 2008) – years of destruction under the Khmer Rouge regime in the 1970s were followed by political upheaval in the 1980s, which devastated the country politically, socially, economically and culturally. The ravages of the Pol Pot regime are still felt deeply within the nation and yet a positive part of that legacy is that those collective experiences created resilience within the communities and a flexibility and openness to new ways of working within the state.

In terms of economic development, Cambodia has been very successful in recent years, achieving substantial growth over the last decade. It is not immune to the effects of the global financial crisis, however— growth reduced from 6.8 per cent in 2009 to −2.6 per cent in 2010, according to most recent estimates (ODI, 2010).

This economic boom was predominantly experienced in the urban rather than rural areas and led inevitably to a flow of poor people into Cambodia's urban areas, in particular the capital Phnom Penh, the focus of this study. This mirrors global trends; as the UN Population Fund (2008) indicates, 2008 was a remarkable milestone in global urbanisation where more than half the human population, 3.3 billion people, were living in urban areas.

The rate of population expansion inevitably meant that the cities were able to offer these new residents little in terms of housing or other support; it is into this context that the Asian Coalition for Housing Rights (ACHR) began its work, knowing that 'Poor people need to be strong, need to know what they want, need to prepare themselves in order to negotiate with the city for what they need and to give the city good reasons to listen to them and become involved' (ACHR, 2001, p 61).

The community organising process began in Cambodia in the mid-1990s in response to the ongoing eviction of the urban poor. As seen in earlier case studies, there was a web of organisations cooperating in the organising process (see Figure 6.1).

One of the organisations involved in the organising process was ACHR, which is itself a coalition of a number of organisations. Its aim is to develop a model of social change that does not rely on Western thinking but is drawn from Asian culture, politics and ways of thinking (ACHR, 2011). Although knowledge and practice are contextualised and shaped within particular historical and cultural situations, the models operated by ACHR do seem broadly similar to approaches we have observed in non–Asian contexts. The sense of what it is trying to do is well expressed by Paa Chan, a community leader from Klong Lumnoon in Bangkok.

> As a member of that national network, I want to tell you that the urban poor in Thailand are rising up, we are capable and we do everything ourselves now: saving, surveying, land negotiations, community planning, housing construction, infrastructure, welfare, income generation, managing funds. I think it is very important for the urban poor in all our countries and all over Asia to link together, because we are the key force that can solve the big, big problems all of you are talking about. And we have many things to share. So how can organizations like ACHR and professionals like you support the poor to be the main actors and the main force to make change in a big way? Ask the community people in the room! (ACHR, 2011, p 3)

Figure 6.1: Organisational structure

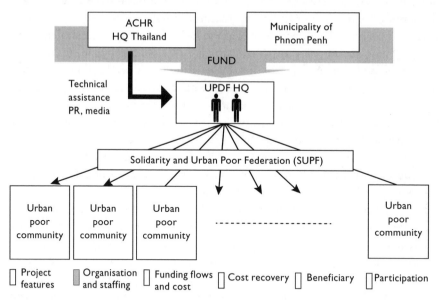

Source: Based on ACHR (2000)

This sense of organised self-help, supported by and in dialogue with professionals, is echoed through all of the SDI-linked organisations.

ACHR provides both funding and a wide range of technical advice and support to local communities involved in the grassroots organisation, the Solidarity and Urban Poor Federation (SUPF):

> SUPF worked to get communities to come together and work out their own ways of solving the problems they all face – problems of insecure land and housing, problems of flooding, inadequate provision for water supply and sanitation, problems of health and education, and problems of finding access to affordable credit for emergencies and for boosting livelihoods. The communities have experimented freely to find solutions that work for them. (ACHR, 2001, p 62)

This grassroots action is supported by another linked partner based in Phnom Penh, the Urban Poor Development Fund (UPDF). It should be noted that SDI also provides direct and indirect support to UPDF.

Phonphakdee et al (2009) describe the genesis and development of the UPDF. Although it was established in 1998 under a Memorandum of Understanding between the municipality of Phnom Penh, the ACHR and the community savings network of Phnom Penh, it built on the earlier work of ACHR who had, for several years, been supporting the establishment of savings networks in Cambodia.

ACHR support participative, solution-focused initiatives aimed at building community capacity and developing productive relationships with the local authorities and wider political processes. These include slum surveys and settlement mapping within which local people are trained and supported to map their own settlements, number their houses, identify common amenities and identify key problem areas. These initiatives helped shift negotiations away from eviction and towards the exploration of in-situ redevelopment and other development possibilities. As part of these negotiations local people produced alternatives to the government's plan that was to resettle informal communities in remote peripheral areas.

Through a series of workshops held between architects and local people, they designed and produced full-scale models of alternative, affordable housing which they showcased to the municipal and national government, demonstrating that they could generate ideas that would help the city solve their housing problems.

They ran national and international exchange visits that involved community leaders and government officers, another example of horizontal learning informing the development process. Phnom Penh's poor communities recognised that they were not alone in their struggle and saw the kind of housing and land solutions that were possible through this partnership approach to development.

From that, they piloted small-scale, community-managed infrastructure improvements, funded both by community members and supplemented by small grants from ACHR and the UN Centre for Human Settlements (Habitat). These included sanitation and drainage improvements, paths and bridges. These demonstration projects built confidence by showing that people could achieve change if they worked together.

UPDF's work is built on a set of operating principles: mutual benefit, collaboration, flexibility, reaching the poorest, a permanent presence and support and involvement in city planning (Phonphakdee et al, 2009). As with the other SDI initiatives, UPDF has sought to develop a partnership with the local authority whereby the poor are at the heart of the development process, offering people-led solutions to the issues of housing and poverty. A parallel intention is that, through the processes of housing development and community upgrading, communities unite and cooperate with one another. This is particularly important in the Cambodian context where recent history has resulted in damage to the social fabric of communities.

One of the compromise solutions that is being negotiated between poor communities and the government is that of land sharing. Rather than the process of wholesale evictions, which was the norm in the 1990s, organised communities have been able to broker deals whereby their self-interest and the self-interest of the government and private developers can be met within the one project.

One example of this is the case of Preah Sihanouk province, a coastal region of Cambodia. Within the province are 19 informal settlements made up of 6,804 households; most of these families work in fishing and construction or are factory labourers or small vendors (ACHR, 2010). Borie Kamarkorn is one of four large informal settlements which occupy a large tract of public land that is partly owned by the National Railways and partly by the Port Authority. The four communities, which are part of the new port project area, have for years been the target of repeated eviction attempts. In September 2009, they achieved a major victory when the Prime Minister announced a land sharing compromise, in which a large portion of the land they occupy (about 10 hectares) was granted to the community to redevelop their housing, in exchange for returning part of the land to the government for its port expansion project. The Asian Coalition for Community Action-supported housing project in Borie Kamarkorn will enable its 117 households to take advantage of this opportunity, upgrade their housing and infrastructure and demonstrate a community-planned and community-implemented model of upgrading which can then be expanded to cover the rest of the settlement – and the rest of the city – in collaboration with the municipality. Although this land concession for poor people's housing is now part of the city's development plan, the tenure details and project parameters are still being negotiated with the local authorities, so the project hasn't yet started.

A further example of land sharing can be found in Borei Keila, an informal settlement occupied by 1,776 poor families in Phnom Penh (UPDF, 2008). This breakthrough project was originally proposed to the government by the UPDF as part of its fifth anniversary celebrations. Essentially, their idea was that, rather than evicting the residents and developing the land privately, the 14-hectare site should be divided, with one half being sold to private developers and the other half being used to construct housing for the current occupants of the site, the apartments to be built and paid for entirely by the private company and given free to the families. The project was eventually approved by the Prime Minister and developed as a collaboration between the community, the municipality and a private developer.

> This land sharing project is a new invention in Phnom Penh, and represents a decent, practical and replicable alternative to eviction. The land sharing strategy represents a kind of cross subsidy, in which the big profits generated by the other part of the site will offset the $7 million cost of building these ten apartment blocks for the community people. People only have to pay for maintenance, electricity and water supply, all of which will be collectively organized through their savings groups. (UPDF, 2008, p 13)

Although the initial focus for the fund was to provide housing loans for communities facing eviction, it has been broadened out to meet a more diverse range of development needs, providing loans for housing, land and income-generation initiatives through the network of savings groups. By using these networks, rather than focusing on loans to individuals, they have also been able to encourage the pooling of resources and efforts in partnership and wider development in the city.

Once some successes had been achieved in reducing evictions and establishing people-led housing developments, the community identified other developmental needs. It was noted that access to business funding for poor people was non-existent and therefore income-generation projects were limited. Each of the seven khans (districts) established a fund for this purpose, partly made up of the savings and also funded by UPDF. Through a series of public workshops and local surveys, each district established its own system for managing the loan repayment process. In addition, they established a loan scheme focused on community food production and another on small transport business loans. Both of these were direct responses to the particular conditions and problems faced by the community at that time.

One example of this loan system in action was a bulk loan to Roessei Keo district to develop the production of prahok, a popular Khmer-style fermented fish (UPDF, 2008, p 7). In 1999, the women's community savings network put together 356 families in 19 riverside communities. Collectively they took out a group loan from UPDF to purchase the fish, crocks, salt and equipment to make prahok. In this way, prahok became a tool for linking communities in the district and for strengthening the community process – and strengthening working relations with the district chief, who was supportive of the process and sat on the committee.

Part of the success of this project lay in the fact that the communities themselves were able to organise the terms of the loan, not by some arbitrary system but around the prahok production cycle. The prahok can ripen anytime between three to eight months, at which point it is sold in the market and the loan repaid in full. This flexibility based on local knowledge and linked to local circumstances demonstrates an innovative approach to finance that meets the needs of the community.

One quote from a local community member, Saman-Srinoh, illustrates how a small input of funding has the power to have an impact on income generation, food production, housing and environmental improvements and transport:

> 'Before we started our savings group, my house was very bad, with walls made of dried leaves, but now it's much improved, with tin-sheet siding and a proper stairway up and a new toilet. I made these improvements using a small housing loan from UPDF which was part of our upgrading project. Early on, we used the profits from prahok to buy a second-hand moto, and so now my husband can make more income as a moto-dub driver, and has also bought a pump and some tools to run a small bicycle repair business when he's not doing the moto-dub business.' (quoted in UPDF, 2008, p 7)

Leh-Sunrah, another member of the women's savings network, highlights the impact that this process has had on both health and education:

'Ten years ago, this was such a poor community. In almost all the houses, if there were three children, the family could only afford to send one of them to school. The others would have to stay home. But today, there is not a single child in Kulalom who does not go to school. And now that the environment is so much better and we have better incomes, the children are more healthy, and we don't have to hesitate to take them to the clinic when they fall sick.' (quoted in UPDF, 2008, p 7)

Reflection on the Slum Dwellers International model

SDI, reflecting on the challenges of achieving meaningful and lasting social change that benefits the poor, identifies three challenges:

- The problem is that the procedure-driven urban governance system inherited from the colonial or pre-urbanisation past – the 'received wisdom' – is inadequate to the challenge of globalising cities in the developing world.
- Engagement must be oriented to *changing the system* so that it works for the poor. This means engaging with politicians and officials with the will *and the power* to change the rules. Engaging the operational-level bureaucracy without explicit, documented, and enforced backing of senior politicians and officials does not produce results.
- This mobilisation must be *permanent*; once it stops, the arrangements achieved by early breakthroughs become institutionalised; and once they are institutionalised, the logic of *the system* soon reasserts itself (SDI, 2008, p 6).

So how do the processes of SDI contribute to both systemic and permanent change?

Dispersed organisation

One of the most striking features of the SDI approach is the lack of a clearly identified, overarching organisation that represents and orchestrates the action. The model it operates has echoes of the virtual team or community of practice that has emerged in the literature and practice since the 1990s. Wenger and Snyder (2000, p 139) discuss virtual teams in terms of communities of practice, which they define as 'groups of people informally bound together by shared expertise and passion for a joint enterprise.' It envisages a 'new workplace will be unrestrained by geography, time, and organizational boundaries; it will be a virtual workplace, where productivity, flexibility, and collaboration will reach unprecedented new levels' (Townsend et al, 1998, p 17). Practitioners in this model choose to develop collaborations based on shared interests and shared values and use that shared endeavour as a way of:

- developing and spreading better practices faster
- connecting 'islands of knowledge' into self-organising, knowledge-sharing networks of professional communities
- fostering cross-functional and cross-divisional collaboration
- increasing ability to initiate and contribute to projects across organisational boundaries. (Kimball, 1997)

Of course it is not without its challenges; collaborating organisations, and the workers within them, need a 'clear mission, an explicit statement of roles and responsibilities, communications options which serve its different needs, opportunities to learn and change direction' (Kimball, 1997). This can be difficult when a range of independent organisations are working together on the same project. Slight differences in focus, agenda and values can cause tension and disruption within the community, resulting in a decrease in the effectiveness of the action.

We also know both from observation of practice and the work cited earlier from de Wit and Berner (2009) that there is often a culture within communities whereby they rely on vertical relationships of patronage in preference to horizontal relations developed through collective action when trying to change their social circumstances. Where multiple, powerful organisations are jointly supporting communities, there is always a danger that local people become passive in the process rather than driving it forward.

Savings

Maintaining high levels of participation and strong accountability is key to the success of any grassroots social movement. De Wit and Berner (2009) surveyed a range of community-based organisations, NGO and local authority development initiatives and discovered that genuine, 'bottom-up CBOs [community-based organisations] may be less widespread than the proponents of community-driven development assume them to be, especially where these are supported, promoted or become an operational need in the context of donor, municipal and NGO interventions' (p 942). However, SDI is highlighted as an organisation that is legitimate because it is accountable and democratic, rooted in communities and whose make-up represents the poor of the global south and not dominated by the west, as is the case with some NGOs (Edwards, 2001).

De Wit and Berner (2009) also discovered that when local women-led savings groups were at the heart of the development process, they provided a foundation for the development of long-term dense webs of mutual support and risk-sharing, which is the basis of collective action at a community level. They noted that the women in these savings groups developed strong relationships in spite of dissimilar incomes and backgrounds, and that they fulfilled an important social role in a wide range of issues including mediating in cases of domestic violence and promoting education.

Horizontal learning

While the embedded use of horizontal learning is an essential, post-colonial reclamation of local knowledge which builds individual and organisational capacity, it must also be recognised that there is a place for more theoretical learning. As previously indicated, the issue is about how that fits and what its status is. Theory that is accessed after a process of reflection by the community and is itself subject to the critical scrutiny of the group can open up new ways of thinking. In the end, if the aim is to not just to change the local but the system that creates the inequality, knowledge which is not purely local will have to be accessed, understood and synthesised into the worldview and practice of communities working for social change.

Co-production

With their focus on developing partnerships with local authorities and others in order to co-produce cities that are inclusive of the poor, 'they have been criticised by rights-based groups for being "too close" to the state' (Patel and Miltin, 2005, p 5). SDI are critical, however, of 'rights-based' approaches since they argue that it places all of the responsibility for development on the state. This leaves no opportunity for the community to develop their own solutions to their own problems.

How does the emphasis on cooperation rather than conflict come out of a context where there has been earlier oppositional social action? In the case of Joe Slovo, participation and partnership came after high profile protests and public disturbances. In the case of Dhavari in Mumbai, there have been ongoing protests about the municipality's redevelopment plans. Perhaps this is another advantage of the organic and dispersed nature of this approach to organising – one organisation's protest lifts the level of tension and threat that in turn makes the local authority more open to the positive, solution-focused approach of another organisation.

Role of women

The centrality of women within the SDI development process is clearly a strength, but it is not without its difficulties. As seen in the Joe Slovo case study, the participation of certain sections of the community was inhibited by the clear leadership roles that women had, and steps had to be taken to draw those sections in. This need to involve the whole community is acknowledged by SDI (Patel and Mitlin, 2011, p 8): 'men belong to the local process, and that women live within a broader community and hence that men cannot and should not be excluded. The process of forming new kinds of relationships will not happen in abstract, rather it can only be realised through tangible and grounded processes that enable new practices and relations to be derived and nurtured.'

Perhaps this is indicative of the dynamics of organising. Conflict models are broadly adopted at times and in cultures where the opportunity to discuss and develop partnerships is debarred to poor communities. As organisations develop and effective practices of research, planning and communication also develop, the opportunity for dialogue and partnership opens up. Perhaps it is a similar case with the role of women in the organising process. At this point in history and culture, where women generally take higher responsibility for family and household expenses, it makes sense for them to be centrally involved in the local savings groups. Similarly, since women are often confined to the domestic and have a limited role in the public realm, it is important to build counter-organisations, such as these, to help shift that position. As situations change, so tactics and forms also change; if they do not, then they are doomed to become part of the problem against which future generations will have to organise against in order to continue the process of developing a more human and more just world.

SEVEN

New models of community organising

The future belongs to those who believe in the beauty of their dreams.
(Eleanor Roosevelt)

In the past few years new community organising networks have been created, the ideas and models of community organising have been widely disseminated, and more fundamental alternatives are being suggested and developed. In this chapter we look at the diversity of practice in the field from an international survey of workers defining themselves as community organisers. We then discuss the work of Gamaliel, a faith-based community organisation in the US. We discuss what could be called the modern manifestation of community organising (or according to some people, its replacement), that of comprehensive community development. Finally, we look at the opposite end of the organising spectrum, that of The Tea Party in the US, and how it uses community organising methods for rather different ends.

Survey of community organisers

As well as the major organisational studies discussed above, we also wanted to develop a sense of the views of community organisers themselves. An online survey form to be completed by people who defined themselves as community organisers was developed from the 11 criteria in Chapter Two. Information about this survey was distributed through the network of the International Association for Community Development (IACD), which has membership in the US, Asia, Africa, Europe and Oceania. The findings from the survey are discussed below. The results should only be seen as generally indicative of a range of practitioner community organiser opinions.

Figure 7.1 shows the distribution of respondents identifying themselves as community organisers. As expected, the largest group were based in North America. Interestingly, Africa and Asia also rated highly.

Question 2 was concerned with the size of the organisations employing the community organisers. The results suggest that the community organisers were generally employed in medium-sized agencies (see Figure 7.2).

In question 3 we wanted to know how community organisers described the main issues worked on by their organisation (see Figure 7.3). Reported activities were sometimes single issue (for example, supporting individuals with intellectual disability) and other times covered a multiple range of issues (for example, malaria prevention, HIV/AIDS and local environmental issues). The organisations could

Figure 7.1: Where organisations are based

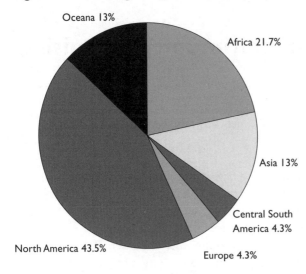

Figure 7.2: Number of employees

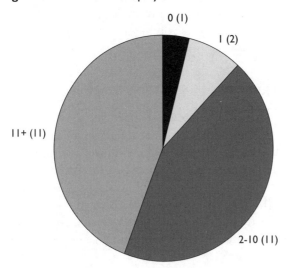

be very broad-based (for example, poverty reduction in Cambodia) to operating in a specific neighbourhood (for example, local repair schemes and violence reduction). Overall, the range of responses could be grouped under the headings listed in Figure 7.3. The main description of the issues being addressed stated, or implied, that the agency response was through some kind of service delivery rather than by campaigning.

Question 4 was concerned with the ways the community organisers and their organisation promoted empowerment with the people they worked with (see Figure 7.4). In general terms most of the replies suggested empowerment was

Figure 7.3: Main issues

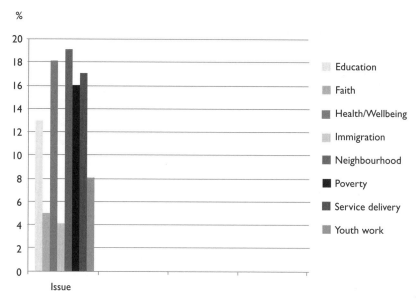

Figure 7.4: How organisation contribute to empowerment

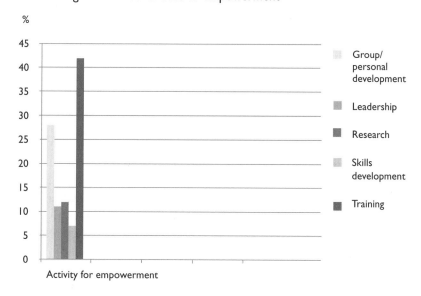

promoted through some kind of educational process. A few respondents talked about listening programmes and visioning which suggests, perhaps, some Freirean-influenced approaches. Linked to these activities, but also featuring more widely, was a significant focus on personal and/or group development. In the descriptions of activities provided by the respondents it was possible to break activities down into more specific categories, with a large general training activity being reported.

Question 5 asked how the community organisations identified and developed leadership within the community. One organiser commented that they identified leaders through the existing roles they currently occupied, for example, a local pastor or village chief. Another respondent said, "They come to me", which may suggest an interesting operational model. All other respondents said that they identified future leaders among the volunteers or from within the wider community and that leaders evolved out of community activity or came via specific leadership courses. Only a minority of replies commented on formal leadership training courses to build leadership capacity. Taken with the replies to question 4 it may be that formal leadership training was not the majority approach, and leadership development was mostly based on experience.

In question 6 we asked if the role of the community organiser was to develop an autonomous group independent of the local state. One respondent commented that it was not, as the organisation was concerned with building an inclusive network. This may reflect a different interpretation to the question than anticipated. Another respondent said that the question was not applicable. All other respondents replied in the affirmative, with some respondents commenting on the US organising models that informed their practice.

Question 7 asked if the community organisers helped in the creation of local assets. All but one respondent replied that asset development was an objective. The nature of these assets varied according to the local context. Examples given of asset development included:

- creating community projects
- providing funding or organising fundraising for local organisations
- training to support project development
- that people were the assets
- creating new community-based organisations
- promoting leadership
- supporting campaigns for more community resources.

Question 8 asked how the community organisers' own organisation helped in the creation of social capital. The largest response to the question was that social capital creation was supported through the activities of the community organisations' membership and/or through involving a wider group of people in local decision making. Some respondents suggested that social capital was promoted through skills development and capacity building programmes. Others perceived it in terms of general relationship building within the community.

Question 9 asked specifically about capability and capacity building within the community. Responses to this question included:

- skills development for volunteers and community activists to run projects
- formal training
- creating employment

- involving people in decision making
- systematic leadership development
- education of potential practitioners
- community awareness campaigns.

In question 10 we asked community organisers how they identified issues and progressed them to the point of action. A majority of responses indicated that issues were identified through listening to people (informally or formally), through dialogue with members, in broader consultation with the community or through discussion at open meetings. A small minority of respondents commented that they identified issues internally through their staff team or organisation.

Question 11 asked how community organisers developed organisational strength when working with marginalised people. For this question respondents came back to training and education programmes to build capacity. One organisation said they used the ACORN organising model for this purpose. Several responses mentioned using participative approaches and capacity building within the community.

Question 12 was concerned with the community organisers' system of communication. A majority of responses indicated face-to-face meetings and individual conversations. This could take place within the membership or wider door-to-door work depending on the nature of the organisation. There was a minority mention of using social events to communicate more widely. A few respondents mentioned newsletters, and others commented that they were thinking about online media. One respondent said that they used emails, and another had a website, but no one else claimed to be currently using the internet/ social media for this purpose, although in answers to other questions it does appear that a couple of respondents did use Facebook.

In question 13 we asked how community organisers recorded and celebrated achievements and victories. A diverse range of responses was recorded. Significant were the number of mentions about celebrations, parties and annual events such as end-of-year picnics. Other comments included:

- through individual learning plans
- written reports and other documents
- posting in public places, flyers, the local press
- newsletter
- website
- recognition ceremonies.

Question 14 looked at the links with national and international organisations and what this added to the overall work of the organisation (see Figure 7.5). The great majority of organisations had national links. These ranged from NGOs, local agencies, trade unions and campaigning organisations. Almost half of respondents had international links. This high return of international relationships may be due to the distribution channel of the survey through IACD. Examples of international

Figure 7.5: Wider links

No such links (8)

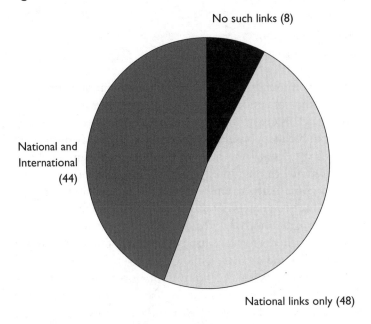

National and
International
(44)

National links only (48)

links included the US Center for Community Change and National People's Action as well as European Community organisations. Interestingly, there was a small return stating no national or international linkages.

In question 15 we asked community organisers how they developed critical thinking in the people they worked with. Some said that people in local organisations had already acquired the faculty of critical thinking. There were some comments that this was part of a Freirean process or due to conscientisation. Other comments included critical reflection on events, training and role-plays. A particular thread in the replies focused on planned analytical work with the membership of the organisation.

Question 16 asked how human rights featured in the work of the community organisation. All respondents to this question said that human rights were either explicitly or implicitly central to the work of the organisation. Sometimes this was a general reference to human rights, in other cases specific rights, such as children's rights or the rights of Indigenous people were the main focus, depending on the nature of the organisation.

In question 17 we wanted to know how the work of the organisation added to the sustainability of the local community. This question led to two different interpretations of what was being asked. The majority of respondents thought of sustainability in environmental terms, while others saw it as sustaining the work of the organisation. In some cases the respondents may have been covering both interpretations. Comments included:

- education on sustainability issues
- capacity building
- helping people to solve their own problems
- networking with other organisations and linking with wider resources
- integrating sustainability into campaigns

Question 18 asked if the community organisation had quality of life, wellbeing and happiness as an explicit goal. The majority of respondents said these perspectives were not explicit goals. Of these replies a significant minority said that these perspectives were outcomes from the work they did, for example, developing play facilities and promoting empowerment would lead to improvements in the quality of life. One respondent mentioned research by Tufts University that showed in a study of post-Katrina New Orleans that ACORN members were more resilient to the social and personal impact of the flooding than non-members.

Question 19 concerned the degree of involvement by organisations in promoting the MDGs (see Figure 7.6). Just under half of respondents to this question said that the MDGs were not relevant to their work. In some case answers to previous questions did suggest that some MDGs could be relevant to their activities, so it is interesting that they were perceived in this way. Around a quarter of respondents thought that the MDGs were implicit in what they did, although they did not explicitly feature in their work. About a fifth of respondents acknowledged the MDGs as being directly relevant to their work. One respondent commented that the MDGs were "empty rhetoric".

Figure 7.6: Working with the Millennium Development Goals

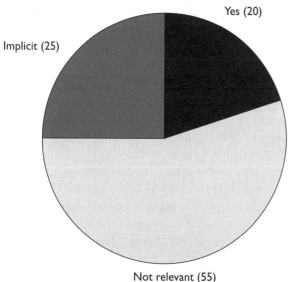

Yes (20)

Implicit (25)

Not relevant (55)

The survey responses show that at a local grassroots level the implementation of community organising can drift away from the tight IAF and ACORN models discussed above, which is probably due to a range of factors, including imperfect knowledge, lack of training, inadequate resources and deliberate decisions to do it differently. Is it only real community organising if it relates clearly to a specific model and the organisation concerned is affiliated to one of the big players? Does this matter if what is being applied works locally?

Gamaliel

On the surface Gamaliel looks to be firmly within the main community organising traditions in the US, especially that of the IAF, but operating within a deeply embedded faith position. It was founded in 1968 in Chicago, a few miles to the west of Back of the Yards and Woodlawn, as the Contract Buyers League. The focus of the League was to support local African-American homeowners against discrimination by local banks, a similar programme to the anti-redlining activities of ACORN, although predating it by several years.

In 1986 the organisation was restructured as a community organising institute. Gamaliel's website (see www.gamaliel.org/Portals/0/Documents/GamalielBrochureforweb.pdf) describes the name of the organisation thus,

> Gamaliel comes from the New Testament. The first Christians were a threat to the established authorities in Israel. The Sanhedrin met to decide the fate of the leaders of the new religion. Some wanted to kill them. But the wise rabbi Gamaliel stood up and said, "Refrain from these men, for if this work be of men, it will come to naught, but if it be of God, ye cannot overthrow it, lest haply ye be found even to fight against God" (Acts 5:38-9). In the Apostle Paul's Letter to the Corinthians, Paul refers to himself as "a disciple of Gamaliel".

The Christian faith is therefore a key underpinning position of the organisation. Gamaliel also sees itself drawing on the Torah, the Qur'an, Catholic social teaching, the principles of US democracy and the Civil Rights Movement. Affiliates tend to have biblical names, such as MOSES (Metropolitan Organizing Strategy Enabling Strength) in Detroit, and ISAIAH in Minnesota.

Gamaliel's mission statement states that it is there to assist community leaders to build and expand powerful faith-based community organisations. The purpose of this is to 'impact the political, social, economic and environmental decisions that affect their lives.' These activities would be supported through leadership training programmes, research and analysis on social justice issues and the creation of a mutual learning network and support to coalitions. Gamaliel currently has 60 affiliates in 18 states, mainly in the north and east of the US, but including California and Hawaii. It also has affiliates in South Africa and the UK. Gamaliel claims to represent over 1,000,000 people. Funding comes from a variety of sources, including George Soros, the Catholic Campaign for Human Development and the Kellogg Foundation.

Gamaliel's current activities include:

Education: the Gamaliel approach to education is derived from the Civil Rights Movement. Gamaliel argues that education is a right, but in the US it is both separate and unequal. Campaigns are focused on increasing the quality of schools, protecting inner-city schools from cuts and reducing the high dropout rate of Black children.

Employment and transportation: Gamaliel suggests that for every US$1 billion spent on highway construction, 48,000 jobs are created. Its campaign is to create local workforce agreements and policies to direct 15 per cent of these jobs to minority communities. Successful agreements have been negotiated in St Louis, Kansas, Cincinnati and Minneapolis. Linked to these employment initiatives are transport-focused policies that argue for an increase of funding to mass transit schemes, transport improvements that reflect the needs of the poor and middle class, and community participation in transport development policies.

Healthcare: Gamaliel says that healthcare is a 'God-given right'. It supports that position with biblical quotations, for example, 'then Jesus called the twelve together and gave them power and authority over all demons and to cure diseases, and he sent them out to proclaim the kingdom of God and to heal' (Luke 9:1-2). Healthcare is a very political issue in the US and, despite the strong faith position, has resulted in Gamaliel being branded on several notable right-wing websites as a communist front.

Several principles are promoted to ensure that there is equal access to healthcare:

* Healthcare coverage should be guaranteed to everyone living in the US
* Healthcare should be affordable and accessible to all, with special consideration for low-income individuals and families
* Healthcare should be cost-effective and sustainable for society
* Healthcare should be of high quality for everyone
* Healthcare coverage should be continuous, regardless of employment status or pre-existing conditions
* Healthcare coverage should be comprehensive, covering all types of illnesses and health conditions, and include preventative care.

Immigration rights: the demand is for comprehensive immigration reform and again, the Bible is invoked as support: 'When a stranger resides with you in your land, you shall not oppress the stranger. The stranger who resides with you shall be to you as the citizen among you; you shall love the stranger as yourself, for you were strangers in the land of Egypt: I am the Lord your God' (Leviticus 19:33-4).

Training: Gamaliel delivers over a hundred training events each year. The focus is on building community power in rural, urban, suburban, white, Black and Hispanic communities. Basic agitational leadership training is offered through seven-day courses. Once a year the top 75 leaders are given a three-day advanced training course. Special training courses are offered to clergy to help them manage their social justice activities alongside their faith commitments. Women-only training is offered through the Ntosake programme (a South African word meaning 'she who walks with lions and carries her own things').

Gamaliel demonstrates the continuing energy and viability of traditional community organising, and that in the US it has become a mainstream development activity that has largely moved away from the confrontational tactics employed by Alinsky in Chicago and Rochester. With its focus on promoting basic rights in poor minority communities, and organising almost exclusively through faith organisations and underpinning its activities with Christian texts, it might be thought that Gamaliel is a non-contentious operation. The first leader of Gamaliel was Gregory Galluzzo, an ex-Catholic priest, and its current leader is Ana Garcia Ashley, who described herself as 'too Catholic to be a liberal'. Nevertheless, the fact that President Obama worked for Gamaliel and that it has links to the IAF and Alinsky is sufficient to have it branded by right-wing commentators as a threat to the US way of life. That Gamaliel supports comprehensive healthcare and immigration reform just adds to that view.

For some commentators on the fundamentalist Christian right it is more than a political threat. In *Rules for radicals* Alinsky said that the first person to rebel against the establishment was Lucifer. This is enough to prove that Alinsky was also a Satanist. By extension, community organisations are seen by some to be anti-Christian, even when in the case of Gamaliel they are clearly operating from a deeply held Christian perspective.

New times, new approaches: comprehensive community development

While in Chicago conducting interviews for this book author Rod Purcell met with a range of community development workers. Some of the interviewees were of the view that the need for traditional community organising was coming to the end of the road. They argued that from the beginning of community organising in the 1940s through to the civil rights protests of the 1960s, adopting an outsider stance to organise poor communities was necessary. Without a local power organisation poor communities would simply be ignored.

In the early 21st century, they suggested, the social and economic climate had changed. It was no longer necessary or effective to focus on single-issue or project-based strategies. What was required was a more holistic approach to communities that understood, and responded to, the interconnected challenges faced by communities.

This new model is still based on citizen engagement and effective local leaders. The difference is that development is focused around a collaborative 'definitive' plan that includes a range of partners and funders to integrate programmes and services to achieve significant improvements to the local quality of life. Two examples given of agencies involved in this approach are the Institute for Comprehensive Community Development (ICCD) and the Local Initiatives Support Corporation (LISC).

Institute for Comprehensive Community Development

ICCD is a support organisation for agencies and communities developing comprehensive development approaches to meet local needs. It describes its core activities as being:

- building the capacity of community development practitioners
- providing on-site support and technical assistance to comprehensive community development initiatives in cities across the US
- applying lessons learned through research and performance evaluation to continually improve ongoing comprehensive community development initiatives and to develop new initiatives
- supporting the development of public policies that integrate government programmes in order to effectively facilitate and support comprehensive community development
- communicating broadly the best there is in practice and theory in the field of community development (www.instituteccd.org).

These activities could be described as modern technical, managerial and planning-driven when contrasted to the on-the-streets organisational building we have been discussing so far. The emphasis here is in developing a research-led understanding of how comprehensive development works, and applying it to cities across the US. As the ICCD says, it is the place where 'practice and theory meet, and where experimentation and innovation – grounded in real world experience – flourish.'

The essential lesson that is being applied is the importance of creating a network that can effectively channel significant public and private funding into a community that enables interconnected issues around education, employment, housing, sports, and so on to be tackled together. It is the scale of the financial investment that creates the tipping point for the community. ICCD brings together community development practitioners, public agencies, foundations, financial institutions and other interested bodies to this end.

There is, of course, a model of how comprehensive community development works. It is described on the ICCD website as:

1) Inventory of community leadership
    a) Citizen/resident leaders
    b) Leaders of agencies, organisations and institutions
    c) Government leader
    d) Private sector leader
2) Engagement of leaders – intentional/deliberate relationship creation
    a) Identification of individual leader self-interest
3) Accumulation and distillation of learning
    a) Analysis
    b) Reporting
4) Gathering leaders together for the first time
    a) Recruiting new leader presenters
    b) Relational exercise
    c) Reporting of findings
    d) Open discussion of meaning (including economy)
    e) Plan/commitment for creation of common vision
5) Second round of intentional/deliberate relationship creation
    a) Newly engaged leaders – engage others
6) Visioning session
    a) Citizen/resident, organisational, government and private sector leaders come together
    b) Creation of long-term community vision: 'What do we want the neighbourhood to be when it grows up?'
    c) Creation, and endorsement, of a communal vision statement
7) Convene smaller planning body
    a) Create plans that will, over time, accomplish the vision
    b) Recruit leaders/sponsors to implement the plan's elements
    c) Begin to seek sources of support
    d) Implement early action projects – 'planning while doing' – proving it is more than just talk
8) Make the plan public
    a) Community celebration
    b) Public rollout assembly – gather the 'who's who' of government officials, funders and corporate actors to fill the seats as an audience for the community's presentation
9) Implement, implement, implement

The common roots with community organising is clear: identify leaders, bring people together and explore issues in terms of self-interest. What is different is the range of people at the table, including significant players from outside of the community, and this raises the question about the relative power distribution. It may be collaboration, but not all collaborators are equal. Who really makes the final decisions, the local community or the external agencies with the money? Does it matter who decides, if the goal of improving local quality of life is achieved?

ICCD provides a wide range of handbooks, templates and manuals to help communities and agencies to apply tested means of researching the area, developing local plans and applying a strategy. A series of case studies from a range of US cities including Boston, Chicago, Phoenix, Pittsburgh and San Francisco illustrate what can be achieved and how it is done.

Local Initiatives Support Corporation

In the 2010 *Annual report* LISC President Michael Rubinger and Chair Robert Rubin commented that when LISC started work in 1980,

> ... top-down government programs could not reverse the slide (into poverty). Individuals could not shift it. And motivated community groups were just barely nudging the needle forward, as most lacked the financial or organizational capacity to enact lasting change. For much of America, the idea of entrenched poverty became just another evening news norm, with blighted neighborhoods viewed as a reality largely beyond our control. (LISC, 2010)

This statement could be viewed as implicit criticism, or simply ignoring the work of the IAF and ACORN. Is it true that all the major community organisations could do is 'nudge the needle forward'?

Rubinger and Rubin believe they have the answer to the way forward. They claim that,

> ... today, we have a comprehensive community development strategy that puts more tools than ever at our disposal. We have a federal government increasingly focused on breaking down silos between programs affecting communities. We have a nationwide base of sophisticated community organizations with the experience and capacity to drive revitalization. And we have a wealth of experience gained from 30 years on the ground in what were once – and in some places continue to be – the most challenged communities in the country. (LISC, 2010)

Since 1980 LISC have:

- invested US$12 billion in local communities, that has leveraged US$33.9 extra funding
- created 289,000 affordable homes
- created 46 million square feet of retail and community space
- financed 153 schools
- renovated 254 playing fields serving 460,000 children.

In 2011 direct investments in communities amounted to US$1.1 billion, with a further US$2.6 of leveraged investment. Income was derived from both grants and loans with major banks such as Citi, Bank of America and Deutsche Bank being major providers, along with the Ford and Rockefeller Foundations among many others.

LISC is currently promoting the building of sustainable communities through:

- Expanding investment in housing and other real estate: this includes developing new affordable housing, public housing and renovating vacant properties
- Increasing family income and wealth: through a mix of improving job skills, job placements and improving financial literacy, encouraging entrepreneurship and supporting small businesses
- Stimulating economic development through local retailers and service businesses to build the local economy and reverse local economic decline
- Improving access to quality education: by investing in Public Charter Schools and childcare centres, breakfast and lunch clubs as well as after-school programmes
- Supporting healthy environments and lifestyles: through environmental improvements, safe playgrounds, walking paths, supporting urban farms and markets, new local grocery stores and community police partnerships to reduce crime.

To further understand the nature of a comprehensive community development, let us take Boston as an example. The strategy has five key interrelated components: catalysing comprehensive community development, building community capacity, supporting affordable housing, greening the neighbourhoods, and leading community development. In more detail, these programmes include:

- Launching a programme called Resilient Communities/Resilient Families, based around ongoing investment for selected Boston communities
- The capacity building initiative supported the Mel King Institute for Community Building to train 400 community development practitioners drawn from 100 organisations. A total of US$250,000 was invested in five years in a Strategic Challenge Fund for non-profit organisations to promote collaboration, strategic mergers and innovative business models
- The housing initiatives include US$1,750,000 for land purchase and pre-development costs for 260 affordable homes, a loan of US$1,000,000 and US$7,000,000 tax credits to promote a mixed community in the Blessed Sacrament Parish, plus other green-related housing investments
- The greening initiative focuses on energy conservation by retrofitting homes. So far US$4,800,000 of funds have been committed on over 2,000 homes. Another 5,000 homes have been identified for energy and water efficiency measures

- In 2008 the Community Development Innovation Forum was launched that explored environmental sustainability and promoted public forums and policy development.

Impressive sums of money are being spent. It is very much top-down investment to buildings from which residents gain benefit. Between 1981 and 2010 Boston LISC and its affiliates provided over US$200 million of direct investment and leverage of almost US$1.5 billion. This created 1.5 million square feet of commercial space (and therefore jobs) and 8,440 affordable homes. This is a degree of investment that most community organisations could not hope to achieve. The nearest IAF can come to this are the Nehemiah Homes projects. ACORN made noticeable achievements through its Housing Corporation and the planning gains from the Atlantic Yards developments, but these are not the norm for community organisations.

However, the role of local people, although one assumes partners in the activity, is not that visible. The capacity building programme is training community development practitioners; it is not training community organisers. Is this just a change in terminology, or is it a significant movement away from the community organising ethos? With community organising local people and local organisers would be the driving force behind development. Is it now the case that they are supporting players while the financial deals for the community are made elsewhere?

On the other hand, if inward investment improves education, creates jobs, increases employment and provides more liveable housing in a safer and greener environment, then people are freer to live their lives and have no need to devote time and energy to campaigning for resources. Personal empowerment can take place in other ways than working in a community power organisation.

The comprehensive community development process is not community organising. Is it the replacement, or something that will co-exist alongside community organising? Can comprehensive community development be active partners with community organisations? Or will comprehensive community development schemes end up being a target for community organisations wanting more control and influence over local developments? Time will tell.

The Tea Party

Community organising, as discussed by Alinsky, is an approach, not just a methodology. There are a range of principles and values that underpin it, a literature that it is examined by, and importantly, it is located within a broader movement for social justice. However, it does contain within it a methodology that, once abstracted from its philosophical and moral context, can be applied by any group of people – people power works.

Even the right wing in the US, with their publicly stated animosity to Alinsky, ACORN et al, has recognised that community organising methodologies are highly effective. One such organisation, which adopts community organising as its underpinning strategy, is The Tea Party.

The Tea Party is an avowed conservative organisation that sees itself as defending the US from leftist threats that seek to undermine its traditional values and practices. In particular it is opposed to all federal government initiatives that could be construed as 'handouts' to 'undeserving' groups; its definition of undeserving seems to be heavily influenced by racial and ethnic stereotypes (Williamson et al, 2011). Its broad concerns are shaped by anxieties about racial, ethnic and generational changes in US society. The Tea Party's 15 non-negotiable core beliefs are:

1. Illegal aliens are here illegally
2. Pro-domestic employment is indispensable
3. A strong military is essential
4. Special interests must be eliminated
5. Gun ownership is sacred
6. Government must be downsized
7. The national budget must be balanced
8. Deficit spending must end
9. Bailout and stimulus plans are illegal
10. Reducing personal income taxes is a must
11. Reducing business income taxes is mandatory
12. Political offices must be available to average citizens
13. Intrusive government must be stopped
14. English as our core language is required
15. Traditional family values are encouraged 16. (The Tea Party, 2012)

Wild Bill for America (wildbillforamerica.com) concludes that the leftist enemies of freedom have used aggressive tactics, and that if conservative America is to save their nation, they must mobilise, be more politically active and prepare for a fight. He is clearly using Alinsky's tactic of polarising the issue in order to stimulate participation.

In much less strident terms, Lorie Medina (2011) draws on church membership and traditions to establish common ground with conservative middle America, and from that place of commonality, goes on to outline The Tea Party's approach to community organising.

She stresses the importance of the local grassroots groups, which can meet in homes, restaurants and church halls, to build the strength of the organisation. They are united because they share the same political ideology and have similar interests and concerns. She sees this as essential to developing relationships and motivating people to act, rather than just being angry about the situation. Since relationships are critical to accomplishing goals, smaller groups are favoured since they create friendly environments and facilitate stronger bonds:

When just one large group represents a large metropolitan area, it often doesn't promote local leadership; in fact, it has a tendency to inhibit future leaders from stepping forward. But with small groups, new leaders will arise. And when people from a nearby neighborhood volunteer to lead, they share their neighbors' concerns; their authenticity also makes for an atmosphere of greater support (Medina 2011)

Leadership is seen as an important aspect of the organising process. Individuals in communities who may not have much of a background in politics or community action but who are highly motivated to achieve change are seen as the ideal leaders: 'The requisite characteristic is passion. Most of the time, these leaders can learn the rest' (Medina, 2011, p 80). They are not, however, considered as solitary figures of power; rather they should exercise leadership in the context of

a leadership team, committee or advisory group composed of trusted individuals, preferably with varying backgrounds and expertise. This small leadership group can provide feedback on initiatives and goals, it can help with the workload and can also lead other small teams that focus on specific projects, such as city hall watchdog, youth outreach and get out the vote. (Medina, 2011, pp 127-30).

The membership of local groups ebbs and flows depending on interest in the issues and the personal circumstances of individual members; it is estimated that approximately every six months, a typical Tea Party group would see about 20 per cent of its members disappear. This means that there is a constant process of identifying and recruiting new members in order to keep the organisation functioning. All members are empowered (sic) to be part of this process and encouraged to use every opportunity to enlist new people. As an example, they are told, 'If you are at a PTA meeting and someone whispers, "What do you think about this new healthcare bill?" that's an opportunity to whisper back, "If you'd like, I can add you to our email list and you can get information about what's going on with health care and other issues' (Medina, 2011, pp 143-6).

Although they get involved in protests, much of their energy is focused on engaging with local political structures. They are specifically local in their focus:

If that member instead uses the time spent on these large global issues attending school board meetings or applying for a seat on the planning and zoning commission, their activism could bring real change to their own lives and the lives of their neighbors. (Medina, 2011, pp 183-5)

Their aim is to develop higher levels of participation in local democratic processes and to build the public sense that they have power. In this way city officials will realise that they don't have free rein over all decisions but they will be challenged by an increasingly aware and active electorate. Again, their strategy to achieve this goal is reliant on activating local micro leaders (a classic Alinsky tactic). Concerned members are encouraged to:

> Identify a few individuals who are interested in knowing more about their city government. Create a city hall watchdog group or civic task force and start by simply attending city council and school board meetings. Read your local newspaper. Sign up for informational e-mail alerts from your city. Watch and listen to see how the city is spending your tax dollars. As mentioned before, when something doesn't make sense, ask a question. (Medina, 2011, pp 193-6)

Summary

In this chapter we have explored some of the ways in which community organising has become embedded in the broader citizenship, social development and political cultures in the USA and other countries. The work of Gamaliel provides a particular example of community organising as a core activity moving out beyond the traditional models of the IAF and ACORN. The survey illustrates how some of the basic principles and ideas of community organising have become part of the everyday world view of diverse groups of practitioners. As we have noted this drift of methods and organising tools into other organisations has both strengths and weaknesses. On the positive side it helps to equip a variety of change focused organisations to better implement their agendas. However, divorced from the underpinning values of challenging oppression and injustice, these methods can be deployed for regressive ends. The Tea Party successfully uses community organising methods, but in this case to promote a political agenda that undermines the poor and disposed communities within which community organising was first developed.

EIGHT

Comparing and contrasting current community organising models

We have it in our power to begin the world over again. (Thomas Paine)

This chapter briefly reviews the key features of the three streams of community organising that we have been considering. While we recognise a broad commonality across each, there are also key differences of emphasis that are key to how they operate and what impact they have at a local level and beyond. We go on to outline the key continuums of practice, and consider where each stream would sit and what the implications of that are.

The key features, developments and innovations of the IAF model can be identified as:

- Being invited into the area by a broad range of organisations
- Being an organisation of organisations, not individual members
- A central role for churches and trade unions
- Money upfront to give operational independence
- Using local issues as a means to build the organisation
- Identifying local/potential leaders and giving them formal training
- Building a local membership base
- The prime objective is creating a power organisation
- Running creative campaigns
- Staying outside formal politics
- Looking for external allies (for example, stockholders).

The key features, developments and innovations of the ACORN model can be identified as:

- Organisers paid a low wage but expected to have high-level education and skills; this means that most organisers have middle-class backgrounds
- Not organising through faith groups and pre-existing organisations
- All leaders come out from the local campaigns, and do not generally include existing leaders from other organisations
- Belief in the inclusive collective leadership model
- Organising national campaigns that local chapters are expected to support
- Campaigns to win elected office
- Establishing a state-based political party
- Organising local unions

- Difference in scale of operation (in 2007 ACORN had 300,000 members)
- Rapid growth and size of the organisation means less time for building internal social capital
- AHC makes deals with the banking sector
- Partner in an urban renewal scheme (Atlantic Yards)
- Changing federal laws – Community Reinvestment Act, National Homesteading Act
- Using referenda at federal elections.

The key features, developments and innovations of the SDI model can be identified as:

- Based on regular savings and credit through local organisation
- Pro-women and faces up to gender issues
- Peer-based experiential learning – horizontal learning
- Against the hegemony of the expert
- No formal leadership training – learning from experience
- Based on partnership with the state, negotiation and dialogue
- Community-driven enumerations
- Mutual self-interest (of all players)
- Dispersed network of organisations – no overarching body; communities of practice.

Each of the main community organising streams that we have been considering vary in emphasis across some fundamental aspects of their practice, and position themselves at differing points on a range of continuums, as shown in Table 8.1.

Table 8.1: Continuum of community organising

Seeking consensus as a way of ensuring the voice of the poor is included	Using conflict as a way of developing power
Working inside the system	Working outside the system
Centralised model of organisation	Dispersed model of organisation
The organisation defines the issues	Local people define the issues
A formalised approach to learning and leadership development	An informal approach to learning and leadership development
Working on local issues	Working on structural issues

Consensus and conflict

The roots of community organising were clearly about building power and encouraging conflict that led to change, but much has changed over the years.

Ed Chambers (2010) still talks in terms of conflict in action – pick a target, personalise and polarise the issue. This approach is reflected in the approach of the Sydney Alliance, but they are very clear that there are no permanent enemies and no permanent friends – conflict and threat are used tactically to reshape the balance of power and to develop a consensus that is more equitable.

In Britain, the Shoreditch Citizens in London, in its assembly in May 2011, agreed that the situation in the area where there was both great wealth and enduring poverty and poor housing was one that should not continue. Noting that individual tenant complaints were being ignored, they decided to take more collective, visible action; they set up their own residents' help desk outside the headquarters of Hackney Homes, the main local provider of social housing, to record and collate tenants' complaints that they would then advocate on their behalf, with the power of the organisation behind them.

In addition to this, they developed a manifesto for long-term improvement, which was developed from the results of a listening campaign previously engaged in with local people, that they called a Commonwealth Agreement, which aimed to share the area's increasing wealth through guaranteeing a set percentage of work opportunities for local people, all paying the London living wage, while promoting better training and apprenticeship options and encouraging a real sense of neighbourliness. They have secured public support for the manifesto from key political figures including Boris Johnson, Mayor of London, and Lord Wei, a champion of community organising processes and adviser to the UK government on their Big Society project. Their long-term ambition is to consign a century-long record of poverty to the history books (UK Citizens, 2011).

From this we can see that conflict was deployed in order to assert people power, although the balance of their overall work was about negotiation and partnership.

The SDI approach is solidly based on consensus rather than conflict.

> SDI has focused on building partnerships with national governments that produce, control or regulate all of the commodities that the poor need for development (land, water, sanitation, electricity, housing finance). Such partnerships are crucial to remind States of their responsibility towards the poor, ensuring that the most vulnerable are not left to the mercy of the market. More recently, however, SDI has also begun to engage on multi-lateral institutions (particularly The World Bank and the UN) bringing the voice of the urban poor to global forums, and attempting to shift policy at the transnational level. (SDI website)

However, as we have seen, conflict is not absent from the SDI processes, although they, as organisations, might not initiate it. In Phnom Penh, Joe Slovo and Dharavi, there has been much protest and direct action carried out by local people and organisations both before and during the interventions of SDI and its related organisations. As such, it could be argued that a broad context of social unrest makes power holders more willing to enter into negotiations with the community or their representatives in order to ensure that a peaceful civil society is maintained.

It is no surprise, given the dispersed structure that SDI operates in, that it is able to concentrate on consensus building while other sections are confronting and agitating. Perhaps in fact this is a real strength of this approach; rather than having one over-arching structure that must compromise between conflict and consensus, separate, although informally related, organisations within a community can ensure that strong conflict and strong consensus-building are mutually reinforcing processes.

ACORN is able to deploy both conflict and consensus-building tactics depending on the situation. An interesting example is the Atlantic Yards redevelopment in Brooklyn, discussed in Chapter Five. In this they demonstrated political power by mobilising voters around their Working Families Party; thereafter they made deals with property developers to get what they thought was the best compromise deal for the community. Although this was controversial, the blending of conflict and consensus clearly won some gains for the community.

In the system and outside the system

The contradictory and conflicting position that community development has had of being both in and against the state has long been recognised (London Edinburgh Weekend Return Group, 1980), and this is no less true for community organising. The state clearly has a role to play in developing long-term strategies to tackle poverty and all that that entails; they control money, the legal system and so on, all of which must be shifted if there is to be a more equitable world. Indeed it could be argued that, given the all-pervasive reach of developed global capitalism, there is not really an 'outside the system' to occupy. Thus organisations find themselves at times working in an oppositional way against the state and at different (or possibly the same) times either in partnership with them or in receipt of their resources and support. The management of these complicated relationships is at the heart of any organising process.

Originally Alinsky saw himself and his organisation as outside agitators, although he always recognised that compromises and deal making were ultimately what would result from the organising process. In a conversation with Michael Gecan, IAF organiser with the East Brooklyn congregations, he described the relationship between the community organising (the third sector), the state and capital, shown in Figure 8.1.

He envisaged a situation where, while recognising the overlapping domains and interest, community organising must remain with its identity intact as a largely separate entity.

In reality, however, the IAF occupies a variety of positions along this continuum. The Sydney Alliance remains broadly outside the system, developing its own research, data and networks which then put pressure on the system to act in their favour. The Woodlawn Organization, on the other hand, from radical and oppositional roots, has developed a much more collaborative approach with city, state and federal agencies. In effect, much of its work is a conduit of state funding to deliver local services. While this is not in itself a bad thing, it does move the third sector more into the state sector that reduces the opportunity for challenge and ongoing change.

Figure 8.1: IAF model

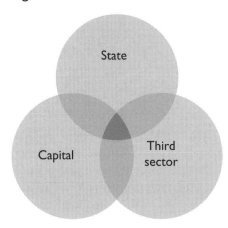

ACORN has historically been involved in overtly political action that places it very much in the system – major voter registration campaigns to put up their own candidates for office (as discussed in Chapter 5). It has also used the legal system by taking out a class action against Household International, a sub-prime lender, in order to fight against foreclosures. And it has established its own labour union. Although oppositional, there is a strong sense of being oppositional within the system, using existing official channels. This is, of course, only part of its work, but it does give ACORN a distinctive feel within the organisations considered here.

SDI is clearly working to be part of the system at local and international levels, and from that position, to achieve long-term change. It has been criticised for being co-opted by the state, but defends its position, saying, 'It is in fact the much more difficult and more transformative route. Instead of seeking safety in affiliation with a particular political party or coalition, SDI develops complex political relationships with the various levels and forms of national and international bureaucracies' (SDI website).

These orgnisations are strongly connected to a range of foundations and international funders, including the Gates Foundation, Ford Foundation, Rockefeller Foundation, Charles Stewart Mott Foundation, Miserior, Cordaid (Catholic Organisation for Relief and Development Aid), the Swedish International Development Cooperation Agency (SIDA), the Sustainability Institute and the International Institute for Environment and Development. They have also taken part in the UN General Assembly on Habitat, and are influencing The World Bank. Strongly connected with people left outside the system and strongly connected to funders, policy makers and power brokers at local, national and international levels is an arrangement that enables information and learning to flow between these two worlds, allows planning and resources to better reflect the interests of the poor and develops models of practice and ways of developing cities that are inclusive of them.

Centralised model and dispersed model

SDI is the most dispersed organisation at a local level. As we have seen, there are always several organisations involved in the action, all with complimentary and sometimes overlapping roles. Indeed at times it is difficult to know who is part of which organisation and which organisations are officially part of the network.

However, this model brings with it a multiplicity of perspectives and resources and there is a synergy that comes from linking groups that are skilled at organising grassroots savings with architects, people with planning experience and people skilled in politics. The challenges here must be both to keep a central set of core values that run across all of the organisations and to ensure that local people remain in the driving seat of the process.

On a broader level the organisation remains cohesive, with high levels of member participation due to its commitment to local and international horizontal learning exchanges. These both build knowledge and confidence and develop a sense of unity of vision and purpose within the wider organisation. This also builds a legitimate platform for SDI to be influential within the global forums discussed above.

Locally, the IAF model is a clearly defined organisation of organisations; there is a visible entity that is made up of but has a separate identity to its member organisations, and this is very useful in situations of conflict. For example, where the target for action is the local state (often a funder of member organisations), the central organisation can spearhead the action and take the reaction, leaving the member organisations free to get funding and remain in partnership.

At a national and international level there are strong connections that seem to be based on relational contacts and that revolve around training. For example, the Sydney Alliance is part of a network that includes community organisations in Washington, Oregon and Canada. It also describes itself as a sister organisation of UK Citizens. Although there is regular contact and sharing of learning, there is little sense of a collective strategy or joint working.

ACORN, on the other hand, has a much more cohesive approach to trans-local action. In 1982 it erected tent cities called 'Reagan Ranches' in 35 cities across the US. This action was part of a campaign to highlight the rights of homeless people. This degree of coordination is rarely seen in the other community organising models considered here. The approach does open up a space for organising on more systemic or structural issues and is therefore a vital component of organising for fundamental and sustainable change.

On a local level, ACORN, unlike the other models, recruits individuals who pay regular subscriptions that pay some (as in the case of India) or all of the organisation's running costs. This gives a very clear sense of what the organisation is, who makes up the membership, and what makes for a tight and accountable structure.

The organisation defines the issues and local people define the issues

Each of the three streams of community organising that we are considering organise around issues that define the action they take. How and who defines those issues varies between each stream.

SDI primarily works on issues around sanitation, housing and land tenure. In a sense these issues are defined neither by the organisation nor by the people, but by the situation that people find themselves in at this point in history.

Their strength in terms of keeping the organisation accountable to the people is their emphasis on exchanges. Maintaining high levels of participation at a grassroots level and keeping the emphasis on locally owned and produced knowledge helps to keep people at the centre of the strategy making and prioritising of action. The challenge may come when, as SDI continues to find favour in the corridors of power, it would be easy to get caught up in the policies of the UN and others and lose its independent focus.

IAF identifies issues by engaging in extensive listening campaigns. The outcome of this is that the issues are identified, not just by people who are interested in or even affected by particular problems that are within the community, but by people who are interested and prepared to do something about it.

The challenge that faces IAF as an organisation of organisations is that there can at times be tension between the aspirations of the IAF organisation, member organisations and individuals. Mechanisms are in place to deal with those tensions, but it requires ongoing vigilance.

ACORN has a mixed approach: some issues are defined through the local organiser analysing local demographics, politics, issues, identifying and developing alliances with existing leaders' identifies and going door to door to discuss their initial thinking and to signing up members. This is quite similar to the approach of the IAF but where it differs is that local chapters are expected to support centralised ACORN campaigns. This is not necessarily in conflict with the issues raised at a local level. As we have seen, the concern of the street traders in India is connected to ACORN's campaign against Wal-Mart, but there can be little doubt that this issue would not have emerged from the people. And so there is the potential here for centralised issues to give a broader dimension and to strengthen local campaigns, but there is also the potential for centralised issues to become dominant. In the latter case the role of local people could be seen as in just making up the numbers in order to add their weight to someone else's campaign.

Formal and informal learning

ACORN in India seems to rely entirely on experiential learning – taking part in action is how you learn about it. Although it does not have any formalised leadership development programme, again relying on experience and learning informally from current leaders, it does hold political discussions around the issues that come up. The danger with this approach is that without systematic reflection, the lessons that have been learned can be easily lost and not easily passed on to the wider constituency. Nor is it possible for ACORN to embed learning organisationally – how, then, can local people own the organisation and effectively input into the strategy for its future development?

IAF has well-embedded processes of learning from action, always reflecting on its roles and performance, its action and reaction by its targets which then shapes future action. These practices were instigated right at the start by Alinsky and strongly feature in contemporary IAF practice.

It also has a very well developed system of formalised training that is at the heart of its development processes. These take the form of leadership institutes that are aimed at new or potential leaders in the organisation, and are run by local networks. They normally last two or three days and cover the basic issues of community organising:

- Why organising matters
- Fundamental organising skills
- Strengthening institutions
- Problems versus issues
- Using relational power in the public arena to negotiate for the common good.

More advanced training tends to take place in the six-day residential programmes. All of the training, although highly participative in style, has a set curriculum and is delivered by trained and experienced leaders. IAF also uses the training as a leadership development process in itself where participants can progress through to increase roles of responsibility in the training planning and delivery.

At the other end of the continuum SDI is committed to processes of horizontal learning where groups of people share their experiences of the development process. While this is no less fundamental to the way the organisation develops, it does not have the same sense of passing down knowledge that has, in a sense, been codified and approved by the organisation. It is, however, intentionally international, giving participants not only a global perspective on their practice but also a sense of solidarity in the struggle.

Local and structural issues

SDI has a very localised focus that is rooted in the savings groups that are the foundation of its organising process, collectivising issues on a very local scale and building high levels of bonded social capital. Its work also operates at the level of the city. Its stated intention of co-producing cities which are inclusive of the poor posits a new model of governance which has greater levels of participation from local people in both identifying issues and developing solutions. Some gains can be pointed to in terms of changes in practice, policy and legislation, but of course, much more is to be achieved.

On a societal level, its claim is that the centrality of women in their processes and structures challenges the prevalent patriarchal mode of society. And again, although this does have an impact on the ground and there have been some gains globally, the fight for a more equitable world for women remains one that has a long way to go.

The foundation that it has established, in terms of good practice and heading up an international network that has high levels of popular support and participation, has given SDI credibility, which in turn has opened up opportunities to be influentially at the highest levels of global power, as discussed above.

ACORN also seems to link local concerns to wider societal or structural issues due to the strong connection between the centre and the member organisations. For example, in Delhi and Mumbai, ACORN is organising groups of pavement sellers who, as well as picking up on local issues, are getting involved in the campaign to keep Wal-Mart out of India in order to protect the traditional modes of shopping on which these small traders rely. Although it would probably take a much more developed network than ACORN is currently able to call on to win on the Wal-Mart issue, this represents a form of organising which has the potential to link the local and the global and by doing so, wield considerable power for marginalised communities.

The IAF tends to focus on local or city-wide issues. This limits its possible impact on wider issues and perhaps linking into networks that have a more global perspective and reach would be to their mutual benefit. This is discussed in more detail in the chapter on Freire and Gramsci's possible contributions to community organising (see Chapter Ten).

NINE

What community organising does and doesn't achieve

> It is difficult to say what is impossible, for the dream of yesterday is
> the hope of today and the reality of tomorrow. (Robert H. Goddard)

In this chapter we explore the contribution that community organising makes to improve the lives of people within poor communities. In doing so we consider the analysis of community organising discussed earlier. As this is only a snapshot of community organising activity, however, our conclusions should be seen as tentative and not definitive.

In attempting to make any judgement of the contribution to social change through community-based activity, the discussion has to deal with questions of process and product. Many people who work in community settings argue that what are important are the products of the work, the tangible gains for the community in terms of money, resources and services. How these gains are achieved is less important than what is achieved. Others take the opposite view, and argue that what is important is how you work with people. Giving respect to diversity, identity and democratic decision making is paramount, and good process should not be sacrificed to achieve outcomes. Ideally, the goal should be about making real gains for the community by means of a democratic and respectful process. In the real world it is seldom that simple, however, and process can be short-circuited to achieve the desired end. On what basis can this be judged as acceptable practice or not?

Community organisations themselves talk about the importance of process, especially internal democracy. SDI, for example is very concerned about improving the role and position of women within the organisation. On the other hand, there are several critics, including Gary Delgado, who have argued that community organisations in the US are often indifferent to 'race', gender, sexuality and identity issues. Overall, we have the clear impression that while a democratic process is fundamental to community organising, it is the success of the campaign that is most important.

Another problem in coming to a judgement on achievements is how community organisations operate. They generally have a campaign for a specific end. But as Alinsky always pointed out, gains come through compromise. Although the stated initial goal is often not reached, things have been achieved. Is the compromise in some sense a failure to reach the initial goal, or was the compromise the real goal of the campaign? Understandably, community organisations do not appear to be very open on this question. They loudly proclaim their successes, but seldom discuss their failures and under-achievements in public.

On balance we have to look at what the IAF, ACORN, SDI, Gamaliel and others have achieved, and can conclude that for the people in the communities concerned, there have been real gains. Whether these gains could have been greater through a different approach is an unanswerable question. The people working for ICCD argue they have a better way. In terms of significant inward investment to communities, they probably do, but that is only part of what poor communities need.

This is a complex question. Let us take the Dharavi slum in Mumbai, India as an example. The local population is at least 600,000 (UNDP, 2006) and the majority live in cramped housing with poor access to potable water and adequate sanitation. Both ACORN International and SPARC work in Dharavi (in fact, their offices are only a short walk away from each other). Vinod Shetty, ACORN International organiser, is clear in his belief that it is impossible to organise the mass of people in Dharavi; what is important is undertaking quality work that may have gains wider than the actual ACORN membership. No doubt this is the only practical way forward. However, Dharavi needs considerable inward investment, not as Mumbai city wants, to knock down the place and rebuild it for new middle-class residents, but to provide infrastructure improvements for the current residents. An ICCD programme would therefore be beneficial, but it would only come through effective community organising campaigning on the ground.

In developed countries the danger with ICCD programmes is that they often only pay lip service to local democracy, and deliver programmes *to* (rather than *with*) local people. Arnstein described this form of participation as tokenism, and there is much of this going on in Western countries. As the Atlantic Yards experience demonstrated, getting involved in large-scale redevelopment has many dangers for community organisations. Perhaps what is required is effective community organising on the ground, to attract ICCD investment and to ensure that it is achieved through genuine partnership with local people.

To broaden out this discussion, in Chapter Two we set out what we believe are some important criteria for community practice today. We identified 11 criteria and return to them now as a framework for discussion on what community organisations deliver. To recap, the criteria are:

- Development of the MDGs
- Promoting organisational development within urban slum and other marginal areas
- Promoting sustainability
- Developing capability and capacity development
- Promoting quality of life, wellbeing and happiness as an explicit goal
- Rights
- Empowering people

- Building social capital
- Building local leadership
- Creating local assets
- Building autonomous organisations.

Community organisations do not, of course, describe their activities in these ways. They operate largely on the basis of campaigns such as the living wage or affordable homes. In our survey of community organisers in Chapter Seven we used the above criteria to try and drill down into how community organisations operate regardless of what the specific campaigns may be. The rest of this chapter continues that analyses.

Development of the Millennium Development Goals

To recap, the UN developed MDGs to tackle global poverty. It comes as no surprise, therefore, that many of SDI's activities fall within the headings of the MDGs (see Box 9.1). These activities are, however, generally described in different ways. And it should not be assumed that the MDGs only apply to the poorest developing countries, although as respondents to the questionnaire pointed out, the MDGs were not generally thought about in community organisation practice. In contrast, Gary Delgado of ACORN frequently expressed the view that parts of the US had poverty levels equivalent to third world nations.

Box 9.1: Millennium Development Goals

Goal 1: Eradicate extreme poverty and hunger

Goal 2: Achieve universal primary education

Goal 3: Promote gender equality and empower women

Goal 4: Reduce child mortality

Goal 5: Improve maternal health

Goal 6: Combat HIV/AIDS, malaria and other diseases

Goal 7: Ensure environmental sustainability

Goal 8: Develop a global partnership for development

If we take these headline statements, then it is clear that much community organising activity in the US does indeed fall within the MDGs. For example, gender equality and the empowerment of women is a basic concern for community organisations. The work to improve primary healthcare fits well with concerns around HIV/AIDS, child mortality and maternal health. Poverty and hunger affect many communities in developed countries, and relate directly to employment creation and living wage campaigns. If we are concerned with developing a globalised understanding of practice, then conceptualising organising activity in relation to the MDGs would help to link community organising in developed countries to that in developing countries.

Promoting organisational development within urban slum and other marginal areas

It comes as no surprise that the example of SDI, and to a lesser extent ACORN International, shows that working in the global mega-slums is a priority for community organising, although there are some differences in approach. ACORN International is concerned with global companies, for example, the penetration of Wal-Mart into developing countries' domestic markets and related trade union issues, alongside the obvious campaigns for potable water, housing improvements and basic schooling. ACORN International generally follows the outsider campaigning approach of traditional community organising.

SDI, on the other hand, concentrates on what it sees is a 'pro-poor' strategy based around savings and the promotion of women as a central plank of organising. The focus of activity is on the key slum issues of housing, land tenure, sanitation, health, employment, savings and education. SDI's underpinning approach reflects the mainstream development paradigm that the solution to the mega-slums, as far as there is a solution, comes through the potential of its residents to organise themselves for development. Within the slums there are social networks, local economies, small-scale capital resources and human capacity that provide the assets to improve what is there. The mega-slums will not go away, but life there could be better. This process is defined and labelled by SDI as 'slum upgrading'. Organisations such as SDI may be the best hope for slum dweller communities.

Unlike ACORN International, SDI therefore sees progress being achieved by working within the system in partnership with city, state and national governments. Funding for its activities come from The World Bank and the Gates Foundation as well as other establishment funders.

Promoting sustainability

Sustainability, in the community context, is something that many people argue for, often in a general and undefined way. It is one of those things that most of us can agree on until we start to define what we mean by it, and recognise the compromises and changes it requires, especially to consumer-orientated societies. For example, do we want local investment in a greenfield manufacturing plant because it creates jobs, or would we prefer to protect the wildlife that lives there?

In considering the campaigns of the IAF, ACORN and SDI, there appears to be little specific focus on environmental sustainability. Housing developments, increased employment, improved schooling and living wages are all traditional development demands. Sustainability may be implied in some of these campaigns. Homesteading, for example, is a more sustainable approach to housing than new build redevelopments, and local employment schemes avoid the environmental costs of commuting, although there is little evidence in most cases that sustainability is included other than by coincidence.

In Chapter Two we took Adams' argument of seeing sustainability as the intersection of social, economic and environmental factors (see Figure 2.1). This model looks for a series of compromise positions, in effect, looking at developments in terms of whether they led to equitable, viable and bearable outcomes such as,

- Social vs economic = equitable
- Economic vs environment = viable
- Environment vs social = bearable

We think that community organisations could do more to promote sustainability as a core focus of their campaigns. In developed countries this could be a challenge, as protecting the environment is something that appeals more to those who already have a comfortable standard of living. If you are poor and unemployed, then a job can seem a good thing even if it comes with local environmental costs. In mega-slums living conditions are so bad it is hard to even think about sustainability – what is there to sustain? Nevertheless, it is an area that community organisations could take more seriously.

Developing capability and capacity development

We take the UNDP's view that capacity development is, 'a long term effort that needs to be embedded in broader change processes that are owned and driven by those involved, that are context specific and that are as much about changing values and mindsets through incentives, as they are about acquiring new skills and knowledge' (UNDP, 2009). Indeed, the experience of being part of a community organisation will undoubtedly build knowledge and skills. However, it is the change in values and mindset that is the essential part of sustaining a development process. People need to believe that change is possible and that can only be achieved if they, together with others, regardless of 'race', religion, sexuality, and so on, work together for the common good. In this way capacity development is embedded within the daily activity of community organising.

This process of capacity development is therefore about developing the skills, knowledge and potential that exists within everyone. It can be achieved in a variety of ways. For example, it can happen through formal and informal training events, reflections on action and focused group discussions. However, it is decidedly not about capacity building where the assumption is that people know nothing, and outside exerts have to train local people with predetermined knowledge before development can take place.

We also take Sen's argument on capability (1985). People need both the motivation and the opportunity to act. The basic idea of community organising is that the individual is often powerless, but the community organisation is powerful. An increase in human capability comes with active membership of a community organisation.

Promoting quality of life, wellbeing and happiness

Community organisations tend to focus on the basic needs of life, such as housing and income. As such, these activities fall within the lower rungs of Maslow's hierarchy (see Figure 2.3) and comprise a minor segment of Max–Neef's model of human scale development (see Table 2.4). The higher and broader levels of social, individual and self-actualisation needs and activities are embedded in various ways in the work of community organisations.

It appears that community organisations do not actively promote these levels of activity as much as they might. While some community organisations do focus on these areas, others start with a campaign heading and simply organise around it. The potential to do more in this area is picked up in the next chapter where we discuss the possible contribution of Freirean thought and practice to community organising activity.

In a similar vein, the ideas of the quality of life, wellbeing and happiness are seldom explicitly explored by community organisations. The respondents in the survey suggested that these factors were outcomes of the work. Our view is that these questions could be posed more directly by community organisations as a central part of planning their activities. It seems reasonable for the community organisation to ask in what ways the current campaign would improve the quality of life, wellbeing and happiness of local people if the campaign was won. Additionally, it could also be asked if the quality of life, wellbeing and happiness would be further improved if the aims of the campaign were modified in various ways.

The value in posing such questions is to avoid the trap that much urban redevelopment activity falls into; namely, assuming that development is automatically good, new housing will always improve the quality of people's lives, and so on. We can illustrate this with a further example from Dharavi. The Mumbai city authorities believe that rehousing slum residents from Dharavi into new tower block apartments away from the area will improve their lives. SDI, in its campaigning, has demonstrated that this is not the case. It has pointed out that moving away from Dharavi is likely to mean the loss of local employment, increased housing costs, reduced social contact and support, and in many cases, a smaller living space, causing increased pressure for an extended family.

Many people think that ideas around quality of life, wellbeing and happiness are esoteric and have little value to a hard-headed campaigning organisation. The alternative view is that improving these things is surely the purpose of community organising. From that position, it seems obvious that community organisations should explore with local people what changes in their community would improve their quality of life, and plan accordingly.

Rights

Alinsky wanted US democracy to work for everyone. For this to happen poor people needed to force their way into the system and reshape the way civil society worked. In effect, people were organising in order to claim their rights as equal citizens. The community organisations discussed in this book all operate on this basis, and the idea of rights underpin and are implicit in what they do, something also reflected in the comments from the survey returns.

Empowering people

The empowerment of poor and oppressed people is the core objective of community organising. Both Alinsky and SDI have publicly said that poverty is the problem of poor people, and that they need to take personal responsibility to solve it. What differentiates community organising from many other forms of intervention is that solutions come from the people organising themselves, not from external agencies delivering services. You simply cannot have a community organisation without empowerment.

Building social capital

We argued in Chapter Two that the existence of social capital is essential for community activities to take place – the stronger the stock of local social capital, the greater the potential for community action, and the better the overall wellbeing of the local community. From our discussions it seems reasonable to suggest that all community organisations create social capital.

The process of creating a community organisation initially depends on some degree of local social capital being in place. For example, with the IAF model the community organiser identifies local leaders (both formal and informal) as initial contacts, disseminates information through their networks and looks for information to flow back. The ACORN model, by contrast, was based on extensive door-knocking activities to make new contacts, which in turn would lead to other people through individuals working through personal social networks.

As the community organising process develops, relationships are built, experiences shared and common purpose created. Through this, bonding social capital is developed. Bridging social capital may also be created through establishing new links between local groups who previously may not have had much to do with each other, but through the community organisation, now have common cause. How far bridging social capital develops will depend on local circumstances, the organising model and the issues being organised. A broad IAF model of bringing together local organisations is much more likely to create bridging social capital than a single-issue group in a particular community. Linking social capital is also likely to be created through developing contacts with external organisations, whether as allies, new partners or in dealing with external power holders and organisations.

Building local leadership

Having effective local leadership is obviously essential to any form of community development activity. As our discussion in Chapter Two suggested, there are different forms of leadership. The most effective leadership approach for community organising appears to be based on the 'enabling model'. All of the community organisations explored in this book fit with this position, albeit in various ways.

Community organisations therefore place high importance on developing local leaders, although they approach this in different ways. The IAF has a fixed view of what constitutes leadership and the methods to be used. Formal training courses are offered to impart this knowledge. In contrast SDI does not consider formal leadership training to be important; rather, people are dropped into leadership roles and learn through experience. It is not clear if experience has shown SDI that this is the best way to develop leadership, or if it reflects a lack of resources to develop and deliver leadership training and/or a reluctance to adopt Western 'expertise'-driven models of development. Either way, leadership development is central to successful community organising.

Creating local assets

In our discussion of creating local assets we noted that one way of conceptualising this was through the 'seven capitals' approach. Specifically:
- Financial capital
- Built capital
- Social capital
- Human capital
- Natural capital
- Cultural capital
- Political capital

We have discussed social capital above and noted that it is inevitably created through the community organising process. Similarly, a successful community organisation will create increased political and cultural capital through its interaction with external power holders. The knowledge and skills being created through community organising activity will generate increased human capital. Depending on the nature of the issues being organised around, there may also be increases in financial, built and natural capital.

There is, of course, a distinction between tangible and intangible assets. To recap, intangible assets can be seen in three ways:

- Individual assets: skills, knowledge, leadership capacities, experiences, personalities, what we have, what we can bring to the group
- Relational assets: networks, relationships, partnerships, friendships, kinships, group ties, associations
- Collective assets: stories, traditions, cultures, institutions, norms, collective experiences

Community organisations are likely to build on all of these through their day-to-day activities.

Building autonomous organisations

In his early days, Alinsky was very clear that community organisations needed to be independent entities able to operate outside of the existing administrative and power structures. He was so committed to this position that the IAF would not enter into an area unless two years of funds were in place to allow complete freedom of manoeuvre.

Today the situation with community organising is less clear. Organisations are autonomous in that they will have their own structures and decision-making processes. On the other hand, community organisations often seek to work in partnership with external agencies of the local state (for example, the SDI model), and in doing so, implicitly accept constraints on their actions. In this way the autonomy of community organisations is, to some extent, voluntarily limited.

In summary, community organisations do well in terms of our 11 criteria, although no single organisation could cover all of these criteria. Different organising models, issues, objectives, local circumstances and so on will shape how the work progresses. It is reasonable to conclude, however, that community organising, both as a process and as a method of delivering products to the community, will, in diverse ways, contribute substantially to these underpinning development criteria.

TEN

Counter-hegemony, critical thinking and community organising

> Power is not an institution, and not a structure; neither is it a certain
> strength we are endowed with; it is the name that one attributes to a
> complex strategic situation in a particular society. (Michel Foucault)

Our position is that community organising is a practice that is strong in terms of its tactics, identification of local issues and mobilising people for change. We think it is less strong in the development of critical thinking and reflection on the one hand, and citing its practice within broader political thinking and political movements on the other. And so this chapter is an exploration of Antonio Gramsci's ideas of hegemony and counter-hegemony, and Paulo Freire's approach to building critical consciousness, which is then used to interrogate the theory and practice of community organising. It provides a critique of community organising and seeks to develop it as a broader and more comprehensive model of practice.

According to Francis Calpotura and Kim Fellner (1996), the common goals that underpin community organising practice are:

- the equitable redistribution of wealth and power to assure each person the necessities of healthful physical survival and the maximal realisation of human potential, in viable communities, on a planet safeguarded from degradation
- a multicultural, communal space where our various identities can shine and interact in an environment of equally shared power and mutual respect. (p 1)

They also ask, however, whether community organising approaches that are based on localised fights for incremental changes necessarily contain, or even lead to, a critique of prevailing social and economic structures; perhaps they only redivide the same pie in other ways. Even the resulting increase in democratic participation is not enough to change prevailing economic priorities and structures since it is all still in the service of capitalism. Calpotura and Fellner call for newer forms of organising that explicitly address identity conflicts, promote multiculturalism and challenge existing cultural frameworks. This opens up a critical organising arena, requiring a more varied palette of approaches, practices and techniques than have been customary in traditional community organising.

We suggest that the two central criticisms inherent within the above, namely, localism and lack of criticality, could be effectively addressed by forms of practice which take community organising and weave in the thinking of Freire and Gramsci. We would argue that Freirean approaches develop critical consciousness essential for sustainable social action, while Gramscian approaches develop concepts of hegemony, counter-hegemony and the war of position, which is a long-term process of building new alliances and developing a new common sense in order that the hegemony of the few becomes the hegemony of the many, thereby giving a theoretical basis on which to build trans-local networks that have the potential to challenge the current dominant order.

We now explore key features of Gramsci's and Freire's thinking, and propose a synthesis between those and community organising approaches in order to suggest a new form of practice that acts on the cognitive/affective, local and structural dimensions of social change.

Antonio Gramsci

As previously discussed, community organising is built on a clear power analysis. Alinsky talked of this in terms of dialectical archetypes – the haves and the have-nots. Ed Chambers (2010) starkly states that the haves never give the have-nots anything that is real (Democratic Promise, 1999). This structural reality of power is played out at a macro level in all community encounters within which community organising takes place. Therefore, in order to understand the dynamics of any situation, it is important to recognise the power dynamics of that situation. All power situations advantage some, disadvantage others and tend to seek to maintain the status quo; it is that reality that community organising seeks to change.

Although community organising recognises and works with this power dynamic at a local level, it is lacking in an analysis of the structural nature of social inequality which, despite an array of local victories, remains broadly unchanged. This understanding of the relative permanence of the prevailing unjust social order is described in Gramscian terms as 'hegemony', a situation where 'Dominant groups in society, including fundamentally but not exclusively the ruling class, maintain their dominance by securing the "spontaneous consent" of subordinate groups, including the working class, through the negotiated construction of a political and ideological consensus which incorporates both dominant and dominated groups' (Strinati, 1995, p 165). Peter McLaren describes the operation of hegemony as, 'The maintenance of domination not by the sheer exercise of force but primarily through consensual social practices, social forms and social structures produced in specific sites such as the church, the state, the school, the mass media, the political systems and the family' (quoted in Darder et al, 2009, p 67).

These social practices give rise to the spontaneous consent of the masses to the general direction imposed by the dominant group (Gramsci, 1971, p 12), and only when this consent breaks down do the coercive forces of the state, police, army and so on have to be deployed. However, this sense of the established order rarely breaks down in reasonably settled society for two reasons. First, because both the dominant and dominated groups within society benefit in some way from the established social order – while the privilege of the dominant group is obvious, the dominated group also gain a variety of benefits such as wages, social security and a sense of acceptance. Second, the status quo is also internalised by people and becomes deeply embedded in their consciousness and their sense of themselves. This phenomenon manifests itself in the experience of 'common sense' whereby the way society operates, its norms and values, appear as natural and not as a product of an ever changing, negotiated social process. In this vein, Leistnya and Alper argue that, 'oppression not only consists of a structural reality built on political and economic processes and relationships, it also relies on symbolic systems to shape the kinds of meaning, identity, desire, and subjectivity that can work to ensure the maintenance of what Gramsci referred to throughout his work as the hegemony of common sense' (quoted in Darder et al, 2009, p 517). Augusto Boal and Lisa Jo Epstein (1990) discuss this phenomenon in terms of 'the cop in the head': 'There are many people who dare not participate in a strike or other political actions. Why? Because they have cops in their heads. They have internalised their oppressions. The cops are in their heads, but the headquarters of these cops are in the external reality' (1990, p 35).

This ably demonstrates the connection between people's inner reality and the societal mechanisms that produce that subjectivity. In effect, people police themselves and each other to ensure that the prevailing order is maintained. Often the greatest resistance to individual and collective change within communities comes from families and peer groups. For example, many of the women whom we have worked with over the years, when beginning to engage in either community development projects or embarking on formal learning programmes, have been resisted most vehemently either by their partners, mothers or by other women within the community. Often the message to them is that they are getting ideas 'above their station' or that learning is not for "the likes of them". This resistance from friends and family, coupled with an already low self-esteem, has stopped many women before they have a chance to embed themselves in a new way of being and acting in their world.

Given this immersion in reality shaped by others, we can see the need for an external intervention to make problematic this common-sense interpretation of lived reality. As von Hoffman (2010, p 23) says, 'the gifted outside organisers do have advantages. They come with fresh eyes and new ideas, enabling them to see possibilities those already there may not realise. They can bring hope and excitement because they are not like the people they have come to organise.'

Within community organising the focus of this intervention is in terms of action, but as Allman (2001) suggests, processes that lead to counter-hegemonic activity must enable people to critically reflect on their socialised roles within wider society as a basis for action. Gramsci similarly argues for a central role for the organic intellectual. He saw that the role of these intellectuals was a crucial one in the context of creating counter-hegemony, for to be without them was to be without 'the theoretical aspect of the theory-practice nexus essential to all effective organizations' (quoted in Hoare and Smith, 1971, p 334). Traditional intellectuals are those who regard themselves as autonomous and independent of the dominant social group, and are regarded as such by the population at large even though they are part of the system that validates and maintains the status quo. They seem autonomous and independent, both of the dominant group and those involved in the struggle to create social change. However, Gramsci, when speaking of organic intellectuals, insisted that, 'The mode of being of the new intellectual can no longer consist in eloquence ... but in active participation in practical life, as constructor, organiser, "permanent persuader" and not just a simple orator...' (Gramsci, 1971, p 10), and that, 'The starting point of critical elaboration is the consciousness of what one really is...' (Gramsci, 1971, p 323). This type of rigorous examination of people's reality and the relationship of that to the wider social world is often missing in community organising practice since its focus is on winnable, local issues. Both Gramsci and Freire point to the centrality of critical reflection and the development of consciousness as a foundation for lasting social change. How this is operationalised is explored in more detail in our discussion of Freire later.

It is important to state that for Gramsci, everyone is an intellectual in the sense that every human being uses their intellect in one way or another (Saavedra, 2010), and so we are not setting up an intellectual/non-intellectual duality. Rather, as with Freire, we see organisers, community leaders and community participants as co-investigators and actors within the world, people who have distinctive and complementary roles. To draw an example from legal critical praxis:

> We have sought to link in common cause with community activists "on the streets" – as well as with critical scholars in other disciplines and agents of social transformation around the world – because we remain keenly aware that we are the representatives of traditionally subordinated communities within the privileged corridors of (legal) academia. We are critically aware of the opportunity and responsibility to combat systems and patterns of subordination within the structures of academia, as well as throughout the general society that they serve. (Valdes, 2003, p 14)

This highlights how different forms of knowing work together in pursuit, not of knowledge for its own sake, but in order to achieve a more just world. Foucault (1979a) made the connection between knowledge co-production and power, 'We must cease once and for all to describe the effects of power in negative terms: It includes, it represses, it censors, it abstracts, it masks, it conceals. In fact power produces; it produces reality, it produces domains and objects and rituals of truth. The individual and the knowledge that may be gained of him belong to this production' (1979a, p 194). He went on to highlight the interrelational nature of how power was achieved, developed and deployed in a way that would chime with community organisers: 'Power is not something that is acquired, seized or shared, something that one holds and allows to slip away; power is exercised from innumerable points, in the interplay of non-egalitarian and mobile relations' (Foucault, 1979b, pp 334-5).

And so this collective process of knowledge production and the power that emanates from that operates in a powerful way at a local level. However, given the structural and globalised nature of social inequality, as described above, local change is not enough. It is into this dilemma that Gramsci spoke about the development of a counter-hegemonic bloc.

Counter-hegemonic bloc

Gramsci analysis was that within developed capitalism the prevailing hegemonic bloc consists of the state, with its practice of political and coercive power and civil society, the media, the church, the education system, families and employers. These diverse organisations mutually reinforce dominant societal values, rewarding compliance and punishing deviance. The common sense that emerges from this arrangement is embedded within language, social practices, media images and people's aspirations; this makes the shifting of the status quo something that is deeply problematic.

This understanding of hegemony operating through a complex web of institutions and organisations further legitimises Alinsky's approach of building broad-based organisations rather than single-issue organisations. A holistic understanding of working with communities recognises the interconnectedness of social phenomena. From this it follows that groups and individuals who are working to solve these problems must link together to create new alliances and networks if our model of society, which is based on different values and assumptions, is ever to emerge. The transition towards this new model must include the linking of individuals and organisations dissatisfied with the current social order and some sense of vision for a more just future. Gramsci states that the 'building of a counter-hegemonic bloc is a long-term task for organic intellectuals working in constant interaction with the groups whose dissent from the established order makes them candidates for inclusion' (1971, p 390).

Carroll (2011) identifies a number of key elements in the development of a counter-hegemonic bloc. It is essentially based on the coming together of class-based political movements and civil society-based democratic and cultural movements at both a national and international level. This is not envisaged as a process of mere pragmatics, but the 'coming together to form a specifically *hegemonic* force involves each group being partly transformed', as it takes on elements of the identity and agenda of other groups and comes to adopt the interest of others as its own (Purcell, 2009, pp 296-7, emphasis in original). This must indicate not only coordinated action, but also a process of reflection and analysis that is embedded within the everyday processes of the network, and ensures cohesion of understanding, of vision and values and common goals.

Even within our current unjust social world, space can be created for radical alternatives to flourish, but on their own, the impact will be limited. A process of unifying dissenting groups into a system of alliances capable of contesting bourgeois hegemony must be developed. Only then will subordinate groups develop capacity for self-governance by creating post-capitalist sensibilities and values, practical democratic processes and a belief in the possibility of a radically transformed future. A new participative version of politics would be 'integrated into the everyday social existence of people struggling to change the world, so that the elitism, authoritarianism and impersonal style typical of bureaucracy could be more effectively combated' (Boggs, 1976, p 100).

In the end it is envisaged that there will be a transition from an economic-corporate phase in which subordinates define themselves and are defined in terms of their usefulness to the current economic system, to an ethico-political phase where identity is produced on a wholly different set of principles and values. This process of moral and intellectual reform not only renovates common sense into good sense, but also incrementally erodes the distinctions between leaders and the led, creating the basis for participatory democracy in a widening sphere of activities.

Some believe that the increasing inequality produced by neoliberalism provides the context for the development of such a counter-hegemonic bloc, 'capable of reversing the trends of neoliberalism, by gradually democratising, with the aid of a coalition of labour unions, NGOs, social and human rights activists, ecologist movements, etc, its institutional organs' (Worth, 2002, p 302). However, this could be considered to be a highly optimistic and almost teleological viewpoint. Take, for example, the emerging anti-globalisation movement. Although underpinned by a profound dissatisfaction with the impact of capitalist neoliberalism, it is disjointed, lacking an overall structure and direction. If processes of community organising could be introduced into this movement, along with an aim to create a cohesive network of alternative political consensus, there would be a much greater possibility of profound change in the social order.

Jørgensen (2001, p 15) describes organising as a process 'which works continuously to establish mutual prediction between multiple fragmented identities and thus between a multiplicity of different intentions and interests embedded in human and non-human agents.' In the end, without an organisation to give predictability to these diverse and disparate elements within this movement, the potential power and threat to the status quo will be dissipated. In fact, hegemony will readjust to allow these tokens of dissent – reclaiming the streets, protesting the G20 summits and the rest – without giving any of its power away, and so action becomes a spectacle, but not an engine that drives forward social change.

Into this context we are seeing the emergence of a potential counter-hegemonic bloc in the form of the World Social Forum which represents today, in organisational terms, the most consistent manifestation of counter-hegemonic globalisation, conceiving of itself as a struggle against neoliberal globalisation (de Sousa Santo, 2008). Started in 2001, it takes the form of an annual international gathering of activists, NGOs, social movements and others organised as a cumulative process, seeking to identify convergences among the movements and to explore the possibilities of communal actions and alternatives. Judith A. Hitchman (2011) describes it as an organisation that 'continues to provide a space for developing connections and dialogue across borders and differences. It may not be a space for action per se, but it does provide the basis for developing actions that reach beyond the few days of the Forum.'

The Forum is organised around 12 complementary axes (Box 10.1).

Box 10.1: Twelve complementary axes of the World Social Forum

• Axis 1: For a human society founded on common principles and values of dignity, diversity, justice, equality between all human beings, regardless of gender, cultures, age, disabilities, religious beliefs, health status, and for the elimination of all forms of oppression and discrimination based on racism, xenophobia, caste system, sexual orientation and others.

• Axis 2: For an environmental justice, for a universal and sustainable access of humanity to common goods, for the preservation of the planet as a source of life, and especially of land, water, seeds, forests, renewable energy sources and biodiversity, guaranteeing the rights of Indigenous, original, traditional, autochthonous, native, stateless, quilombola and riverain peoples and the rights on their territories, resources, languages, cultures, identities and knowledge.

• Axis 3: For the applicability and effectivity of human rights – economic, social, cultural, environmental, civil and political rights, including children's rights – particularly the rights to land, food sovereignty, food, social protection, health, education, housing, employment, decent work, communication, cultural and political expression.

• Axis 4: For the freedom of movement and establishment of all, especially migrants and asylum seekers, trafficked people, refugees, Indigenous, original, autochthonous, traditional and native peoples, minorities, for the respect of their civil, political, economic, social, cultural and environmental rights.

• Axis 5: For the inalienable right of people to the cultural patrimony of humanity, for the democratisation of knowledge, cultures, communication and technologies, valuing common goods in order to make subjugated knowledge visible, for the ending of private and hegemonic knowledge, and for a fundamental change of the system of intellectual property rights.

• Axis 6: For a world freed from the principles and structures of capitalism, of patriarchal oppression, of all forms of domination from financial powers, transnational corporations and unequal systems of trade, neocolonial and debt domination.

• Axis 7: For the construction of a social, solidarity and emancipatory economy, with sustainable modes of production and consumption and with a system of fair trade that puts an end to productivism and putting at the heart of its priorities the balance of all living beings, the fundamental needs of peoples and the respect for nature, ensuring systems of global redistribution with global taxes and with no tax havens, and for a mode of food production and

---

consumption based on food sovereignty that resists the industrial model, the monopolisation of land and the destruction of peasant seeds and local food markets.

• Axis 8: For the construction and expansion of democratic, political and economic structures and institutions, at a local, national and international level, with the participation of the peoples in decision making and in the control of public affairs and resources, respecting people's diversity and dignity.

• Axis 9: For the construction of a global order based on peace, justice and human security, the rule of law, ethics and sovereignty, condemning economic sanctions and for the self-determination of peoples, specially peoples under occupation and those in situations of war and conflict.

• Axis 10: For the valuing of the skills, histories and struggles of Africa and the diaspora and their contribution to humanity, and for the recognition of the violence of colonialism and neocolonialism.

• Axis 11: For a collective reflection on social movements, on the World Social Forum process and on the perspectives and strategies for the future, guaranteeing their contribution to the effective achievement of another possible and urgent world for all.

• Axis 12: For the inter-learning of alternative paradigms for the crisis of hegemonic civilisation of modernity/Eurocentric coloniality, through decoloniality and socialisation of power, especially in the relations between state-market-society; the collective rights of peoples; the decommodification of life and 'development'; the emergence of alternative subjectivities; and epistemologies for racism, Eurocentrism, patriarchy and anthropocentrism.

Structure, agency and the possibility of change

Ed Chambers (2010, p 137) calls for a new politics for the 21st century: 'the century's refounders must create new instruments for public life based on technology science but on communal habits of the heart. New radical, nonpartisan, international assemblies must be created and fostered as countervailing institutions.' Perhaps the World Social Forum or something similar is one of those new instruments. Although it may not be a forum for action per se, perhaps it does represent an opportunity for community organisations to collectivise action on a global scale. The linking of local action into a global network that is consciously based on a set of principles and values that is oppositional to the prevailing hegemonic order offers community organising the long horizon to allow its actions to progressively work for fundamental social change. For the Forum, having networks of power-conscious, grassroots organisations bridges the gap between discussion and action; a dialectical approach that fuses the global and the local opens up the possibility for radical social justice for all.

There are reasons to be hopeful that there may be the possibility of community organising networks getting involved in the Forum or something like it. First, it is clear that building coalitions and internationalisation is in their organisational DNA. The IAF, ACORN and SDI all see the power that comes when organisations collaborate, and even though much of this has a local focus, they also have an international dimension to their work. They all have international networks that bring people together and share ideas and training. ACORN International takes that a stage further, and links up internationally on campaigns that have global resonance, such as the campaign to control the corporate behaviour of Wal-Mart, which is ongoing in the US, South America, India and China. It would be easy to imagine that community organisations may see the opportunity for an even more broad-based organisation to have a more profound impact on the way the world operates.

However, the linkages are currently mostly strong within the networks but weak between and beyond them. It would be fair to say that even with some of the networks, the linkages could usefully be developed. Take the case of Chicago where the Back of the Yards and Woodlawn neighbourhoods are very close geographically but have little contact and no collaboration. This leaves a situation where one organisation is strong and well resourced while the other is lacking.

The big problem seems to be in collaboration across these streams. Take the Dharavi slum as an example of localised practice. Both ACORN International and SDI currently have programmes running in this slum. The People's Responsible Organisation of United Dharavi (PROUD) is also a community organisation at work in Dharavi that was at least influenced by the work of Saul Alinsky when it set up in the late 1970s. Roma Chatterji (2007) identifies PROUD's role within Dharavi as forging links of solidarity by turning civic problems into social causes:

> At the beginning PROUD was concerned about issues like water, drainage, garbage, pollution, etc but in the first week of February 1980, when the Municipal Authorities served a verbal notice to some eighty families that their houses would be demolished within a week, on the same night "Temporary Planning Committee Members" of PROUD met together and formed the PROUD Land & Housing Committee. (Chatterji, 2007, p 208)

It can clearly be seen from this that they occupy the same social terrain as ACORN, SDI and IAF, and yet there are no joint strategies or programmes.

We also met with members of PUKAR, an independent research collective and an urban knowledge production centre that provides a platform for cross-disciplinary, multisectoral, community-based research for issues related to urbanisation and globalisation, working in Dharavi. Their aims are to democratise research and to broaden access to knowledge among disenfranchised or weakly institutionalised groups and to create a space from which their non-traditional and non-expert knowledge can contribute to local, national and global debates about their own futures. Again, this is an organisation that is working to similar ends and values, and yet there seems to be little contact with ACORN or SDI, let alone a joint strategy and programmes.

Perhaps if community organisations saw their work in terms of counter-hegemony and not just mobilising people to tackle poverty and how it affects them, then there would be a greater chance of local and global partnerships. Until then, localised action can only result in zero–sum gains with more organised sections of the community gaining resources and influence at the expense of others, and as long as that is the case, there will be little change in our globalised world which is predicated on domination and exploitation.

Paulo Freire

Social change is not just about people becoming organised to change external circumstances in order to better the situation of the marginalised; it is also a process whereby those on the margins learn anew what it is to be more, to have a voice and to reshape their relationship with the world. This is why we consider it to be imperative that community organising is seen in terms of praxis and not just action, where praxis is critical reflection and action to humanise the world (Wingeier, 1980). Alinsky himself noted that, 'Happenings become experiences when they are digested, when they are reflected on, related to general patterns and synthesized' (1971, p 70), and yet critical reflection which goes beyond the task at hand is sometimes weak within community organising practice.

Domestication or liberation?

At the heart of Freire's analysis of education is the claim that all education is political; it either domesticates people, thereby supporting the status quo, or it liberates them to challenge and change the existing social order. We seek to widen that analysis to encompass all social intervention, including community organising.

There are many organisations and projects that seek to improve the lot of marginalised people. However, many of them have adopted an approach that does things *for* people or *to* people rather than doing things *with* people. In this model of practice all of the power remains with the workers, and even though goals may be successfully achieved, the community is not empowered because they have been passive objects through the process. Freire analyses this dynamic very well in the context of education, but the lessons for practice are far wider.

Many educators, even with the best of intentions, further disempower the people they are working with essentially because they fail to recognise the power dynamic at work within the educational exchange and the centrality of relationships within that exchange – the relationship between teacher and learner and the relationship between learners and knowledge. As a result, much of what purports to be learner-centred, progressive or radical approaches to education ends up being banking education in a thin disguise. It is therefore important that we now outline those central dynamics and relationships, and go on to make an application specifically to community organising.

In traditional forms of education, described by Freire as 'banking education', the teacher has power by gift of their institutional and social position, experience, subject-specific knowledge and control over the mechanisms of assessment and validation. From this position of power they set the curriculum, delineate the acceptable scope of discussion, predetermined outcomes, pose questions and define the correct answers. In this form of education, the role of the learner is one that is largely defined by lack of power and passivity. It is clear that in an educational exchange, where the teacher makes all of the major decisions, this can only reinforce the learners' sense of powerlessness and inadequacy.

Within the banking model the focus is pre-existing knowledge; its task is effective transmission of this knowledge by the teacher and effective retention and repetition of this knowledge by the learners. The relationship between learners and knowledge is static. There is no assumption that new knowledge is created; only that existing knowledge is consumed. Freire talks about the possibility of new knowledge, the possibility that people can name and rename their world.

This must cause us to reflect on the relationship between the community organiser and the community itself. Organisers have power in similar ways to teacher power, as described above. There is a great danger in this situation given that within our current social relationship we are constructed to defer to power. It is therefore perfectly feasible that situations of collusion will arise wherein organisers will exercise power and communities will acquiesce to that. Even if the organisation gains initial victories, the overall effect on individuals is disempowerment. If the organiser decides what the starting points are, what tactics are to be used and what the outcomes should be, then this only substitutes one form of oppression for another; the community is still the passive recipient of an outsider's expert analysis and solutions. If participants have not engaged in rigorous processes of reflection on what their situation is, what the causes are and what the solutions might be, then they are no better able to deal with their lives than they were before the organising process began. Inevitably, at the point when the organiser moves on, the organisation will collapse because they never really owned their own power but rather were the mechanism for someone else's agenda.

The strength of the community organising approach is the clarity of the model and the legacy of a rich range of tactics. However, given the discussion above, this can also be seen as a potential weakness. Communities may be steamrolled by this powerful, predefined process. In order to avoid this, communities must be given the space to be critical about everything, including organising processes and tactics themselves. This demands great humility on the part of the organiser, no matter how experienced. They must recognise and hold strongly to the fact that no one knows anything fully, there is always a new chapter to be written. As one participant in a Freirean process states, 'adopting this new value base and belief system, which encourages critical thinking and self-awareness of your own position in society, the natural progression is to challenge, ask questions, reason and search for solutions' (Beck, 2012, p 121).

The Freirean process

The Freirean process of education outlined below could usefully be incorporated into community organising practice. This would ensure that critical reflection was an integral part of the action guarding against the situation where leaders analyse and plan and local people do.

Listening survey

Hope and Timmel (1995) outlined the nature of a listening survey. Teams of workers, often made up of a mixture of development workers and local people, sought to identify the issues within the community that people had the strongest feelings about. The process was to find situations where people were involved in informal conversations – shops, bars, outside schools, waiting rooms and so on – and to listen for the issues about which people were worried, happy, sad, angry or fearful about. In particular the team listened for issues that related to six themes that were common to groups of people living together:

1. Meeting basic physical needs
2. Relationships between people
3. Community decision-making processes and structures
4. Education and socialisation
5. Recreation and beliefs
6. Values

The key issues or generative themes were then presented back to the community by the use of codes; these are discussed in detail below, which led to critical reflection and collective action.

Generative themes

There are parallels to be drawn between community organising's central practice of identifying and developing issues, and Freire's idea of the generative theme. 'A "generative theme" is a theme that elicits interest from the participants because it is drawn from their lives' (Peckham, 2003, p 231). These themes are powerful because they 'speak to the social, political and economic conditions' of communities and thereby generate both a critical curiosity and an impetus for action (Cammarota and Aguilera, 2012, p 492).

Where the issue, in Alinsky's terms, is the external, winnable goal that coalesces individual self-interest, investigation of the generative theme has both an external and internal dimension. To investigate the generative theme is to investigate people's thinking about reality and people's action on reality, which is their praxis. For precisely this reason, the methodology proposed requires that the investigators and the people (who would normally be considered objects of that investigation) should act as co-investigators. The more active an attitude men and women take in regard to the exploration of their thematics, the more they deepen their critical awareness of reality and, in spelling out those thematics, take possession of that reality (Freire, 1972, p 78).

Wingeier (1980, p 564) stated that taking this approach to reflection went beyond just understanding what the needs and issues were within a community; rather it enabled participants in the process to de-mythologise their world, that is, become able to penetrate and expose the myths by which their oppressors had interpreted reality to them, and then remythologise it in terms of the generative words and themes by which they came to perceive and interpret it through their conscientised eyes.

Codification

Within Freire's approach to education, these generative themes are explored dialogically through a process of codification and de-codification. The generative theme is presented back to the community in concrete form; this could be a photograph, a video, a short play or a piece of text. The idea of the code is to present aspects of people's lived reality as a problem. Issues that have become invisible due to their ubiquity and as such seem to be unchangeable are seen with new eyes. They become the focus of critical dialogue by the learning group consisting of both leaders and participants.

Participative research and codes

Photovoice is a method of using photography to develop codes to critically examine people's lived conditions that result in collective action (see Purcell, 2009). An example of this is the work documented by Wang et al (2004) in Flint, Michigan. They describe Photovoice as participatory action research methodology based on the understanding that people are experts on their own lives. Using the Photovoice methodology, participants allow their photographs to raise the questions, 'Why does this situation exist? Do we want to change it, and, if so, how?'

In this situation they worked with 40 people from their neighbourhood and professional photographers to document the impact of violence on community life. An example of what was produced was an iconic photograph entitled 'Exploded frustration' taken by Eric Dutro, a 17-year-old participant, which featured a bullet hole on his bus. Eric wrote, 'I can tell that the bus I ride in is always different because the bullet holes are always in different windows.' These images and text then became the object of the group's reflection. These reflections happened around the mnemonic 'SHOWED':

- What do you **S**ee here?
- What is really **H**appening?
- How does this relate to **O**ur lives?
- **W**hy does this problem or strength **E**xist?
- What can we **D**o about it?

From these dialogues community themes emerged; they defined a 'theme' as having at least four compelling photographs and stories that emerged during group discussion. These themes were then presented to policy makers and community leaders and had an impact on public policy and levels of community engagement within that neighbourhood (Beck and Purcell, 2010, p 88).

Action

While Freire is very clear that discovery cannot be purely intellectual but must involve action (1972, p 65), much of the practice we have observed which has been inspired by Freire's work has been strong on developing generative themes and engaging people in dialogue which developed critical awareness of the issues that the community faced but have often been less strong in organising to take action. It is here that we can see a perfect partnership between Freirean education and community organising.

Freire's clear analysis of the power dynamic within practice and the possibility of either domestication or liberation enables practitioners to clearly understand the dialectical nature of that relationship, and engaging the struggle necessary to develop processes of democratic co-investigation.

His approach to understanding the generative themes within communities reminds the practitioner to go deep into their examination of the themes and issues. These not only consist of poor housing and inadequate services, but also include the internal processes and methodologies that hold people in a place of subjection. Without processes to deal with these boundary issues, it is all too easy for people to default to a discourse of dependency and powerlessness. On the other hand, these issues also link to structural forces, economics and politics. Without connections to these broader issues, all action becomes localised, the structure of society remains unchanged and therefore all gains will be temporary since the forces that created the initial problems will, in time, reassert themselves.

Finally, Freire's use of problem posing through codes offers a mechanism of democratic engagement where local people can define and analyse the issues and develop their own solutions to meet those challenges.

Conclusion

It is interesting to think that Alinsky thought that the life of an organisation should be about five years, and that before his death he was considering sending in organisers to organise people against the organisation that he had set up years before! I think he understood the way that hegemony operates to turn dissention into consent through threat and force if needed, but more subtly and effectively through incorporation. Alinsky (undated) says that if you are on the inside, you get knocked off or co-opted. Carroll and Ratner (2006) warn that as groups begin to exercise power, they face two challenges to maintaining counter-hegemonic activity. These come in the form of marginalising and colonising moves by both capital and state. In the first move, access to funding and places at the negotiating table are denied. If this fails and the organisation continues to grow in power and influence, the state will try to mainstream the organisation, paradoxically trying to give funding while at the same time neutralising their effect through bureaucracy, policies and constricting guidelines.

This must serve as a warning to community organising that is increasingly taking a place in the mainstream. While this is certainly a great step forward, the danger of becoming part of the problem rather than the solution is a clear and present danger.

Without an analysis of the world that takes as a starting point its essentially unjust nature and recognises the hegemonic web that keeps that unjust order in place, the chances are that community organising will become another well-intentioned project that keeps people busy, tinkering on the edges while not changing the substance of their oppression.

Similarly, as we have seen, community organising, rather than being a social movement, is a patchwork of networks and interventions that do not strategise or collectivise their efforts. Surely this flies in the face of basic community organising thinking, that to collectivise people power is the only way to take on political and economic power. To have an understanding of community organising as being involved in developing a counter-hegemonic bloc pushes organisers and organisations to always be looking for the next step, the next connection, as they seek to develop a new common sense based on alternative values and practices.

It is very easy to see how Freirean approaches could usefully combine with some of the community organising approaches we have been considering. The listening campaign that the Sydney Alliance engaged in in order to generate both the issues that they would take on and people's participation in those issues has many of the features of the Freirean approach. This is also coupled with a long-term, strategic aim to have an impact on the political and economic life of the city and beyond. If this process of dialogue, creating a vision, taking action and reflecting is maintained, then perhaps we are seeing the emergence of a model that brings together the best of both these approaches. Inclusion of specific training on Freirean approaches for organisers and leaders would ensure that, in terms of analysis and practice, their processes lead to liberation and not domestication.

Similarly the horizontal learning embedded within SDI approaches offers a space in which Freirean approaches could offer real benefits. The strength of that approach to learning is that it is highly participative and rooted in people's knowledge and experience. Currently, however, the focus just on issues of practice is perhaps too narrow if people are to conceptualise and create a radically different world. Educational approaches which link people's knowledge and experience to wider theories and modes of analysis help to challenge collectively held assumptions which limit choice and creativity. It also gives people the tools they need to be analytical about the things that are said to and about them. Finally, it enables them to distinguish fact from opinion and to develop sound theories and strategies for themselves based on credible evidence.

Within ACORN, as observed in India, learning seems to be by immersion in experience, and yet, as already noted, Alinsky himself stressed that experiences were only useful to people when they were digested, when they were reflected on, related to general patterns and synthesised (1971, p 70). Without those reflective processes participants will tend to be reliant on the leaders of the organisation for direction, analysis and the development of alternative models and actions. This is particularly true in societies where the dominant discourse is one of knowing your place and deferring to authority figures. Without the struggle to transform those ingrained social relationships, little fundamental change in the long term will be possible.

Endnote

In the last paragraph of his book, *Rules for radicals*, Saul Alinsky wrote,

> We have forgotten where we came from, we don't know where we are, and we fear where we may be going. Afraid, we turn from the glorious adventure of the pursuit of happiness to a pursuit of an illusionary security in an ordered, stratified, striped society. (1971, p 196)

Sadly, these words, written a generation ago, are for too many people still true today. Alinsky described community organising as the 'democratic promise', that it would be a vehicle for the poor and dispossessed to claim their rights, improve their lives and become fully part of mainstream society.

Since 1939, when the Back of the Yards Neighborhood Council (BYNC) pulled together diverse trade union, religious and ethnic interests in the Stockyards area of Chicago, community organisations have developed into a diverse movement across the US, and have spread into Western Europe, Asia, Africa, South America and Australia. Although community organisations have not transformed the world, they have improved the lives of countless people, built houses, increased wages, improved schooling and healthcare. More importantly, perhaps, community organisations have given hope and a belief that a better world is possible.

This route to a better world can be travelled along different roads, and community organising provides both a map as well as some roads to follow. Community organising as an activity is not perfect; sometimes it fails, changes and needs to constantly learn from experience and adapt to new circumstances. It provides those of us wanting progressive social change with options that we would be well advised to explore. As US Senator Paul Wellstone commented, "What makes community organising especially attractive is the faith it places on the ability of the poor to make decisions for themselves."

The last words go to the one time anti-war activist, Abbie Hoffman, who said,

> The key to organising an alternative society is to organise people around what they can do, and more importantly, what they want to do.

That is both the promise and the raison d'être of community organising.

References

Abrams, M. (2010) 'When the past stands in front of the present so we can't see the future', in V. Ivanova and M. Klingenberg (eds) *Closing the Books or Keeping them Open?*, International Perspectives on Education series, pp 29-41.

ACHR (Asian Coalition for Housing Rights) (2000) 'Urban Poor Development Fund', Bangkok: ACHR (www.achr.net).

ACHR (2001) 'Building an urban poor people's movement in Phnom Penh, Cambodia', *Environment and Urbanization,* October, vol 13, no 2, pp 61-72.

ACHR (2010) ACCA in Cambodia, Bangkok: ACHR.

ACHR (2011) A report on the Regional Meeting of the Asian Coalition for Housing Rights, 27-30 January, Menam Riverside Hotel, Bangkok.

Adams, W.M. (2006) *The future of sustainability: Re-thinking environment and development in the twenty-first century. Report of the IUCN Renowned Thinkers Meeting*, 29-31 January, Gland, Switzerland: International Union for Conservation of Nature and Natural Resources.

Alinsky, S.D. (1971) *Rules for radicals: A pragmatic primer for realistic radicals,* New York: Random House.

Alinsky, S.D. (1989) *Reveille for radicals*, New York: Vintage.

Alinsky, S.D. (undated) 'Saul Alinsky explains community organizing as an outside agitator' (www.youtube.com/watch?v=pQtwo8lp_E8).

Allman, P. (2001) *Critical education against global capitalism: Karl Marx and critical revolutionary education*, Westport: Bergen and Garvey.

Anderson, P. (1966) 'Making trouble is Alinsky's business', *The New York Times Magazine*, 9 October.

Arnstein, S. (1969) 'A ladder of citizen participation', *Journal of the American Institute of Planners*, vol 35, no 4.

Atlas, J. (2010) *Seeds of change: The story of ACORN, America's most controversial antipoverty community organizing group*, Nashville, TN: Vanderbilt University Press. Kindle edition

Ayton-Shenker, D. (1995) *The challenge of human rights and cultural diversity*, Department of Public Information, New York: United Nations.

Baptist, C. and Bolnick, J. (2012) 'Participatory enumerations, in situ upgrading and mega events: the 2009 survey in Joe Slovo, Cape Town', *Environment and Urbanization*, April, vol 24, pp 59-66.

Bardlow, B. (2011) 'Between the "informal" and the "formal": slum upgrading in South Africa', SDI: Cape Town, www.sdinet.org/blog/2011/06/

Barr, A. (1991) *Practicing community development*, London: Community Development Foundation.

Barr, A., Hasegan, S. and Purcell, R. (1996) *Monitoring and evaluation of community development*, Belfast: Northern Ireland Department of Health and Social Security.

Bass, B.M. (1999) 'Ethics, character and authentic transformational leadership behaviour', *Leadership Quarterly*, vol 10, no 2, pp 181-207.

Batten, T. (1967) *The non-directive approach in group and community work*, London: Oxford University Press.

Beck, D. (2007) 'Adding some glue to the pot: community development, education and the development of social capital', *Learning Communities: International Journal of Learning in Social Contexts*, November, pp 78-108.

Beck, D. (2012) 'Community of strangers: Supporting drug recovery through community development and Freirean pedagogy', *Journal of Progressive Human Services*, May, vol 2, pp 110-26.

Beck, D. and Purcell, R. (2010) *Popular education practice for youth and community development work*, Exeter: Learning Matters.

Becker, G. (1976) *The economic approach to human behaviour*, Chicago, IL: University of Chicago Press.

Bischof, L. (2009) *Community organizing as an instrument of change management*, Wisconsin: Comm-org Papers (http://comm-org.wisc.edu/papers2009/bischof. htm).

Bishop, D. (2007) 'Unintentional leadership', *Integral Leadership Review*, vol vii, no 4, August.

Boal, A. and Epstein, S. (1990) 'The cop in the head: Three hypotheses', *The Drama Review*, vol 34, no 3, Autumn, pp 35-42.

Bobo, K., Kendall, J. and Max, S. (2010) *Organizing for social change: Midwest Academy manual for activists*, Santa Ana, CA: The Forum Press.

Boggs, C. (1976) *Gramsci's Marxism*, London: Pluto Press.

Bolnick, J. (1993) 'The people's dialogue on land and shelter: community-driven networking in South Africa's informal settlements', *Environment and Urbanization*, vol 5, no 1, April, pp 91-107.

Brood, P. (1986) 'The forms of capital', in J.G. Richardson (ed) *Handbook of theory and research for the sociology of education*, Westport, CT: Greenwood Press, Chapter 9.

Bourdieu, P. and Waquant, L. (1992) *An invitation to reflexive sociology*, Chicago, IL: University of Chicago Press.

Brazier, A. (1969) *Black self-determination*, Grand Rapids, MI: William B. Eerdmans.

Briggs, S.M., Tyler, J. and Mullineaux, D.R. (2003) 'Communications to the 12th Commonwealth International Sport Conference', *Journal of Sports Sciences*, vol 21, no 4, pp 340-65.

Brown, T.F. (2002) 'Theoretical perspectives on social capital', Beaumont, Texas: Lamar University.

Bunyan, P. (2008) 'Broad-based organizing in the UK: reasserting the centrality of political activity in community development', *Community Development Journal*, vol 45, no 1, January, pp 111-27.

Burra, S., Patel, S. and Kerr, T. (2003) 'Community-designed, built and managed toilet blocks in Indian cities', *Environment and Urbanization*, October, vol 15, pp 11-32.

Calpotura, F. and Fellner, K. (1996) *The square pegs find their groove: Reshaping the organizing circle*, Madison, WI: COMM-ORG, Online Conference (http://comm-org.wisc.edu/papers96/square.html).

Cammarota, J. and Aguilera, M. (2012) '"By the time I get to Arizona": Race, language and education in America's racist state', *Race, Ethnicity and Education*, vol 15, no 4, pp 485-500.

Carroll, W. (2010) 'Crisis, movements, counter-hegemony', *Interface: A Journal for and about Social Movements*, vol 2, no 2, November, pp 168-98.

Carroll, W. and Ratner, R. (2001) 'Sustaining oppositional cultures in 'post-socialist'times: a comparative study of three social movement organisations', *Sociology*, vol 35, no 3, pp 605-29.

Catholic Culture (www.catholicculture.org/culture/library/view.cfm?id=2885).

CDP (Community Development Project) Inter-Project Editorial Team (1976) *Whatever happened to council housing*, London: CDP Information and Intelligence Unit.

CDP Inter-Project Editorial Team (1977a) *The costs of industrial change*, London: CDP IIU.

CDP Inter-Project Editorial Team (1977b) *Gilding the ghetto*, London: CDP IIU.

Chambers, E (2010) *Roots for Radicals: Organizing for Power, Action, and Justice*, New York: Continuum International Publishing Group

Chandler, D. (2008) *A history of Cambodia*, Boulder, CO: Westview Press.

Chatterji, R. (2007) 'Plans, habitation and slum redevelopment: production of community', *Dharavi, Mumbai, Contributions to Indian Sociology*, vol 39, pp 197-218.

Coleman, J. (1988) 'Social capital in the creation of human capital', *American Journal of Sociology*, vol 95, S95-S120.

Conservative Party (2010) 'Big Society, not big government' (www.conservatives. com/news/news_stories/2010/03/~/media/Files/Downloadable%20Files/ Building-a-Big-Society.ashx).

Cooke, I. and Shaw, M. (1996) *Radical community work: Perspectives from practice in Scotland*, Edinburgh: Moray House Publications.

CORC (Community Organisation Resource Centre) (2009) *Joe Slovo household enumeration report*, Cape Town: CORC.

Cortes, E. (1986) 'Organizing the community', *The Texas Observer*, 11 July.

Craig, G. (2007) 'Community capacity-building: Something old, something new...?', *Critical Social Policy*, vol 27, no 3, pp 335-59.

Darder, A., Baltodano, M.P. and Torres, R.D. (2009) *The critical pedagogy reader*, New York: Routledge.

Davis, M. (2007) *Planet of slums*, London: Verso.

DCOC (Drumchapel Community Organisations Council) (1993) *Mercat forces: An exercise in community management for urban regeneration*, Drumchapel: DCOC.

Democratic Promise (1999) 'Democratic Promise: Saul Alinsky and his legacy', Chicago Video Project, co-produced by Bruce Orenstein.

de Wit, J. and Berner, E. (2009) 'Progressive patronage? Municipalities, NGOs, CBOs and the limits to slum dwellers' empowerment', *Development and Change*, vol 40, issue 5, pp 927-47.

Delgado, G. (1986) *Organizing the movement: The roots and growth of ACORN*, Philadelphia, PA: Temple University Press.

Delgado, G. (1999) *Beyond politics of place: New directions in community organizing*, Berkeley, CA: Charndon.

Department of Local Government and Housing (2009) *Western Cape provincial master plan 2008-2014*, Cape Town: Department of Local Government and Housing.

de Sousa Santos, B. (2008) 'The world social forum and the global left', *Politics & Society*, June, vol 36, pp 247-70.

Dow, G. and Lafferty, G. (2007) 'Decades of disillusion: Reappraising the ALP-ACTU accord 1983-1996', *Australian Journal of Politics And History*, vol 53, no 4, pp 552-68.

Edwards, M. (2001) 'Global civil society and community exchanges: a different form of movement', *Environment and Urbanization*, vol 13, no 2, October, pp 145-9.

Egan, J. Very Rev Msgr (1965) 'The Archdiocese responds', *Church Metropolis*, Summer, p 16.

Erickson, F. and Vonk, J.A. (2006) *If The World Were 100 People*, University of Wisconsin – Green Bay

Foucault, M. (1979a) *Discipline and punish: The birth of the prison*, Harmondsworth: Penguin.

Foucault, M. (1979b) *Excerpts from 'The history of sexuality: Volume 1: An introduction'*. Harmondsworth: Penguin.

Freire, P. (1972) *Pedagogy of the oppressed*, Harmondsworth: Penguin.

Freire, P. (2001) *Pedagogy of freedom: Ethics, democracy and civic courage*, London: Rowman & Littlefield Publishers.

Galloway, S. (2006) *The benefits of culture and sport: Literature review*, Edinburgh: Scottish Government (www.scotland.gov.uk/Publications/2006/01/13110743/0).

Gaynor, N. (2011) 'In-active citizenship and the depoliticization of community development in Ireland', *Community Development Journal*, vol 46, no 1, pp 27-4.

Global Footprint Network (2008) *The ecological footprint atlas 2008*, Oakland: GFN

Goff, C. (2007) 'An interview with Sheela Patel', *The Internationalist Magazine*, issue 398.

Government of India (2001) *Census of India, 2001*, New Delhi.

Gramsci, A. (1971) *Selections from The Prison Notebooks*, London: Lawrence & Wishart.

Gray, H. *Chicago organizing: Tough, cat-clawing, bloody* (http://hunterbear.org/chicago_organizing.htm).

Green, J. and Chapman, A. (1992) 'The British Community Development Project: Lessons for today', *Community Development Journal*, vol 27, no 3, pp 242-58.

Gulbenkian Committee (1968) *Community work and social change*, Harlow: Longman.

Hanifan, L.J. (1916) *The rural school community centre*, Boston, MA: Silver Burdett.

Hansard (1948) *Parliamentary debates*, 3rd series, vol 97, col 122.

Harriss, J. (2002) *Depoliticizing development: The World Bank and social capital*, London: Anthem Press.

Henderson, P. and Salmon, H. (1995) *Community organizing: The UK context*, Belfast: Churches Community Work Alliance.

Hitchman, J. (2011) 'The Social Forum movement in Africa', World Social Forum (www.forumsocialmundial.org.br/noticias_01.php?cd_news=3044&cd_language=2).

Hoare, Q. and Smith, G.N. (eds) (1971) *Selections from the prison notebooks of Antonio Gramsci*, New York: International Publishers.

Hofstede, G. (1984) 'The cultural relativity of the quality of life concept', *Academy of Management Review*, vol 9, no 3, pp 389-98.

Hoggert, P., Mayo, M. and Miller, C. (2009) *The dilemmas of development practice*, Bristol: Policy Press.

Hope, A. and Timmel, S. (1995) *Training for transformation. Vols 1, 2, 3*, Gweru, Zimbabwe: Mambo Press.

Horwitt, S.D. (1989) *Let them call me rebel: Saul Alinsky – His life and legacy*, New York: Alfred A. Knopf.

Hunter, F. (2010) 'Some insights into community adult education in South Africa', *Adult Education and Development*, no 74.

Iveson, K. (2010) 'Seeking spatial justice: Some reflections from Sydney', *City: Analysis of Urban Trends, Culture, Theory, Policy, Action*, vol 14, no 6, pp 607-11.

Jacobs, J. (1961) *The death and life of great American cities*, New York: Random.

Jones, M. (2006) *The American pursuit of unhappiness – Gross National Happiness (GNH) – A new socioeconomic policy*, Nevada: International Institute of Management (www.iim-edu.org/grossnationalhappiness/).

Jordhus-Lier, D. (2011) 'Local contestation around a flagship urban housing project: N2 Gateway and the Joe Slovo community in Cape Town', European Association of Development Research and Training Institutes/ Development Studies Association Conference, 19-22 September, York.

Jørgensen, K.M. (2001) *Power, knowledge and organizing*, Aalborg: Centre for the Interdisciplinary Study of Learning, Aalborg University.

Kaufman, M. and Alfonso, H.D. (1997) *Community power and grassroots democracy: The transformation of social life*, London: Zed Books.

Kimball, L. (1997) Keynote address, Team Strategies Conference, Toronto, Canada.

Knight, B. (1991) *Community organizing in Britain: The first two years of the Citizen Organizing Foundation*, Critical Review of International Social and Political Philosophy.

Kretzmann, J. and McKnight, J. (1993) *Building communities from the inside out: A path toward finding and mobilizing a community's assets*, Chicago, IL: ACTA Publications.

Lane, P. (1939) *The Lane report: The field of community organization*, Buffalo, New York: National Conference on Social Welfare.

Ledwith, M. (2011) *Community development: A critical approach*, Bristol: Policy Press.

Lees, R. (1975) *Research strategies for social welfare*, Boston: Routledge and Kegan Paul.

Ley, A. and Herrle, P. (2007) *Report on the evaluation of SDI strategies to secure land and basic services in South Africa and Malawi*, Cape Town: Oikos Human Settlements Research Group.

LISC (Local Initiatives Support Corporation) (2010) *Annual report* (www.lisc. org/annualreport/2010/message/message.shtml).

London Edinburgh Weekend Return Group (1980) In and Against the State, London, Pluto Press

McGaffey, R.J. and Khalil, H. (2005) *Alinsky in the age of neocolonialism* (http:// ibible.enablepassion.org/Writing/school/06%20nyu%20gallatin%20fall%2005/ alinsky.pdf).

Makau, J., Dobson, S. and Samia, E. (2012) 'The five-city enumeration: the role of participatory enumerations in developing community capacity and partnerships with government', *Uganda Environment and Urbanization*, April, vol 24, pp 31-46.

Maslow, A. (1943) 'A theory of human motivation', *Psychological Review*, vol 50, no 4, pp 370-96.

Max-Neef, M.A., Elizalde, A. and Hopenhayn, M. (1987) *Human scale development*, New York: The Apex Press.

Meadows, D. (1990) Returning Peace Corps volunteers of Madison Wisconsin, Unheard voices: Celebrating cultures from the developing world Donella H. Meadows, *The global citizen*, 31 May 1990.

Medina, L. (2011) *Community organizing for Conservatives: A manifesto for localism in the Tea Party movement (Voices of the Tea Party)*, New York: HarperCollins, Inc. (Kindle edition).

Miller, M. (2010) 'Alinsky for the left: The politics of community organizing', *Dissent*, vol 57, no 1, pp 43-9.

Miller, M *Beyond the politics of place: A critical review* (http://comm-org.wisc.edu/ papers96/miller.html#interest).

Mitlin, D. (2008) 'With and beyond the state – Co-production as a route to political influence, power and transformation for grassroots organizations', *Environment and Urbanization*, October, vol 20, pp 339-60.

Muller, A. and Mitlin, D. (2007) 'Securing inclusion: Strategies for community empowerment and state redistribution', *Environment and Urbanization*, vol 19, pp 425-39.

Navarro, V. (2002) 'A critique of social capital', *International Journal of Health Services*, vol 32, no 4, pp 629-56.

Norman, J. (2010) *Big society: The anatomy of the new politics*, Buckingham: University of Buckingham Press.

Nussbaum, M.C. (2000) *Women and human development: The capabilities approach*, Cambridge: Cambridge University Press.

O'Leary, T. (2011) *Appreciating assets*, Fife: International Association for Community Development.

O'Malley, J. (1977) *The politics of community action*, Nottingham: Spokesman Press.

Obama, B. (1988) *Problems and promise in the inner city*, Springfield, IL: Illinois Issues (http://illinoisissues.uis.edu/archives/2008/09/whyorg.html).

Obama, B. (1990) 'Why organize? Problems and promise in the inner city', in P. Knoefle (ed) *After Alinsky: Community organizing in Illinois*, Springfield, IL: Sagamon State University, pp 35-40.

ODI (Overseas Development Institute) (2010) *Cambodia: Case study for the MDG Gap Task Force Report*, London: ODI.

PACSW (Provincial Advisory Council on the Status of Women: Newfoundland and Labrador) (2012) 'About us', www.pacsw.ca/about-us/provincial-advisory-council-on-the-status-of-women/

Patel, S. and Mitlin, D. (2001) *The work of SPARC, the National Slum Dwellers Federation and Mahila Milan*, London: Human Settlements Programme, International Institute for Environment and Development.

Patel, S. and Mitlin, D. (2002) 'Sharing experiences and changing lives', *Community Development*, vol 37, no 2, pp 125-37.

Patel, S. and Mitlin, D. (2005) *Re-interpreting the rights-based approach: A grassroots perspective on rights and development*, Working Paper Series 22, Oxford: Global Poverty Research Group.

Patel, S. and Mitlin, D. (2011) *Gender issues and slum/shack dweller federations*, London: International Institute for Environment and Development (http://pubs.iied.org/pdfs/G03089.pdf).

Peckham, I. (2003) 'Freirean codifications: Changing walls into windows', *Pedagogy*, vol 3, no 2, pp 227-44.

Phonphakdee, S., Visal, S. and Sauter, G. (2009) 'The Urban Poor Development Fund in Cambodia: supporting local and citywide development', *Environment and Urbanization*, 1 October, vol 21, pp 569-86.

Pitt, J. and Keane, M. (1984) *Community organizing – You've never really tried it: The challenge to Britain from the USA*, Birmingham: J&P Consultancy.

Purcell, R. (2005) *Working in the community: Perspectives for change*, Raleigh, NC: Lulu Press.

Purcell, R. (2009) 'Images for change: Community development, community arts and photography', *Community Development Journal*, vol 44, pp 111-22.

Purcell, R. (2011) 'Community development and everyday life', *Community Development Journal*, February, vol 47, no 2, pp 266-81.

Putnam, R.D. (2000) *Bowling alone: The collapse and revival of American community*, New York: Simon & Schuster.

Raff, C. and Sobrado, M. (2000) *A future for the excluded: Job creation and income generation by the poor, Clodomir Santos de Morais and the Organization Workshop*, London: Zed Books.

Reeler, D. (2005) *Horizontal learning: Engaging freedom's possibilities*, Cape Town: Community Development Resource Association.

Reissman, F. (1967) 'The myth of Saul Alinsky', *Dissent*, July–August. [Reprinted in J. Natoli and L. Hutcheon (eds) (1993) *A postmodern reader*, New York: State University of New York Press, pp 333-41.

Rodham, H. (1969) 'There is only the fight: An analysis of the Alinksy model', Wellesley College thesis (www.under-dogma.com/HillaryClintonThesisSaulAlinsky.pdf).

Saavedra, M. (2010) 'Engaged intellectuals: Comments on the crisis of the Latina/os public intellectual', *Journal of Gender, Social Policy & the Law*, vol 18, no 3, pp 811-23.

Schalock, R.L. (2000) 'Three decades of quality of life', *Focus on Autism & Other Developmental Disabilities*, vol 15, no 2, p 116.

Skocpol, T. (2003) *Diminished democracy: From membership to management in American civic life*, Norman, OK: University of Oklahoma Press.

SDI (Slum Dwellers International) (2008) *The challenge of engagement: The South African process*, SDI: Cape Town (www.sdinet.org/media/upload/countries/documents/the_challenge_of_engagement__the_south_african_process.pdf).

SDI (undated a) *Making cities inclusive* (www.sdinet.org/videos/72/).

SDI (undated b) *A miracle rising out of the ashes: SDI partners in South Africa respond to the fire at Joe Slovo, Langa, Cape Town* (www.sdinet.org/).

Sen, A.K. (1985) *Commodities and capabilities*, Oxford: Oxford University Press.

Sen, A.K. (2001) *Development as freedom*, Oxford: Oxford University Press.

Sen, R. (2003) *Stir it up: Lessons in community organizing and advocacy*, San Francisco, CA: Jossey-Bass.

Shekhar, K. (2000) *Murder of the mills: A case study of Phoenix Mills*, Mumbai: Girgangaon Bachao Andolan (Movement to Save the Mill District).

Silberman, C. (1968) *Crisis in black and white*, New York: Random House.

Singhal, A. (2001) *Facilitating community participation through communication*, New York: UNICEF.

Sivanandan, A. (1990) 'All that melts into air is solid: the hokum of new times', *Race and Class*, vol 31, no 3, pp 1-30.

Slayton, R. (1986) *Back of the Yards: The making of a local democracy*, Chicago, IL: University of Chicago Press.

Slum Dwellers International (undated) 'What we do,' www.sdinet.org/about-what-we-do/

Smith, M.K. (2000-09) 'Social capital', *the encyclopedia of informal education*, London: INFED (www.infed.org/biblio/social_capital.htm).

Smock, K. (2004) *Democracy in action: Community organizing and urban change*, New York: Columbia University Press.

Sokupa, M. and Adlard, G. (2010) Report on visit to Mumbai and Pune at the invitation of the Community Organisation Resource Centre, 14-21 April (www.sdinet.org/media/upload/countries/documents/REPORT_ON_VISIT_TO_MUMBAI_FINAL1.pdf).

SPARC (The Society for the Promotion of Area Resource Centres) (2009) *Annual Report 2008-2009* (www.sparcindia.org/files/Annual%20Report%20SPARC_2009.pdf).

Speech to the House of Commons (1 March 1848) *Hansard's Parliamentary Debates*, 3rd series, vol 97, col 122.

Stoecker, R. and Stall, S. (1997) 'Community organizing or organizing community? Gender and the crafts of empowerment', *Gender & Society*, vol 12, pp 729-56.

Stokes, P. and Knight, B. (1997a) 'A citizen's charter to save our cities', *The Independent*, 1 January.

Stokes, P. and Knight, B. (1997b) *Organizing a civil society*, Birmingham: Foundation for Civil Society.

Strinati, D. (1995) *An introduction to theories of popular culture*, London and New York: Routledge.

Suet-Lin, S.H. and Kwok-Kin, F. (2010) 'Organizing women for policy advocacy in Hong Kong: identities and perspectives of women organisers', *Community Development Journal*, vol 45, no 4, pp 423-38.

Tattershall, A. (2010) *Power in coalition: Strategies for strong unions and social change*, Ithaca, NY: Cornell University Press.

Tattersall, A. (2011) Canadian Union of Public Employees National Municipal Sector meeting, 'Power of coalitions', Keynote address, 16-18 February, Toronto: Sheraton Hotel.

Tea Party, The (2012) *What is The Tea Party?* (www.theteaparty.net/).

Tedmanson, D. (2005) 'Whose capacity needs building? Open hearts and empty hands: reflections on capacity building in remote communities', Paper presented at the Fourth International Critical Management Studies Conference, 4-6 July, University of Cambridge, UK.

Thenextright.com (2008) 'Obama – ACORN: The root cause of the mortgage crisis' (www.thenextright.com/ozarkguru/obama-acorn-root-causes-of-mortgage-crisis).

Townsend, A.M., DeMarie, S.M. and Hendrickson, A.R. (1998) 'Virtual teams: Technology and the workplace of the future', *Academy of Management Executive*, vol 12, no 3, pp 17-29.

Tully, J. (2005) *A short history of Cambodia: From empire to survival*, Sydney: Allen & Unwin.

Turner, J.F.C. (1976) *Housing by people: Towards autonomy in building environments*, London: Marion Boyars.

Twelvetrees, A. (1989) *Organizing for neighbourhood development: A comparative study of community development corporations and citizen action organizations*, Avebury: Ashgate.

UK Citizens (2011) 'Community organizing' blog (http://communityorganizing. tumblr.com/).

United Nations Department of Economic and Social Affairs (2012) *World urbanization prospects: The 2011 revision*, New York: United Nations.

UNDP (United Nations Development Programme) *Human development and human rights: Report on the Oslo Symposium, 2–3 October 1998*, New York: UNDP.

UNDP (2006) *Human development report*, New York: UNDP.

UNDP (United Nations Development Programme) (2009) *Frequently asked questions: The UNDP approach to supporting capacity development*, New York: UNDP.

UNPD (2012) Fast Facts: Millennium Development Goals, www.undp.org/ content/dam/undp/library/corporate/fast-facts/english/FF-Millennium-Development-Goals.pdf

UNFPA (2008) *State of world population 2007* (www.unfpa.org/swp/2007/presskit/ pdf/sowp2007_eng.pdf accessed 16/02/12).

UNGA (United Nations General Assembly) (1987) *Report of the World Commission on Environment and Development: Our common future,* Transmitted to the General Assembly as an Annex to document A/42/427 – Development and International Co-operation: Environment.

UN (United Nations) Habitat (2008) *State of the world's cities 2008/09 – Harmonious cities,* Nairobi: UN-Habitat (www.unhabitat.org/pmss/listItemDetails.aspx?publicationID=2562).

UN Habitat (2009) *Statistical annex, Part VI* (www.unhabitat.org/downloads/docs/GRHS2009/GRHS.2009.6.pdf).

UPDF (Urban Poor Development Fund) (2008) UPDF Newsletter, May 2008.

Valdes, F. (2003) 'Legal reform and social justice: An introduction to latcrit theory, praxis and community', *Griffith Law Review*, vol 14, no 2, pp 147–73 (http://www.worldlii.org/au/journals/GriffLawRw/2005/13.html).

Valley, C. (2008) 'Alinsky at 100', *Journal of Community Practice*, December, vol 16 no 4, pp 527-32.

von Hoffman, N. (2010) *Radical: A portrait of Saul Alinsky,* Philadelphia, PA: Nation Books.

Waddington, P. (1983) 'Looking ahead – Community work in the 1980s', in D. Thomas (ed) *Community work in the eighties,* London: National Institute for Social Work, pp 66-81.

Wang, C.C., Morrel-Samuels, S., Hutchison P.M., Bell, L. and Pestronk, R.M. (2004) 'Flint Photovoice: community building among youths, adults, and policymakers', *American Journal of Public Health*, vol 94, no 6.

Watanabe, Y. (2008) Urban Poor Development Fund (http://web.mit.edu/sigus/www/NEW/LIHCourse/Cambodia/cambodia-presentations.pdf).

Weil, M. (1986) 'Women, community, and organizing', in N. van den Bergh and L.B. Cooper (eds) *Feminist visions for social work,* Silver Springs, MD: National Association of Social Workers, pp 187-210.

Wenger, E.C. and Snyder, W.M. (2000) 'Communities of practice: the organizational frontier', *Harvard Business Review*, vol 78, no 1, January-February, pp 139-45.

Wenocur, S. and Reisch, M. (1989) *From charity to enterprise: The development of American social work in a market economy,* Urbana, IL: University of Illinois Press.

White, A. (2007) *A global projection of subjective well-being: A challenge to positive psychology?,* Leicester: University of Leicester.

Wilcox, D. (1995) *The guide to effective participation,* York: Joseph Rowntree Foundation.

Williamson, V., Skocpol, T. and Coggin, J. (2011) 'The Tea Party and the remaking of Republican conservatism', *Perspectives on Politics*, vol 9 , pp 25-43.

Willis, J. (2012) 'The geography of community and political organisation in London today', *Political Geography*, vol 31, issue 2, February, pp 114-26.

Wingeier, D.E. (1980) 'Generative words in six cultures', *Religious Education*, vol 75, no 5, pp 563-76.

Woolcock, M. (2001) 'The place of social capital in understanding social and economic outcomes', *Isuma: Canadian Journal of Policy Research*, vol 2, no 1, pp 1-17.

World Bank, The (2000) *World Bank Development Report 2000/01*, New York: Oxford University Press.

World Bank, The (2010) *World Bank Development Report 2010: development and climate change*, Washington: World Bank.

Worth, O. (2002) 'The Janus-like character of counter-hegemony: Progressive and nationalist responses to neoliberalism', *Global Society*, vol 16, no 3, pp 297-315.

Xiaorong, L. (1999) 'Asian values and the universality of human rights', *Business and Society Review*, vol 102, no 1, pp 81-7.

Zangmo, T. (2008) *Psychological Wellbeing Survey Report*, The Centre for Bhutan Studies (www.grossnationalhappiness.com/surveyReports/).

Selected website links

ACORN International http://acorninternational.org/

Back of the Yards Neighbourhood Council http://bync.org/

Citizens UK www.citizensuk.org/

Community Healing Network http://communityhealingnet.com/

Dharavi project – ACORN Foundation India www.dharaviproject.org/

Gamaliel www.gamaliel.org/

Industrial Areas Foundation (IAF) www.industrialareasfoundation.org/

Local Initiatives Support Corporation www.lisc.org/

Slum Dwellers International www.sdinet.org/

SPARC www.sparcindia.org/

Sydney Alliance www.sydneyalliance.org.au/

The Woodlawn Organisation http://twochicago.org/

UN Millennium Goals www.un.org/millenniumgoals/

Urban Poor Development Fund www.achr.net/updf.htm

Index